I Needed This

I NEEDED THIS

Allan W. Cates

I NEEDED THIS

iUniverse books may be ordered through booksellers or by contacting:

iUniverse
1663 Liberty Drive
Bloomington, IN 47403
www.iuniverse.com
844-349-9409

Because of the dynamic nature of the Internet, any web addresses or links contained in this book may have changed since publication and may no longer be valid. The views expressed in this work are solely those of the author and do not necessarily reflect the views of the publisher, and the publisher hereby disclaims any responsibility for them.

Any people depicted in stock imagery provided by Getty Images are models, and such images are being used for illustrative purposes only.
Certain stock imagery © Getty Images.

ISBN: 978-1-6632-7029-0 (sc)
ISBN: 978-1-6632-7031-3 (hc)
ISBN: 978-1-6632-7030-6 (e)

Library of Congress Control Number: 2025900701

Print information available on the last page.

iUniverse rev. date: 01/22/2025

PREFACE

The book you are about to read, or toss, defies categorization. Of the millions of books that have been written or compiled and copyrighted, each has fit into one or more of the thousands of categories that are only understood by a select number of people in the so-called Library of Congress somewhere up north.

This book is unique. It is a compilation of anecdotes, thoughts, and meanderings. Some articles might be as short as a paragraph, others might qualify as essays, and you will even encounter a short story now and then. Approximately 86.7% (my estimate) of the articles are autobiographical, and the remaining percentage may or may not contain a modicum of truth. It will be up to the reader to try to discern the truth from fiction.

It is also a word study to further discourage any efforts to classify and catalog the text. For the benefit of my deeper-thinking friends, I have provided a vocabulary word with a brief dictionary definition ahead of each article. I have chosen these words to be commonly used and understood in everyday conversation but not normally written in everyday life. Therein, we see that each of us has at least two vocabularies, one spoken and one written. I am providing you the opportunity to elevate a couple hundred words from your spoken vocabulary to your written vocabulary. I might toss in a sleeper occasionally. You may want to keep a pocket dictionary handy.

I think it will be fun. At least it has been for me.

A Dropout in College

**Abhorrent: inspiring disgust
and loathing; repugnant**

In the late summer of 1964, I found myself living in Ventura, California, while working as a drywall finisher in new housing tracts around the Ventura, Oxnard, and Santa Barbara area. A couple of my co-workers were attending evening classes at Ventura College, a community college established in 1925 on a pleasant 112-acre campus not ten blocks from my apartment. In conversation with Jim and Gary, I learned that Gary, like myself, had not graduated high school. It piqued my interest. Might I be able to attend college courses in Ventura? Back in Arkansas, I had been told that because of my being a non-high school graduate, I could not enroll in college.

I drove out to the campus, found the enrollment office, and strode in. The enrollment officer I spoke with assured me that I could enroll as a student in a remedial curriculum. I was elated. The next course that was available was an evening class in the second summer term. That was perfect because I was plenty busy taping sheetrock during the daytime.

It was late July or early August when I attended my first college class. I was almost petrified with apprehension as it had been a full ten years since I had been in a classroom. Moreover, I had only attended a few months into the 11th grade back in Arkansas before

I dropped out and joined the army. I was also intimidated by the thought that my classmates had just graduated from high school a few months earlier. Their knowledge would be fresh. I hoped that I could make it.

It was during this time when the Vietnam War had been raging for years. The student movement arose at the University of California at Berkeley in 1964 when students involved in civil rights activism started protesting the war and the university's sudden attempt to prevent them from organizing politically on campus. The activists zeroed in on the Vietnam War, military conscription, and the right to protest.

Students protesting the draft were chanting, "Hell No! We won't go!" There were pockets of social unrest erupting in university campuses nationwide. On the Berkeley Campus, just up the coast from Ventura, students had barricaded themselves inside some of the classrooms. They were destroying property and throwing desks out the windows. I suspect the damage ran into the millions of dollars. I felt it was <u>abhorrent</u> that they would do that, costing enormous sums of money from taxpayers' earnings. I was even more astonished that my professor, a man whom I had highly respected, spoke out in agreement with the so-called free speech movement that it had become called. I never had quite as much respect for my teacher from that point on.

Oh yes, I found that I did well and made an A in my first college course. It turns out that the class, English 101, was the remedial class. It was called "Bonehead English." My fellow classmates were in it because they were too dumb to pass the entrance examinations. I had thought I was pretty smart until I learned that the ones I outdid were borderline morons.

It pays not to get too cocky.

Bugless Nevada

Lanai: A porch or Veranda

It was early June 1992, and I had been assigned to a construction project near Indiantown, Florida. I would just be in Florida for a year or so. Therefore, I wouldn't consider buying a house. So, I went shopping for a rental home. I located an ad for one on Thornhill Drive in Port St. Lucie. I was told that it was a relatively new three-bedroom home with a two-car garage and a lanai. I had to ask, "What is a lanai?" The owner said it was a large patio enclosed by screen wire.

I checked out the home, loved it, and leased it for a year. The lanai was as the owner had described it. I muttered to myself, "We would call it a screened-in back porch in Arkansas. If he had called it that, I would have understood." However, over time, I learned to call it a lanai. It is a pleasant-sounding word, kind of Hawaii-like. It had a nice hot tub, and the screen protected us from the umpty-squat billions of bugs that Florida is known for.

A decade later, we were adding a bedroom to our home in Texas. I told the contractor that I also wanted to add a lanai. He said, "What's a lanai?" I described it and said that I wanted a place for a hot tub in it. "Oh, so you want a hot tub room?"

"Okay, call it what you will."

A few years ago, my daughter bought a home on a canal on

Marco Island, Florida. Naturally, it had a lanai. Every modern home in Florida seems to have a lanai, and no one has to ask, "What is a lanai?"

Now I live in Las Vegas, Nevada, where the only bug between here and Santa Monica is an old Volkswagen. I can drop "lanai" from my vocabulary. Nobody in this vast Mojave Desert has ever heard of one.

Jobsite Seminary

Apocryphal: of doubtful authenticity, although widely circulated as being true

Several years ago, I worked in East Arkansas on a flood control project for the Memphis District of the US Army Corp of Engineers. Some of my co-workers and I routinely discussed religions, especially denominations in Christianity. My wife, at that time, was a Catholic, and I began attending Mass with her. My co-workers were from various denominational backgrounds; Noel was from the Church of Christ, Donnie attended the Church of God, and John was a Jehovah's Witness. They compared the wording of passages of scriptures from their Bibles: the King James Version (KJV), the Revised Standard Version (RSV), and the Jehovah's Witness bible, the New World Translation of the Holy Scriptures. (NWT) We found that the KJV and the RSV substantially agreed; however, they were in a different style of English. The Jehovah's Witness was different. Then, my friends asked me about the Catholic Bible. How was it different from the Protestant Bibles? I didn't know, but I vowed to find out.

After some months of study and research, I felt enlightened and ready to share my new knowledge. In the year 382, Pope Damasas II commissioned Jerome and his staff to compile the various Hebrew and Greek scriptural writings into one book. It took Jerome 20 years to complete the task. His finished work, the very first complete bible, became known as the Vulgate Bible. Jerome translated the Hebrew and Greek texts from the Alexandrian Canon of Scripture. It covered biblical history from creation to the first century of the Christian Era. It is still the official bible of the Catholic Church.

When protestants started compiling their own Bibles around the 15th century, they initially translated from the Vulgate Bible. Later, when translating from the Jerusalem Canon of scriptures, they set aside the scriptures covering the three centuries immediately preceding the Christian Era. Those they labeled as "Apocrypha." Eventually, they deleted them altogether from the printed bibles.

So, there is a most significant difference between the Catholic and Protestant Bibles. They are similar, except the protestant bibles have deleted the books that cover some three hundred years immediately before the Christian Era and see them as apocryphal. The Catholic Bibles include those seven books. Rather than apocryphal, they are known as the Deuterocanonical books. They are interesting reading because some interesting historical events occurred during that period. We might never have known about Cleopatra, the Ptolemaic Kingdom, or Alexander the Great if it weren't for the original bible, the Vulgate, and the many Bibles that were translated from it.

I tried to explain all of this to my Protestant co-workers. I don't think they were ready for it.

I DIDN'T CLIMB
MOUNTAINS EITHER

Arduous: involving or requiring
strenuous effort; difficult and tiring

I first arrived in the Northwest in the spring of 1957. I was 19 years old and working as a drywall finisher in Southern California when an Arizona company retained me to tape the drywall on a military housing project at Fort Lewis, Washington. I arrived in Tacoma on March 10th and went to work on March 11th, and it sometimes seems that I worked every day for the next 45 years. Most of my years as a young adult were spent in the Tacoma and Puyallup areas. I lived there, off and on, for a dozen years. It was early 1969 when I left the region for the final time.

The major outdoor activities of western Washington had to do with the mountains. The Cascade Mountains were an ideal range for skiing. I never skied. I was always too busy working. Besides that, many skiers seem to get laid up with an ankle in traction until they are healed enough to return to work. I couldn't afford that. A person working construction work to provide for a wife and family cannot afford to risk his livelihood.

Another big sport that was popular among an elite segment of the population was mountain climbing. Seattle was a hotbed of professional mountain climbers, including some of the most famous in the world. They included Scott Fischer, Greg Nance, and the Whitaker Brothers, Jim and Lou. You have heard of Jim Whitaker. He became the first American to reach the summit of Mount Everest as a member of the American Mount Everest Expedition led by Norman Dyhrenfurth; they ran out of oxygen but managed to reach the summit. That was May 1st, 1963.

I didn't climb mountains either, for some of the same reasons that I didn't slide down them. Another reason was that it simply didn't make sense to spend that kind of time and effort just because the mountain happened to be there.

My youthful years, filled with agility and energy, are way behind me now. My mountain now is to walk across the parking lot from the car to the grocery store on a hot summer day without panting bulldog style. That is as <u>arduous</u> a task as I will ever need.

Southern Cross

Austral: Relating to the southern hemisphere.

It was about the time when Jesus's apostles started to spread the Gospel of Christ. Claudius Ptolemy studied the Southern Cross from his home in Alexandria, Egypt, and documented it in his notes. Fourteen Centuries later, Amerigo Vespucci used the constellation to navigate the <u>Austral</u> seas. Another 500 years later, the United States acknowledged it when it was embroiled in a fight for its life against the Imperial Japanese Army.

It was on May 27th, 1942, on the island of New Caledonia, that the United States Army activated a new 23rd Infantry Division. They called it the Americal Division and designed the Southern Cross shoulder sleeve insignia showing the four stars of the Southern Cross on a field of deep blue. I was honored to wear that insignia for eighteen months while serving in the Americal Division in the Panama Canal Zone in the mid-1950s.

The Southern Cross is meat for legends, myths, poetry, and songs. We cannot see it from the United States. In fact, I could not see it from Panama when I was in the Southern Cross Division. I was still in the northern hemisphere.

Five decades later, when I cruised around the southern tip of South America, I first had the opportunity to see the Southern

---

Cross. It was a thrill that I had anticipated for years. During world cruises in 2008 and again in 2020, those opportunities repeated many times, and I never got tired of scanning the <u>austral</u> skies at night for the Southern Cross.

UPSTATE

Impregnable: strong enough to resist or withstand attack; not to be taken by force; unconquerable.

After a plane change in Baltimore, we flew into Albany, New York, arriving in the early afternoon. A friendly fellow we met on the plane was excited to meet folks from Texas coming to tour his part of the world. He lived in Saratoga Springs, which was on our route northward.

We picked up our rental car and drove north. At Saratoga Springs we stopped for dinner at Sperry's, the fine-dining restaurant our fellow plane traveler had told us about. Yes, like he said, Sperry's was very good. Costly too. Oh well, we are on vacation.

We continued north and checked into a Hampton Inn on the western shore of Lake George. This country is even more beautiful than I had expected.

The following morning, right outside our hotel, there was a big celebration and a reenactment of a battle from some foregone century. We enjoyed talking with the costumed re-enactors and marveling at the extent to which they go for these historical observances. Those were serious people. I asked one of the sutlers what Revolutionary War battle they were reenacting. He looked at me like I had just spit in his mess kit and informed me that it was from the French and Indian War. I decided against asking any more questions.

11

I hated to leave town, but we had much more to see, and I am eager to see Plattsburgh again and revive a couple of memories from nearly 50 years earlier.

We stopped for a tour of the great Fort Ticonderoga. This giant fort played a crucial part in several wars and battles. The French built it at a "narrows" on Lake Champlain's south end and Lake George's north end. Manned by upwards of 4,000 soldiers, it was impregnable. No enemy vessel could get past it or effectively attack it. The fort is in beautiful condition, including the surrounding 2,000 acres declared America's Most Historic Landscape.

We left the lake and drove high into the Adirondacks to Lake Placid. Lake Placid and nearby Saranac Lake have hosted the 1932 and 1980 Winter Olympics. At 1,800 feet high, the air was crisp and clean. From the looks of the homes and the boats, Lake Placid is not a place for paupers.

It was only another hour north from Saranac Lake, through Ausable Chasm to Plattsburgh. My mind quickened as we drove into the beautiful town sitting on the west bank of giant Lake Champlain. I remembered the little cabins beside the water where I stayed in June 1958. I remembered strolling along the water's edge and looking across the lake at the Vermont shoreline.

We checked into our previously reserved Best Western and found a nice restaurant overlooking the lake. It had been a big day. A good dinner and a bottle of Northern New York burgundy was an excellent way to wrap it up.

The following morning, we found a lakeside park, perfect for strolling, relaxing, and snapping pictures. I'm still thinking back to 1958 and those little white cottages down behind the Noah's Ark Restaurant. The image is still in my mind, but five decades of new development have long since wiped out the scenes that I recall.

I would be happy to hang in for about a week and explore the rest of the Adirondacks. But that could not be. We were headed for Quebec.

IRA HAYES,
THE PIMA HERO

**Intriguing: Intriguing is rousing one's
curiosity or interest; fascinating.**

The story of Ira Hayes is as <u>intriguing</u> as it is sad. His story is
told in a song by Johnny Cash in The Ballad of Ira Hayes, recorded
and made popular in 1961. Its words tell the story of Ira Hayes, one
of the six marines who became famous for having raised the U.S. flag
on Mount Suribachi during the Battle of Iwo Jima in World War II.

On November 10, 1954, he attended the dedication of the
Marine Corps War Memorial in Arlington, Virginia, which was
modeled after the photograph of Hayes and five other Marines
raising the second flag on Iwo Jima.

Ira Hamilton Hayes was a Pima Indian born at Sacaton, Arizona,
on 12 January 1923. He was an Akimel O'odham Indigenous
American. He was an enrolled member of the Gila River Indian
Community in Pinal and Maricopa counties in Arizona.

Hayes was commemorated in art and film, before and after his
death. In 1949, he portrayed himself raising the flag in the movie
Sands of Iwo Jima, starring John Wayne. He was the subject of an
article by journalist William Bradford Huie, which was adapted for
the feature film The Outsider (1961), starring Tony Curtis as Hayes.

In 2006, Hayes was portrayed by Adam Beach in the World War II movie Flags of Our Fathers, directed by Clint Eastwood.

After the war, Hayes suffered from post-traumatic stress disorder and descended into alcoholism. Following a night of heavy drinking on January 23–24, 1955, he died of exposure to cold and alcohol poisoning. He was buried with full military honors at Arlington National Cemetery on February 2, 1955.

We drove up from Obregon, in southern Sonora, Mexico, on April 6th, 2006, and toured the Gila River Indian Reservation and the town of Sacaton. Our visions of the features of the little desert town were rendered unclear by our misty eyes as we reflected upon it being the homeplace of an American hero, Ira Hayes.

Hershel

Loquacious: tending to talk a great deal; talkative

My friend, Hershel, was a talker, the most <u>loquacious</u> among our little circle of friends. That's not all bad. One was never bored around Hershel. We just didn't know if half the tales he told were true, but now and then, one would be provable. That's what kept us on our toes.

Hershel liked to go down to the La Jolla Cove on weekends when he wasn't busy at the junkyard. He was a lover of seals. He said he could sit all day watching his seals play. He assumed them to be harbor seals, but he didn't know. He was fascinated at how they could swim up to a rock at top speed and just seem to leap out of the water onto the rock.

One day, as Hershel was enjoying his pinnipeds barking and cavorting, he spoke to a passerby about how much he loved to watch his seals. But Lo! The local fellow who walked the cove every morning told Hershel, "I hate to be the one to break it to you, but those are not seals. They are sea lions." Hershel was shattered! He made up his mind on the spot that he would never visit the La Jolla Cove again. He now makes pilgrimages up the coast to Point Reyes, where the rocks are laden with speckled harbor seals.

THEM OLD COTTONFIELDS

Malodorous: smelling very unpleasant

It was in the early 1950s, and I was about 14 years old, give or take. My best friends in those days were the Cox family. In the early fall, Mr. Cox decided to take his family to pick cotton for a week near Charleston, in southeast Missouri, right on the Mississippi River. Charleston is in the Bootheel.

Missouri's Bootheel is that little chunk of southeast Missouri that hangs down in what should be Arkansas. The Bootheel was created as an indirect result of a massive earthquake back in 1811, but that is another story.

The cotton was better in the Bootheel than what we had closer to home, and the owner there was paying 4 cents per pound for picking the cotton, which was about a penny more than we were getting in Randolph County, Arkansas. I was invited to go along with them. I could make some money for school clothes.

The farmer we worked for provided an old sharecropper house that sat at the edge of the cotton field for us to stay in. It was an old wood frame house with four rooms. The utilities were a pitcher pump in the front yard and an outdoor toilet in the back yard, with no electricity or running water. Furnishings were nil. We slept on blankets that we laid on the rough wooden floor.

In addition to Mr. & Mrs. Cox, Virgil, and Effie, the Cox Family included Leo, the twins Leon and Levon, and the girls Merlene and Earlene. Both Merlene and Earlene were, at separate times, objects of my affection, but those are other stories.

We were all hot and dirty all week. It's hard to bathe at an outdoor pitcher pump under any circumstances. One afternoon after we had finished work, one of the twins suggested that we walk to the Mississippi River, about a half-mile away, and take a bath by swimming in the river. We walked about a mile before we found a bank that was clear enough to get to the edge of the river. We then waded through sticky, black, wet mud up to our ankles, getting to the water. Both the mud and the water were about as <u>malodorous</u> as a St. Louis sewer might be. In fact, that's likely where the water got its terrible stink. Our swim didn't last long. We waded back through the mud, and by the time we got back to the house, it was dark. We were muddy and sweaty, and needed the pitcher pump bath twice as bad as we had needed it before. It is hard to bathe in darkness in cold water pumped out of the ground while swatting mosquitoes.

Many memories were made in the cotton fields of my youth. When we were young, we couldn't wait to get away from that work. Now, I look back with fondness on those memories. Can memories from fast food joints and video parlors compare? I don't think so.

STORM IN BARCELONA

**Ma'am: a term of respectful or polite
address used for a woman.**

It was our first auto-tour trip to Europe, and we planned it down to the last detail. However, when we landed in Barcelona, somehow, our bags were still on the tarmac back in Frankfurt, Germany.

There's one constant about touring in Europe. Prepare to be unprepared.

I supposed Barcelona would be as good as any place to lay in for a couple of days. We would pick up our Peugeot rental and start trying to learn road signs in Catalan and Spanish. We negotiated an extension of our reservation at the Barcelona Hilton and canceled our reservation at Toulouse, France, our first intended stop heading north for the Normandy Coast.

Our seventh-floor room at the Barcelona Hilton was spacious and tidy. The lights were some kind of 220-volt fluorescent things of a type that I'd never seen before. I never did understand the TV remote control. The third night we were there, we went to a Flamenco show that lasted until midnight. (I've never figured out when Europeans sleep.)

Back at the hotel, we'd hardly gone to sleep when a violent thunderstorm rolled through the city. Lightning was constant. We were sound asleep when suddenly the TV was blasting at the volume of an above-ground nuclear test, and all the lights were flickering on. I managed to find the controls and get everything turned off, and get my heart rate back down to about 155 when suddenly it happened again. During the next two hours, every time the lightning flashed, there would be a loud crash of thunder, and the same thing would happen again. I tried to unplug the TV, but it was wired direct. I didn't get much sleep that night.

We went downstairs for breakfast at 8:00 AM. The smiling little Spanish desk clerk greeted us, "Good morning, Sir. Did you sleep well?" I mumbled, "Yes, ma'am." I was too tired to try to explain it.

TUCKER PRISON FARM

Misanthropy: A dislike of humankind.

Wayon was an average kid in grade school. By the time we got into high school, there seemed to be a mean streak deep inside him that welled up occasionally. When I came home on leave from the army, my former girlfriend, Merlene, asked me what I thought of Wayon. I told her she would be better off staying away from him. Did she? The next time I came home, following my discharge, I found that Merlene and Wayon were married and that he was in prison at Tucker Prison Farm down below Pine Bluff.

Some years later, Wayon was out of prison and I spent an afternoon with. He told me at least a hundred tales about his experiences and misadventures at Tucker Farm. I could see that Wayon harbored a streak of mistrust and <u>misanthropy</u> toward everyone. I had never faced misanthropy before. It was unsettling. Apparently, Wayon had been so incorrigible in the prison farm that the guards told him that he had better not come back to Tucker and that if he did, they would kill him.

I never saw my old classmate again. I learned later that he violated parole by some misdeed and was sent back to Tucker Farm to serve out his time. I learned also that shortly after he went back to Tucker farm, he was dead. The official cause of death, by the Prison officials, was recorded as pneumonia. His body was returned to his family for burial in a sealed casket. Family members had to bury him without seeing his body. There was never a doubt, by his wife and siblings, nor by me, for that matter, about Wayon's cause of death. The guards said they would kill him, and they did.

CALIFORNIA SMOG

**Omnipresent: Widely or constantly
encountered; common or widespread.**

We often hear about the smog problems in our major cities, with the Los Angeles, California, area winning the prize as the poster child for smog problems. Californians now pay some of the nation's highest gasoline prices due to the production costs for the pollution control components in the fuel. It remains a mystery how the residents can contend with the air pollution continually.

Back in 1964, I was working as a drywall finisher in Southern California. Occasionally, I would be assigned a house – mansion, I might say – to tape and finish high on a hill in Burbank. It was an experience not soon to be forgotten. From midmorning, I could look out across the valley at the yellowish-brown blanket of smog that was <u>omnipresent</u> throughout the valley. As the hours passed, the insidious blanket of smog started to rise. By about 2 PM, it reached the houses where I worked. Some people could stand it. I could not. I suppose my eyes are hyper-sensitive. Anyway, the burning was untenable. As a remedy, I started arising at 3:30 am in my Ventura apartment in order to start work in Burbank at 6 am. That way, when the smog reached the elevation where I was working, I was through for the day. During the six decades since, I have never had to endure such air pollution.

No wonder Californians build houses out in the mountains where periodic forest fires come through and burn them all down. The answer? Move to Texas! And they are doing it.

Piazza San Marco

Palmiest: glorious, prosperous, or flourishing

Anyone who has visited Venice will acclaim its beauty and magnificence. Indeed, Venice was haughty and powerful for nearly 1400 years. Its armies compelled the world's applause, and its navies ruled the oceans. Those were its <u>palmiest</u> days. They are no more. Venice has fallen prey to age, neglect, and the forces of nature.

One can cruise into the Grand Canal on a cruise ship or travel overland by auto and train. We have done it both ways and cannot find fault with either. On one occasion, we used our hotel in Cittadella as a home base and drove to the rail station in Venezia Mestre, where there was adequate auto parking. Then, we rode the train a short four miles to the train station in Venice. From there, one can catch a vaporetto, a kind of marine taxi, to anywhere in the city.

There's much to see in the city, but St. Mark's Square, or Piazza San Marco, is a central feature that attracts every tourist. St. Mark's Square is dominated by St. Mark's Basilica, from which the piazza gets its name. The Cathedral is built entirely of precious marble brought from the Orient. A tour of the Basilica's interior and the Doge's Palace immediately adjacent to the Basilica is a must.

St. Mark's Basilica was built in the ninth century to contain and preserve the remains of St. Mark, the Disciple and Evangelist. One might wonder how the bones of the Evangelist got from the Holy Land to Venice. I wondered also.

St. Mark, known universally as Mark, the Evangelist, and historically recognized as the author of the Gospel of Mark, lived in Alexandria, where he founded the Episcopal See of Alexandria. As an evangelist, Mark busied himself preaching the Gospel of Christ and converting Alexandrians to Christianity. Much like the Pharisees in Jerusalem, the pagans of the city resented his efforts to turn the Alexandrians away from worshipping their traditional gods. In AD 68, they placed a rope around his neck and dragged him through the streets until he was dead.

During the next several hundred years, Venetians made numerous expeditions to Alexandria to recover the Saint's remains, but time after time, the efforts failed. In 828, Venetians learned that the Alexandrian church that housed the Saint's bones was designated to be torn down by the Muslims (which it was) and the materials were to be reused to build more mosques. (which they were) They devised a stratagem. They stole the bones from the church, separated them, and packed them in cases of pork lard. The Muslims abhorred anything associated with pigs, so they refused to even look at the cases of lard. In this manner, the bones of St. Mark were taken to Venice and have rested in the Basilica ever since.

Yes, the old city is decaying and slowly being claimed by rising waters in the lagoon. We see it in the daytime, and it can be depressing. In the evening, however, when the tourists return to their cruise ships, the crowds are gone, and the magic of Venice returns. This is the time to board a sleek jet-black ornamented gondola and tour the city.

COMPUTERS

Perplexity: A state of confusion or a complicated and challenging situation or thing

Whether we talk about it or not, my Facebook friends and I have had some similar experiences. In the last three or four decades, we have all bought computers. We have had to learn how to use them. We had to learn DOS, and then everything changed to Windows. We learned WordStar, and then we had to learn WordPerfect. That was not a keeper, so we had to learn Microsoft Word. We have had to learn Facebook. We have had to deal with hackers. The perplexity of it becomes overwhelming. And the worst of it is when we try to get something done, and the program tells you that you have entered an incorrect password. The overwhelming exasperation is that you cannot argue with the blasted thing.

MISS JUANITA

Preceptor: a teacher or instructor.

It is a rare few in Randolph County, Arkansas, that could remember the days before "Consolidation," when all the rural one-room schools in the area were shut down and students began being bussed into town to the big school. Richardson School, the school where I started, was one of those schools.

Richardson School sat, appropriately, on Richardson Road. I was five years old when I started there. It was summer school. No, summer school was not for dummies who couldn't pass their classes. In those days, summer school was part of the regular school term. Classes started early during the summer months and then curtailed during the cotton-picking season, as everybody had to pick cotton in those days. It was a way for kids to make money to buy school clothes. When a kid goes barefooted all summer, he outgrows the shoes that he wore to school last spring.

Richardson School had eight grades in one room, and our single <u>preceptor</u> was Miss Juanita Kerley. Miss Kerley remained Miss Kerley all of her life as she never married. After consolidation and the Richardson School closed, Miss Kerley started teaching in Maynard School, and for the next half-century, she taught virtually every student who attended Maynard High School. She is fondly remembered by hundreds, if not thousands.

Richardson School was more than a mile, maybe two, from our home, back through our farm, through woods and fields, and across another property to Richardson Road, where the school was located.

My sister, Jo Ann, was just three years older than I was. She and I rode our horse, Old Ribbon, to school. Hallie and Elsie Brooks had their house and a little store near the school. My mother made arrangements with Hallie, and he allowed us to keep Ribbon in his pens during the day. Then, we would bridle her and ride her home after school. We didn't have a saddle. Hallie and Elsie's daughter, Joyce, was my age and my classmate. She became my friend and my playmate.

My friend Joyce grew up and became the postmaster in my hometown, and she served in that function for 40 years before retiring. She kept track of our Maynard High School Class of 1955 alumni and was always my source of information when I wanted to inquire about some former classmates.

Some years after Richardson School closed, Hallie Brooks bought the building and moved his store into it.

I was notified in the summer of 2024 of the passing of my friend, Joyce. I know that many people remember Joyce, but how many remember that the aging white building, Hallie Brooks's Store, on the hill on Richardson Road, used to be the Richardson School?

BIRTHPLACE OF PIZZA

Brioche: a light, sweet yeast bread typically in the form of a small round roll

It was January 17th, 2020, and in the early weeks of our intended four-month, around-the-world cruise. In the city of Messina, on the island of Sicily, I enjoyed a <u>brioche</u> and caffè latte at an al fresco café while doing some people-watching, one of my favorite pastimes.

I engaged in a discussion with a couple from Peekskill, New York. In conversation, I shared that I was disappointed that we did not go to Naples and that we stopped in Messina instead. I wanted to visit Naples and have a pizza in the hometown of pizzas, the place where they originated.

The lady told me: "You'll have to be careful. Their pizzas are not like ours." I didn't say it aloud, but "Hey, lady! Do you think pizzas started in New York and eventually spread to Italy? And maybe the recipe got corrupted before it got to Naples?"

Yes, people are funny.

JEFFERSON CITY, OR CHESTERFIELD?

Prerogative: a right or privilege exclusive to a particular individual or class.

It was the spring of 1983. I had fallen in love with a lady in Jefferson City, Missouri. I had been divorced the previous year and felt that the time was right to marry once again. I was 46 years old. Sue Gardner was four years my junior and had been divorced a couple of years. Sue's divorce had been a painful experience, not of her choosing. She was a Christian lady and strongly believed marriage should be a lifetime commitment. Her husband had felt no such responsibility. The whole affair was distasteful and saddened Sue greatly. As our romance grew, we decided to set a date for marriage. It would be June 24ᵗʰ, 1983.

Sue was a longstanding member of Capital City Christian Church, which was just a couple of blocks from her house. As Christians, we both preferred to be married in a church, and the obvious choice would be the church down the street where she attended and sang in the choir. She talked to her pastor, Gary Baker, about it and then brought me the troubling news. She was almost distraught that Pastor Gary told her that he would not marry us. It seems that Pastor Gary thought that I had too many Catholic leanings. I suppose that he thought I would pollute her mind, maybe even jeopardize her salvation.

Having been married previously to an Independent Christian Church preacher, Sue knew plenty of pastors around the Missouri area. She had a pastor friend in Chesterfield, Missouri, who was glad to perform the ceremony for us.

I felt more than a little miffed that Pastor Gary thought I wasn't good enough to marry in his church. As the pastor, it was his prerogative to marry us or not. Thank goodness, it didn't detract us from the happiness that we shared for the next 20 years before cancer took her away from me.

Is there a modern Nostradamus?

**Prescient: Having or showing knowledge
of events before they take place.**

It is difficult for folks like me to take people seriously who claim
to see into the future. There have been too many uneducated and
unlearned preachers who have forecast the end of the world. They
don't count. They are just inferring something from the scriptures
that the scriptures didn't say. On the other hand, there are those who
claim to have intuitions or visions. They are the fortune tellers, palm
readers, and such. It is hard to take them very seriously.

But then there are those who have made their mark in the
world. The renowned French astrologer and seer from the 16th
century, Nostradamus, continues to captivate the world even 500
years after his death. His mysterious writings, compiled in 1555
as Les Propheties, have been analyzed and debated for centuries.
And then there was Jeane Dixon, who predicted the assignation
of President John F. Kennedy. Richard Nixon created a cabinet on

counterterrorism based on Dixon's recommendations. Dixon was also an advisor to Nancy Reagan.

So, it appears that the gift is real. If Nostradamus and Jeane had true <u>prescient</u> powers to foretell future events, who's to say that others don't have the same gifts?

TOWER DOGS

___

**Bravura: Great technical skill and brilliance
shown in a performance or activity**

I lived in Texas for about half of my adult life. In Texas, we like
to talk about what is biggest, prettiest, sometimes the flattest, or the
highest. Many folks are surprised to learn how many mountains and
mountain ranges are within the Texas borders.

The highest natural point in Texas is Guadalupe Peak, at 8,751
feet. The tallest building is the JPMorgan Chase Tower, at 1,002
feet. But that is not the tallest manmade structure in Texas. In fact,
it's only half as tall as the tallest structure in Texas, the Liberman
Broadcast Tower in Era, which is 2,000 feet – more than one-third
of a mile high and 200 stories. And some brave workers climb those
kinds of towers as part of their daily work.

A couple of such workers were Boyce and Eugene. I met them
on the island of Adak, about 1,500 miles out on Alaska's Aleutian
Island Chain. We were all construction workers on Adak that
summer in 1965. I would say we were all good at what we did, or
our bosses wouldn't have paid the big bucks to send us out there. We
were building a large administration building and air terminal. We
were carpenters, pipefitters, plumbers, electricians, drywall hangers,
finishers, painters, etc. There is nothing exciting about any of it.

___

Then Boyce and Eugene showed up. These guys were different. "What do you guys do?"

"We are tower climbers." Well, that didn't help much.

Here's the story. Boyce and Eugene were "Tower Dogs," as they call themselves. They erect towers, and they climb them to do repairs and maintenance. They came from Texas, where there are dozens of towers that are up to 2,000 feet tall. They were journeymen, not fazed by our 1,200-foot-tall towers on Adak. Their boss had a maintenance contract for some of the Adak towers. Boyce and Eugene would climb the towers daily until they checked and tightened every bolt, and then the painters would come.

I admired Boyce and Eugene for a couple of reasons. First off, these Panhandle boys (I think they were from Lubbock) brought their lizard-skin cowboy boots with them. After work, they showered up and looked like they were ready to go to a dance hall rather than slouching around in coveralls as the painters did. But secondly, it was their work that fascinated me. You have to picture this. First off, The Aleutian Islands have some of the rottenest weather on the planet. Half the time, there is a fog (or clouds) that blankets the ground early in the morning and then only lifts a couple of hundred feet as the day wears on.

Every time those tower dogs strap on their safety harness and then grab hold of the steel at the base of the tower, they display an indisputable level of <u>bravura</u>. I remain impressed to this day. I have watched these guys disappear into a cloud only a couple hundred feet from the ground and not see them again until evening. I don't know how much these guys got paid, but whatever it was, they earned it.

So, friends, the next time you drive past a steel tower sticking more than a quarter-mile straight up, think about the men who have been at the top of that tower, then imagine yourself up there.

Arabs and Berbers

**Profanation: Profanation is the act
of saying or doing something terribly
offensive or blasphemous.**

It was smack on 7:30 AM in Gibraltar when I paid my fare and climbed aboard the big trimaran ferry. I watched the other passengers as they followed. There were people of about every stripe and race, almost invariably much darker of skin than I. It might be hard for me to appear to fit in today. That is what a tourist must try to do in a foreign country, especially a country that the United States routinely issues travel warnings about.

To say I was excited would be a gross understatement. I had had Tangier on my radar for a long time. In other countries, I have found foreign-looking things and foreign-looking people, but always with things and people intermixed that we were familiar with.

When I go to a foreign country, I want to get away from people who look like me and talk like me. If I wanted to see my kind of people, I could stay at home. No! There is no novelty in that. I want to go to a place that is thoroughly and uncompromisingly foreign, with nothing about it to compromise its foreignness – nothing to remind me of any other people or any other land under the sun. And this is it! Tangier is my destination – my mecca! Tangier is a foreign land if there ever was one.

Ashore, on the north coast of Africa, I was soon amidst every kind of humanity that I could imagine. One doesn't doubt the city's reputation: it is a giant nest of spies, romantics, and villains. This is the infamous Barbary Coast, from which, for centuries, Barbary pirates terrorized the northern Mediterranean coast, ravaging towns and carrying off the comely maidens to take home and sell to the wealthy Arabs. These people are from every stripe and ancestry. Some trace their blood and culture back to the Canaanites that Joshua chased out of Jericho nearly four thousand years ago. Others still wear the Moorish garb and resentment from being chased off the Iberian Peninsula by Ferdinand II and Isabella I some five hundred years ago. They trace their history back to the night of time. Then there are the Jews. When the Christian crusaders chased the Moors back across the Strait, back to Africa, they rounded up the Jews and evicted them, too.

And then there are the rest – the Arabs and Berbers. Once bitter enemies, now one can hardly tell them apart. And, there are the swarthy Riffians from the mountains – born cutthroats and real genuine African Negroes, as black as anthracite.

I wondered what they were thinking as I walked among the kaftan-clad men in yellow slippers and the burka-shrouded women. What was their life like? Did the men never see the faces of their wives until they married? Had the woman, who opened one eye just enough to see a person with white skin, ever been seen by a man? Do I dare look at one? I already know that, as a Christian infidel from America, if I were to set foot in a mosque or a Muslim household, I would have defiled the place, and I would never see my family again.

As I gingerly descended the concrete steps down to the subterranean Medina, taking one step at a time as there were no handrails and nothing to hang onto, I thought of my wife safely enjoying an aperitif back in the hotel in Gibraltar. She had told me, with her practiced disapproving scowl, that I could take my life into my own hands if I wanted to, but she was sure as blazes not going to Tangier. She had seen enough of the Arab world on our visits to Casablanca.

I thought of my wife's admonitions as I roamed through the souks and stalls of the Medina. There were hawkers of every stripe. There were shops selling fish from both the Atlantic and the Mediterranean. There were markets with dozens of kinds and colors of olives. Then, the spice markets looked like they had fifty different spices in different colors. Who could know what they all were? The sights and aromas were beyond description.

There were dozens of stalls, no bigger than a shower stall in a Super 8, where an angry-looking Arab sat cross-legged on the floor and could reach every item, whatever they happened to be, if somebody wanted to buy one.

As I walked among the shops and stalls, as well as the Arabs, Berbers, Riffians, and Bedouins from the desert, I felt enveloped by a culture that I had heretofore never imagined. It would have been a profanation to have laughed in jest or bandy or engaged in frivolous chat with anyone that I encountered in this strange world.

I survived the Medina and caught a cab to take me to Hercules Cave, just a few miles from town facing the Atlantic. Tangier is where Hercules, supposedly clad in his lion skin, landed four thousand years ago, came ashore, met his enemy, Anitus, and brained him with his club. The cave was a great visit. Hercules's writing is supposedly still on the cave walls, although I didn't see it. I did not know that Hercules could write and what language it would likely be in.

I made a brief visit at Cap Spartel, a lighthouse on a promontory looking out over the entrance to the Strait of Gibraltar, a full thousand feet above the surf. From the northernmost point in the African continent, the commanding view is breathtakingly awe-inspiring.

Back across the Strait, in the safe and sanitary surrounds of Gibraltar, I knew that I had truly been in a foreign country.

THE TEXAS JEWBOY

**Provocateur: a person who provokes trouble,
causes dissension, or the like; agitator.**

Texas, far beyond any other state, I believe, has produced some unforgettable characters. I don't mean they were unforgettable because of their accomplishments, but rather because they were, well, different. The most famous in our generation is, by far, Willie Nelson. But there have been others. Hondo Crouch. Hondo was a writer, humorist, and owner-self-proclaimed Mayor of Luckenbach, Texas. Who could suspect that Hondo had been an All-American swimmer at the University of Texas? And then there's Ray Wylie Hubbard. His song, "Up against the Wall, Redneck Mother," is autobiographical: "He's not responsible for what he's doin', his mother made him that way."

And there's Kinky Friedman and his band, the Texas Jewboys. Kinky Friedman is undoubtedly the most unique Jew who ever moved from Chicago to Texas. His band members were almost as kinky as the Kinkster himself. They included Little Jewford, Big Nig, Panama Red, Wichita Culpepper, Sky Cap Adams, Rainbow Colours, and Snakebite Jacobs. Kinky and the Jewboys recorded such songs as "They ain't making Jews like Jesus anymore" and "Get your biscuits in the oven and your buns in the bed,"

Some of the quotes that Kinky left us were as unique as the Texas Jewboy himself.

Here's one: "Well, I just said that Jesus and I were both Jewish and that neither of us ever had a job, we never had a home, we never married, and we traveled around the countryside irritating people."

I only met Kinky one time. He was sitting on a picnic table under the live oak trees at Luckenbach playing his guitar and sucking on a Lone Star longneck. That was probably forty years ago.

Yes, Kinky was indeed a <u>provocateur</u> extraordinaire. He will not soon be forgotten.

THE HOE

Publican: One who owns a pub

We country folks, having grown up in the dry hills of north Arkansas, didn't know anything about pubs; probably never heard of one. There were bars, taverns, and honkytonks above Missouri's state line, but none in our "dry" county. Tavern owners in Ripley County, Missouri, liked to laugh and say, "Missouri gets the money. Arkansas gets the cans." It was true. The roadside between my hometown and the state line looked like it was outlined with neon lights at night as the headlights reflected on the empty beer cans that had been tossed from the cars.

I was finally introduced to pubs when visiting England. In the coastal town of Plymouth, we trekked to the Pub on the Hoe for dinner. I had to ask Burley, the <u>Publican</u>, what the menu item "Bangers and Mash" was. He simply answered that they were sausage and mashed potatoes. That was simple enough.

You might wonder about the Pub on the "Hoe." The Plymouth Hoe, referred to locally as the Hoe, is a large south-facing open public space in the city of Plymouth, overlooking the Plymouth Harbor. The origin of the name is a little hazy. The name derives from the Anglo-Saxon word hoh, a sloping ridge shaped like an inverted foot and heel.

Incidentally, this is the harbor from which a shipload of Puritans on the Mayflower last saw land as they set out for the New World on September 16th, 1620.

There's a lot of history on The Hoe.

An hour before
Daylight

**Relinquish: Voluntarily cease
to keep or claim; give up**

I suppose the last Democrat I voted for was Jimmy Carter. I don't apologize for voting for a Democrat even though, in the eyes of noted Republicans, Jimmy was not a good president. I voted for Jimmy Carter because I liked him. I still like him.

Several years ago, I was introduced to "An Hour Before Daylight," written by Jimmy Carter. The memoir is a poignant journey through the heart and soul of a bygone era, masterfully told by a statesman whose roots run deep in the fertile soil of rural Georgia. Having grown up in a rural environment, I saw dozens of anecdotes and descriptions in his young life that paralleled those of my own. It gave me the confidence I needed to start my own autobiography, which I finished and printed in 2005.

But I am a firm Republican now. You can <u>relinquish</u> any thoughts to the contrary.

MISS NORTHERN SUNSHINE

**Resplendence: Resplendence is a quality
of almost unbelievably majestic beauty**

It was my third long day of driving the Alaska Highway. This is
the same highway that American and Canadian military forces built
to connect the new frontier, an area threatened by Japan's Imperial
Army during World War II. It was initially named the Alaskan-
Canadian (Alcan) Military Highway.

It was in the spring of 1964. Back then, there were no satellite
radio stations, nor were there even tape players in cars. The signal
from Prince George, British Columbia, radio stations hardly reached
past the city limits. From there, I faced over a thousand miles of
gravel road with nothing to listen to except the road noise.

When I was about fifteen miles short of Whitehorse, Yukon, a
young native woman flagged me down. She was going to Whitehorse
and needed a ride. I thought this could be interesting. I was a young
single man. How could I ask for a better stroke of fortune? She was
probably in her late twenties and was either Eskimo or Indian. It's
hard to tell the difference. As she got in the car, I could see she was
already missing a few teeth, and she smelled as though she had just
climbed out of a tank of walrus grease. I rolled down my window,

and we took off for Whitehorse. At least I would have someone to talk with. I'd been talking to myself for two days.

Miss Sunshine Nushagak, or something like that, asked if I had a bottle. I didn't have one, so she said she knew a place where I could buy one in town. She inquired as to how long I was going to be there. She indicated that with a bottle now and then, she could take care of any and all my needs for as long as I wanted. I lied and said I was married. She wanted some vodka anyway. I lied again and said I didn't drink. She then asked, "Are you a preacher?"

I changed the subject. "Can you see the Northern Lights from here," I asked Miss Northern Sunshine.

She said, "The Northern Lights are bad spirits, especially when they are howling."

"Howling? What do you mean, howling?" She didn't want to talk about the spirits. I wondered if the bad spirits ever spoke to her about soap.

We arrived in Whitehorse, and I said "Goodbye" to Miss Northern Sunshine in front of the Klondike Hotel, and she shuffled across the street to the corner saloon. For the cost of a bottle of vodka, some old stampeder was going to have his needs taken care of tonight. It would not be me.

A few months later, I was on a night flight from the Aleutian Islands. The pilot announced that a beautiful display of the Aurora Borealis could be seen from the plane's left side. I moved to a vacant seat next to a window and watched the Northern Lights for nearly two hours. The <u>resplendence</u> was beautiful beyond words.

Most of the world's population has never beheld the Aurora Borealis, and they never will. I felt particularly blessed to sit in comfort, watch out the window of the old Douglas DC-6 airplane, and see such dazzling beauty.

SEBASTIAN LAMAR
OUTLAW

Retribution: punishment inflicted on someone as vengeance for a wrong or criminal act

Sebastian Lamar Outlaw was a Texas Ranger, a Deputy U.S. Marshal, and a gunman of note. He was also my cousin – third cousin, once removed, as I recall. Sebastian's father, Meshack Napoleon Outlaw, nicknamed his son "Bazz" when he was growing up in the cotton-growing region in Georgia, and the name stuck. He has been written about as "Bass" Outlaw and "Baz" Outlaw, but we think "Bazz" is most likely the correct moniker.

Bazz Outlaw has been the subject of a great number of printed articles and, in fact, one book, Whiskey River Ranger, written by Bob Alexander in 2016. Whiskey River Ranger is available from Texas A&M University Press and Amazon books.

Bazz was known as an excellent Ranger, known to be fast with a gun, with a deadly aim, and most of all, fearless in a battle. Importantly, as they said, "He had never come out second best in a gunfight." Captain Frank Jones, a famed nineteenth-century Texas Ranger, said of his company's top sergeant, Bazz Outlaw (1854-1894), "A man of unusual courage and coolness and in a close place is worth two or three ordinary men."

Although notable in many arrests and enforcement actions, Bazz had one significant flaw. He was a drinker, and when he was drunk, he was dangerously unpredictable. In fact, while stationed at a Ranger encampment in Alpine, Texas, Bazz was found to be drunk on duty and was fired from the Rangers.

Following his termination, Bazz learned that he could earn twice as much pay by working as a hired gun escorting loads of silver bars from a mine in Mexico's Sierra del Carmen Mountains west of Minas De Barroterán. Outlaw and two fellow Rangers, who resigned from the force, struck out for Mexico. Their jobs were to escort wagon loads of silver bars from Frontieriza Mining Co. near Santa Rosa to the railroad station at Barroterán. The 160-mile route through mountains and desert was known to be the home turf for cutthroats and unscrupulous co-conspirators who had been plaguing the shipments. It was a dangerous job, but it paid $2 per day instead of the $1 they received as Texas Rangers.

The Mexicans didn't like the Pistoleros, and they particularly didn't like the Diablo Tejanos – the Texas Devils – as Texas Rangers were known. Things went well for a couple of months with few incidents. The hired guns were doing their job.

The problem didn't occur on the trail. It happened in town. Outlaw was drinking in a cantina in the village, some arguments started, and a Mexican came at him with a knife. Bazz whipped out his six-shooter and shot the Mexican. He knew he was in a precarious situation. These cantina patrons were not his people. He lined up the other hombres against the wall and made them toss their weapons in the middle of the floor. He proceeded, gun in hand, to back out the door and hurry back to camp. Back at the cabin, Bazz and his compadres successfully stood off the dangerous mob.

Bazz soon decided that Mexico was not for him. He went back to Texas.

In early 1894, U.S. Marshall Dick Ware hired Bazz as a Deputy U.S. Marshall in transporting a prisoner to El Paso. In El Paso, Bazz got drunk and was causing a stir at Tillie Howard's Sporting House on Utah Street. In the flurry of activities, Bazz and a young ranger named Joe McKidrict drew their guns, and McKidrict fell dead. Constable John Selman stepped to the brothel door and shot it out with Outlaw. Selman was hit twice in the thigh. Bazz was fatally wounded. His law enforcement career and his life ended that evening in El Paso.

The marshal of El Paso gave the coroner Bazz's guns to pay for his burial. His grave can be found in Evergreen Cemetery. His tombstone reads: "B. L. Outlaw, 1854-1894, 1st Sgt Co D. F. B., State Forces, Dpy U.S. Marshal."

The story doesn't end there. Selman was a blowhard and a killer. He killed the infamous gunman, John Wesley Hardin, to enhance his own name as a gunfighter. Fact is, though, he ambushed Hardin and shot him in the back of the head.

But then: A new lawman came to town. George Scarborough was a Deputy U.S. Marshall who had previously served and scouted with Bazz Outlaw. They were friends. Scarborough and Selman were not friends. George blamed Selman for the killing of his friend, Bazz, although Selman had been acquitted in court.

On April 5th, 1796, on the second anniversary of his friend Outlaw's death, Scarborough supposedly called Selman into the alley behind the Wigwam Saloon, where two men argued and fought. Scarborough claimed both drew their guns. John Selman fell dead. Scarborough was acquitted of murder in the killing of Selman, but locals knew that he had done it in <u>retribution</u> for the killing of his friend, Bazz Outlaw.

Incidentally, in recent years, the matched set of Bazz's Colt pistols, beautifully engraved, have been sold and resold by Merz Antique Firearms of Minnesota. Photos and descriptions of the guns can be found on the web.

SINGING RIVER

**Riverine: relating to or situated on
a river or riverbank; riparian.**

Rivers are fascinating. They are alluring. and they are everywhere. Nearly every major city not situated on a seacoast sprang up on or near a river. Rivers are the stuff of legends. Rivers are the subjects of songs, movies, and Broadway shows. Who has not heard of "Old Man River" or "Moon River?" "Big River," a Broadway musical with music by Roger Miller, ran over 1,000 performances starting in 1985. And, of course, who can forget "River of No Return," the song and the movie starring Robert Mitchum and Marilyn Monroe?

But how about a river that can sing its own music? The river with the sonic reputation is the Pascagoula River near the Mississippi Gulf Coast, and the source of the Singing River Legend is somewhere deep in the ancient culture of the Pascagoula people.

The history of the Pascagoula people is shrouded in as much mystery and legend as the river itself. Although the origin of the Pascagoula people is unclear, they were one of many smaller bands, like the Biloxi, who lived together along the riverine systems of Mississippi and Louisiana, spilling into the Gulf of Mexico.

According to legend, the Biloxi and Pascagoula Tribes had co-existed for centuries before a split between the tribes resulted in the disappearance of both tribes from the region.

Altama, Chief of the Pascagoula, was in love with Anola, a Biloxi princess who was promised to the Chief of the Biloxi, going against traditional protocols. Altama and Anola wanted to be together regardless of the outcome. In response, the Biloxi made war on the Pascagoula, killing and taking them as slaves for the decision Altama had made. The Pascagoula were outnumbered and feared what the future held for them. Loyal to Altama, they decided as a group that it would be better to die at their own hand than become slaves. They would be reunited in the afterworld and live in a perfect world. Altama, Anola, and the Pascagoula people chose to drown themselves in the river, and while singing their death song, they joined hands and walked into the waters. According to local legend, the disappearance of the Pascagoula people directly connects with the sounds they hear from the water.

Back in the early 1980s, I lived on the Mississippi Gulf Coast near the Singing River Hospital—our electrical power came from Singing River Electric Cooperative. We even had a Singing River Market and a Singing River Brewing Company.

Nearly five decades have passed since I sat on the banks of the Singing River and listened to the night sounds. There was the normal gurgling of the current pushing the flowing water toward the Gulf. But I had heard it before. All the rivers sounded that way. This river, though, was known to be different. It was called the Singing River. I had heard drum drumming in the gravel in the shoals of Current River, but I had never heard a river sing.

So, what does the river sound like? It's been described as "flute-like." It's also been compared to the sound produced by rubbing the rim of a crystal glass.

The origin of the sound is unknown; however, what is known is that the river has been "singing" for a very long time. French settlers heard the river as early as 1699 and wrote about it.

MEALTIMES IN THE PAST

Supper: the evening meal, especially when dinner is eaten at midday

We haven't heard the word "sup" lately. In fact, I cannot remember when I have heard it, although it is a good word. It has a couple of meanings. The thought of it reminds me of life nearly a century ago when most of our population led agrarian lifestyles.

Back on the farm in Arkansas, many words and terms were used that we no longer see today. Naturally, we don't see terms like single tree, neck yoke, or trace chains, and I don't suppose we ever will again unless we go back to plowing fields with horses, which isn't very likely. So, we lose those words due to attrition. No great loss. We lose other terms, though, because we simply quit using them.

In the most recent past century, spring and summer days would find the farmer/dad working in his fields. He got up long before dawn, and by the time the sun came up, he had eaten breakfast and harnessed his mules for a day of fieldwork. His several hours of work in the sun made a long morning. At noon came dinnertime. You have seen it in old movies, and I am sure it has happened many times in real life. Mama rings the dinner bell to signal to Dad to unhook the team tie them where they would have shade and water, and come to the house to eat dinner.

Dinner was the main meal in the farmhouse. After dinner,

51

Dad would take his team and go back to the field. If he needed to, he would work until darkness came. If he were not being pushed, he might just work a couple of hours, then put the mules away and avoid working in the sun during the hottest hours of the afternoon.

As evening approached, it would soon be suppertime. That's the time when the kids playing outside had to come in for the evening meal. The supper would be something light. I recall that many evenings, it was simply cornbread and milk. The farmer had to bed down early, sometimes immediately after nightfall. As suppertime approached, if a neighbor had dropped by for a visit, he would be invited to "sup" with the family.

We didn't hear much about lunch in those days. The exception was the lunches for school days. Most kids had lunch pails to carry their small lunches in. Additionally, if the folks were doing day labor for other farmers, like chopping or picking cotton or making hay, they might pack a lunch to avoid having to come back to the house to eat. Thus, were some of the standard practices in the Midwest and South in the early 20th century as well as in previous centuries.

As time passed and agrarian life lessened, people lived and worked in urban environments. Dinnertime moved to the evening after the completion of the workday. The noon meal became a light meal during a lunch break, which was a brief thirty minutes for many. Eventually, supper, as a word, became all but forgotten. It is a good word, though, with a lot of history. Remember our Savior, Jesus. He and his disciples shared the famous "Last Supper" on a Thursday evening prior to his death by crucifixion the following day, on Good Friday.

Give it some thought. Retired folks are increasingly moving their noontime meal to earlier or middle afternoon and having only a light snack before bedtime. Folks, that is breakfast, dinner, and supper.

BLACK JIM WALL

Turned: Past tense of turn, which is to revolve, go around, rotate, or spin

Deep in the northern Ozark Mountains of Missouri, I found the cemetery where my grandmother, Clemmie Wilson, was buried and found the headstone that my grandfather, I.T. Wilson, had placed over a hundred years ago. The location was in the hilltop churchyard of Curry Church, the same church that I.T., Clemmie, and their three children attended in the early 20th century.

Southern Miller County is stunningly beautiful, picturesque, and interesting because of the history deep in those hills. I love to visit my grandmother's grave, scan the countryside, and ponder that murky history.

The Curry Church Cemetery and Clemmie's headstone face a beautiful broad valley of scattered meadows and wooded glades. In this valley 150 years ago lived James M. Wall, better known as Black Jim Wall, and his wife, Mildred. Black Jim and Mildred James had met and married in Virginia before moving to Missouri in the 1860s. On a creek in the valley floor, Jim had built a primitive home, a trading post, and a grist mill and named his little community Faith.

Frequent customers to Black Jim's grist mill were area settlers who would bring sacks of grain, usually by horseback, to have Jim grind it into wheat flour or corn meal. Jim bartered a small portion of each customer's grain in exchange for his services. That way, he usually had a supply of products for those who wished to purchase them at his trading post.

It was first come – first served at his mill, and people had to wait in line, sometimes overnight, during the busiest season. They waited to have their grains <u>"turned"</u> by the mill's grinding stones, giving rise to the term "wait your turn."

In the 1870s and 1880s, the backwoods country around Faith became a common place for the notorious James brothers (Jesse & Frank) to visit. Mildred James Wall was a cousin to these famous outlaws, and they were known to travel to these parts to spend time with their kinfolks. Local historians tell that Black Jim kept several horses in his stables, and the James brothers and their gang would sometimes trade horses in order to have fresh mounts. Rumor has it that after Jesse's death, his older brother, Frank James, often returned to the area. He would sit under a tall shade tree and play his fiddle as the country folks gathered to listen.

When I visited my grandmother's grave, I always took some extra time to look to the northwest, across the little one-lane gravel road, and let my eyes scan the broad valley. I could easily picture the James brothers on their fresh horses following the creek up the valley on their way back to their homes in Clay County.

Black Jim's and Mildred's graves are side-by-side, not far from my grandmother's grave. Now that I am "up in years," as they say. I will not likely visit southern Miller County again. I trust that some of my descendants will now and then visit Clemmie's grave and leave a flower or two.

LUKE WILLS

Wonderment: amazement, awe, bewilderment, curiosity, a state of awed admiration or respect.

A couple of years ago, I wrote and posted on Facebook a short bio-vignette about Luke Wills, a younger brother of the famous pioneer of western swing music, Bob Wills.

Luke Wills was born September 10th, 1920, near Memphis, in Hall County, Texas, just across the Prairie Dog Town Fork of the Red River from the town of Turkey, where his older brother, Bob Wills, was learning to be a barber.

Luke was the seventh of the Wills' family children. He was so different from the rest of the family that it was a family joke that his mother had picked up the wrong baby after one of the many social dances held in the area.

Like his other brother, Johnnie Lee Wills, Luke learned to play tenor banjo. He made his musical debut in 1937 when he was 17, doing his first show with Bob's Texas Playboys band in Cain's Academy in Tulsa, Oklahoma. Luke even signed his first Social Security card in the office at Cain's. Luke continued his career later as a bass player in the second Wills band, led by Johnnie Lee Wills, called the Rhythmaires. In the early 1940s, when Bob left for Hollywood to make western movies, he took Luke and several other Texas Playboys with him. Together, they made several theatrical shorts and features while Johnnie Lee took over the Cain's broadcasts and dances.

In 1943, Luke joined the US Navy. After WW II service, he led Bob's second band and covered the dance circuit of northern and central California, appearing first as Luke Wills and the Texas Playboys Number 2, but to avoid confusion, this soon became Luke Wills' Rhythm Busters. He recorded for King and RCA-Victor in the late 1940s.

Following my posting of the above bio article, my former teen sweetheart and first wife, Elaina, living in Las Vegas, Nevada, whom I had only seen a few times in the previous half-century, saw my posting on Facebook. In her <u>wonderment</u>, she read about her dear friend from several years earlier. When Elaina worked at the Thunderbird Hotel and Casino on the Las Vegas Strip, she became friends with Luke Wills. The former great musician and band leader, now in his advanced years, worked at the Thunderbird as a security guard. Elaina was astonished at her former husband's words as they told her about her dear friend from years earlier, Luke Wills.

Luke Wills lived out the last 35 years of his life in retirement in Las Vegas and died there on October 21st, 2000, at the age of 80. He was the last living member of the great family that made up Bob Wills and the Texas Playboys. Their western swing music will live on forever in the Texas dance halls.

Rural Mount

**Derelict: in a very poor condition as
a result of disuse and neglect.**

Colonel Alexander Outlaw was an American frontiersman and politician. He was also my 3rd great-granduncle. Public records show him as a member of Safety Committees in 1775. He was a Captain in the Duplin County, North Carolina, militia service, served on an "expedition against the insurgents" with Col. James Kenan in 1776, and was in the battle at Moore's Creek Bridge. He later moved to Washington County, where he served as militia Captain, Major, and Lt. Colonel, and magistrate. In 1780, he fought alongside Colonel William Campbell in battle at Kings Mountain, SC.

Following the war, Col. Outlaw settled on the Appalachian frontier. There, he and his friends carved off a big chunk of North Carolina where he lived and named it Franklin. They later changed the name to Tennessee. Colonel Outlaw represented Jefferson County in the Tennessee House of Representatives during the First and Third General Assembly (1796–1801) and was elected Speaker. After his senate term, he focused primarily on land speculation and law. He is recognized as one of the founders of the state of Tennessee.

In 1799, Colonel Alexander Outlaw built a stone mansion in the Nolichucky River bottoms as a wedding gift to his daughter and son-in-law. The two-story home and the 3,000+ acres were named "Rural Mount."

The Rural Mount home is now on the National Register of Historic Places. It has not been occupied in several years and is now <u>derelict</u> and in disrepair but protected by the National Registry.

It was a beautiful day in late May when my wife and I set out from Sevierville in Tennessee's Smoky Mountains. We were searching for the landmark home that had been built by my distant uncle more than 200 years earlier. I had a brief description of the location from a family record. It was described as being on private property in the Nolichucky River bottoms in Hamblen County.

We drove every road in the region without success and sought help in Morristown, the county seat of Hamblen County. I first tried the county fire department as I figured they knew every road in the county. No luck. They couldn't help me but suggested that I check with the sheriff's office.

At the sheriff's office, I explained to the dispatcher that I was looking for a historic home that my ancestor had built. Captain Vodra Moore, from back in the station, heard my query and beckoned me to a chair at his desk. He said he thought he remembered such a house. He opened up a Google satellite map on his computer, and we started searching the farmland in the river bottom. Pay dirt! We found the house about a quarter mile off a county road on a farm. Captain Moore knew the farmer, so he picked up the phone and called him. His friend answered, and the captain explained that I was a relative of the man who had built the house and that I wanted to go see the house and snap some photos of it. The farmer – I didn't write his name down, and now I cannot remember it – said it would be fine, "Just remember to close the gates."

It was a great and memorable experience to see the mansion structure that my distant uncle had built so long ago. The two-story building was constructed with ashlar stones circa 1799 by frontiersman Alexander Outlaw for his son-in-law, Joseph Hamilton.

It was designed in the Federal architectural style. It has been listed on the National Register of Historic Places so that it will enjoy some degree of protection. It comforts me to know that it is still standing, and I hope it will be restored someday.

The Nicene Creed

Whence: from what place, source, or cause

We church-goers are all familiar with some form of the Nicene Creed or the less widespread Apostles' Creed. "We believe in one God, the Father, the Almighty, Maker of heaven and earth, of all that is seen and unseen — etc." We take it for granted because we have heard it all of our lives. We seldom give a thought to whence it originated.

In the first couple of centuries of the Christian Era, the Bible had not been compiled, and there were some wild and crazy ideas about what exactly Christians should believe. So, the Church decided to settle the arguments.

Roman Emperor Constantine I called for a council of Christian bishops to assemble and work it out and cement in place exactly what Christian belief should be. Companies and organizations in the modern business world attend seminars and formulate "mission statements" in much the same way.

The Christian bishops convened the First Council of Nicaea in the Bithynian city of Nicaea (now İznik, Turkey.) The Council of Nicaea met from May until the end of July 325. On the 19th of June, they formulated what became, from that time forward, the core of Christian belief. That is when the Nicene Creed, as we know it, came into existence.

So, the next time you recite your Profession of Faith in your local church, just stop and reflect on how many of us believe exactly the same thing about the Holy Trinity: God, Jesus, and the Holy Spirit, and how long we have believed it.

Down with Drugs

**Abstemious: not self-indulgent,
especially when eating and drinking**

My wife is possibly the most impressive person that I have ever met. I should have let her influences rub off on me years ago. I am confident that it would have made me a better person. From the very beginning, she has eschewed both tobacco and alcohol. Not I! I have never had the willpower to be that <u>abstemious</u> about anything.

My weakness is single-malt Scotch Whiskey, and I have avoided being over-served, at least most of the time. But that's the limit of my loose living. I quit tobacco more than 40 years ago, but not soon enough. My doctor assures me that the COPD that I deal with currently is a direct result of my nicotine days.

I am adamantly opposed to the use of illegal street drugs. I have visited countries where the selling of street drugs is a capital offense. By strict enforcement of those laws, they have virtually eliminated illegal street drugs. Thus, they have put an end to the ready availability of addictive substances that tempt young people and lead to their eventual destruction.

If our country would do the same, innumerable lives would be saved. Execute a couple of dozen drug dealers, and the others would see reasons to change their ways. It would save the lives of hundreds of thousands.

ROCK OF GIBRALTAR

Surfeit: An excessive amount of something, more than needed

It was in the early morning when the word went out, "Land Ahoy!" Excursionists swarmed to the outer decks, binoculars dangling, to see land, although at that time, it was a misty outline that was rising from the flat horizon at an almost imperceptible rate.

We chuckled that these same people who eagerly signed on for the cruise to get to sea and away from land are now eager to see Mother Earth again. That is the natural reaction when one who has lived as a landlubber is separated from hard dirt for ten days. He feels he has seen nothing but sea for a month, even though he just spent two days ashore in the Azores less than a week ago. That doesn't count. The Azores are mere islands. Harvey, from Wichita Falls, wants to see the European continent he has heard of since grammar school.

Within two hours, we had passed Cap Spartel, Morocco's fortress, and the lighthouse that shines its beacon out over the great Atlantic from Africa's left shoulder. As we entered the legendary "Strait," on our left were the olive-tree-covered hills of Spain. Strung out along that same coast were the Moorish stone towers, erected centuries ago for protection from Moroccan rascals who ravaged Spain's coastal settlements, carrying off the prettiest girls to sell to the wealthy Arabs. We cruised into the Strait, and there they were: the Pillars of Hercules and the Rock of Gibraltar.

The Rock of Gibraltar cannot be missed. Ancients thought it was the end of the world, which it was at that time. They had no idea that a beautiful continent like ours was just beyond the horizon. The great Rock dominates every view, standing over a quarter of a mile high and reigning supreme over everything in sight.

"The Rock," as it is known, is the only distinguishing feature of the British territory of Gibraltar. It is so tiny that one can hardly swing a dead cat without hitting someone or getting hung up on a cannon, of which there are thousands. There is only one road into town. People driving to or from Spain must drive straight across the airport runway.

Our little excursion bus labored all the way to the summit of the Rock as our ears were crying for mercy. From sea level, it is almost like being shot into the clouds. Once at the summit, however, the excursionist surfeits himself with solitude while watching the ferries from Tangiers threading their way between the giant ships that are making their way to and from Mediterranean ports from countries half a world away.

We were in no hurry to leave a place with such a commanding view, but the romantic cities of North Africa are just across this busy 13-mile-wide channel. Now that we can see them, we are impatient to get there.

LESTER

Raconteur: a person who tells anecdotes in a skillful and amusing way

Our friend, Lester, was a constant source of amusement. As a raconteur, he could tell a story and describe the details, regardless of how trivial, down to the tiniest nuance, whether it was true or not. Lester's tales were never immune to embellishment and exaggeration. By the time he had limned a scene to the last minuscule feature, he had us hooked. We didn't believe it to be the truth, but he did.

When he told how he had won a fight as a middleweight boxer, Herb told him, "Now come on, Lester. The only boxing you ever did was boxing apples over in Yakima." Lester didn't miss a stride. He just simply went on to a new story.

Lester could tell you about his caribou hunt and advise how you get an antler trophy. He said that when there is a group of them, they always walk in a straight line. You simply pick out the one that stands taller than the rest and shoot it. It sounded believable until he mentioned that he hunted them in the valley near El Paso.

"Those were not caribou, Lester. They were antelope."

"Oh, I hunted them too." Then, he would go on to the next tale.

Winston Salem

Abattoir: A slaughterhouse

It was back in 1961. I was eager to take my young wife on an exciting trip all the way across the country. We had been married for a couple of years. Elaina was 19 years old, and I was 23. She and I lived on the outskirts of Tacoma, Washington, near where she had grown up.

We had started dating when she was 15, and I was 19. These days, folks would point an accusatory finger at me and say I should be locked up. And likely I would be. But it was acceptable in society at that time and entirely natural for the two of us.

I had been "out west," as they say, for five years. That meant I had not seen my hometown in Arkansas, my friends, or even my mother for that time.

My eldest sister and her family lived in North Carolina, all the way across the country, and I had not seen her since I was in the army. I was eager to introduce Elaina to my family. As I look back, I scratch my head, trying to think of any good reason to embark on a trip like that in the middle of the summer in a car with no air conditioning.

We were excited to be setting out for an all-new adventure. We were young lovers just living for the moment.

We first headed east for White Pass in the Cascades. We made a quick stop in the town of Randle to surprise Elaina's grandparents and tell them about our exciting excursion.

The plunge down out of the eastern Cascades to Yakima only took an hour and we were soon motoring down through the "hop" country heading for the Columbia River crossing at Umatilla.

The Yakima Valley is U.S. hop country. The valley's hop growers keep the craft beer industry brewing! The Valley is one of the most essential hop-growing regions in the world, harvesting 75% of the nation's hops. The hops are grown on overhead trellises created by thousands of 20-foot-tall hop poles connected by wires that support the hop vines 18 feet above the ground. The sight of such a field is not soon forgotten.

From Pendleton, we continued driving southeast through the picturesque Wallowa-Whitman National Forest. The 2.4-million-acre forest is home to the Wallowa Mountains, Hells Canyon National Recreation Area, and Snake River canyon country, and its elevation ranges from 875 feet in Hells Canyon to 9,845 feet. The mountain range and National Forest cover a big chunk of northeast Oregon and lap over into eastern Washington and western Idaho. We were agog with scenery and sites totally new to us.

We crossed the corner of Idaho near Nampa and drove across the "Potato Belt," the Snake River Plain, where a third of the nation's potatoes are grown. The highway was crowded with open trucks hauling potatoes and sugar beets—another new and interesting sight.

At Salt Lake City, we turned east. U.S. Highway 40 would be our home for half of our trip across the country. Shortly after Salt Lake City, we were climbing the western slope of the Wasatch Range when we came to the first of many stops. Recent rains had caused several portions of the highway to slough off into the adjacent canyons. There would be traffic delays all the way to the continental divide.

Climbing the steep slopes of the mountains started causing our engine to overheat. Stopping for delays in the July heat just made things worse. Finally, with the temp gauge topped out in the red zone, the engine simply stopped. We coasted backward to a wide spot on the shoulder while other motorists, already mad because of the closures, threw some choice words at me as they sped to catch up to the next car ahead, which was already stopped.

What shall I do? The little bit of water that was left in the radiator was still boiling and spewing out the overflow and vent pipes. It would soon be empty, and there was nothing that I could do about it. I recognized that the fuel pump had vapor-locked.

Years earlier, I had owned a flathead Ford that vapor-locked every time it got hot. There is no cure or fix other than wait for it to cool down. There was a mountain stream flowing westward in the canyon alongside the highway. I didn't have any kind of container to carry water in.

I found a hubcap about a hundred feet back down the hill that someone had lost. I saw that it would hold water, so I thanked the unknown motorist who had lost it. With the hood up to aid cooling, I started the first of about two dozen trips down the steep slope to get a hubcap full of cold water to refill the radiator and pour on the hot fuel pump. Elaina was helpless to do anything but wait in the car under the boiling hot sun.

We finally got cooled down and were on the road again. The highway construction workers quit for the day. The car was breathing better in the cool nighttime air as we crossed the continental divide and headed down through the Front Range.

Soon, we could see a glow in the eastern sky. It was a glow from the millions of street lights and neon signs of Denver. Finally, at a sharp left curve in the road, the full array of the city lights of Denver appeared far below us ahead; an unforgettable sight.

I was a closet nostalgist in my early days. My "coming out" of that shadow would be spread over years and decades. However, my early experiences in the city of Denver trigger a touch of sentimentality to this day.

My mind raced back to the summer of 1953. I was 15 years old. My brother and his wife were living in Denver. They had visited my mother and me in Arkansas, and when the visit was over, I rode with them back to their home to spend the rest of the summer in Denver.

To make some money to attend an occasional movie, I learned

to be a pinsetter in the local bowling alley. In those days, Bowling alleys didn't have automatic pin-setting machines. Every lane had a pin-boy at the back of the lane.

I would sit on the backboard and raise my feet to keep from getting hit by the bowling ball or the flying pins. Sometimes it worked. I particularly recall that bowlers liked to blame the pinsetter when the pins didn't fall to suit them. If the bowler was drinking, which was often the case, his bowling was worse, and the shouted expletives filled the air. I had words and names shouted at me that still won't be found in a dictionary.

That was in 1953. Fast forward four years and I had spent two years in the army and learned to be a qualified drywall finisher. By the summer of 1957, I had taped gypsum wallboard in Illinois, California, and Washington and had built a good reputation.

I was offered a job in a development in Denver so I left my girlfriend in Tacoma and drove to Denver to work for a season. The big city was exciting, and I spent my 20th birthday there before going back to Tacoma.

These are some of the memories that I shared with Elaina as we spent the early hours of the night driving through Denver and Aurora and out into the wheatlands east of the city. There are stretches of highway out there that will try to convince a driver that the world is flat.

Elaina and I were young and tough. We dealt with the difficulties and kept going. When one of us got tired of driving, we simply switched places. We didn't give a thought to renting a motel room.

It was 2 AM and Elaina was driving while I slept in the back seat. We topped a long hill near Cheyenne Wells, Colorado, and were greeted with the sight of a mile-long string of vehicle taillights. Elaina woke me, and we tried to figure out what to do. There was nothing we or anyone else could do. We were in the middle of a very dark nowhere.

One must keep in mind that there were no interstate highways out there in 1961. The two-lane road was a parking lot for hundreds of cars and trucks. An 18-wheeler up ahead had hit a bridge banister and was on its side from one side of the bridge to the other. The driver was lying dead on the grass, and his badly injured wife was asking about him. I remember the sinking feeling in my heart when I saw the Arkansas license plate.

Looking back from my modern-day vantage point, I remember the multitude of fatal accidents on those old two-lane highways. Travel was difficult and dangerous in the 1940s and 1950s.

After a delay of nearly two hours, we were on the move again. We crossed into Kansas and pressed on eastward. It was nearing daybreak when we drove through the sleeping little town of Sharon Springs, hardly noticing it. We didn't know it as we approached the little prairie town, but Sharon Springs would rest in our memories for the rest of our lives

We were no more than ten miles east of the town when the big Coupe de Ville simply stopped running. The 1956 Caddie was a beautiful car, but it was jinxed. Later that summer, I renamed it Coupe de Lemon and got rid of it before winter came.

There was virtually no traffic at 4:30 AM, and certainly, no one was going to stop in the darkness to help. What could they do, anyway? We had passed a farmhouse about a quarter mile back, so I struck out walking.

The farmhouse was no more than 40 yards from the highway. The giant cottonwood and oak trees in the front yard bore witness that the farmstead had been there for a long time. The roadside mailbox just said BUXTON in bold upper-case letters. I wondered if the car-tire swing hanging from a sturdy oak tree was for an elderly Mr. Buxton's grandkids or might I be greeted by a younger man of the house.

I stepped as quietly as I could upon the wooden board porch that reached the front corners of the house in both directions. What a comfortable place! A porch swing hung near one end of the porch. I always wanted a porch and swing like that.

I opened the screen door and knocked on the wooden door of the house, tense with anxiety about who might open the door. Would he have a shotgun close at hand?

———

The old fellow who answered my knock looked like I had just awakened him. Quite likely, I had done just that. He looked at me like I was a side dish that he had not ordered. His brow furrowed as I explained my predicament and said I needed to call a garage.

He let me use his phone to call a garage in town. He recommended Smith Motors, so I called them. They said they would send a tow truck, so I handed Mr. Farmer the phone to explain where we were.

I walked back to my car. Traffic on the highway was picking up as folks were hurrying to their jobs.

It was about 8 AM when Kevin arrived with a tow truck. Smith Towing Company was painted in big letters on the door of the truck. Kevin invited Elaina and me to ride in the cab with him into town and to the garage at Smith Motors.

The service manager understood that we were traveling and said he would get us back on the road as quickly as possible. I asked him where we should wait, and he pointed to Smith's café across the street and said they serve a good breakfast. It sounded good. We were hungry. I wondered, does Smith own the whole town?

As we crossed the street and started walking up the sidewalk, it sounded like we were walking on eggshells. "What is that?" It was bugs! Thousands of them, maybe millions. Even yet, I have never seen so many bugs in my life. Some were dead, others were alive, and some were crawling on their last legs. There were grasshoppers, crickets, katydids, locusts, and anything else that would crunch beneath our footsteps.

We opened the screen door and ducked in quickly. An "Aunt Bea" looking lady was standing with a broom at ready to sweep back out any bugs that tailgated in the door behind us.

With time to kill, we enjoyed a leisurely country breakfast. We sat next to a window where we could watch the town coming alive and the bugs. We could also watch the garage where our car was hopefully being restored to life.

Sharon Springs typified a small town in the breadbasket of our country. The people were just as typical. There were seasoned farmers in their John Deere hats. Younger men wore western straws that looked like they had done time in the cattle pens. We could suspect that some of them were in town to pick up parts for their farm equipment.

The local wheat harvest was in full swing. Most wheat farmers didn't own their own combines. Custom harvesters cranked up their equipment in North Texas in the early spring and worked the wheat harvest all the way to the frosty fields of northern Montana in October.

We finished our breakfast and a waitress cleared our table, but we still didn't have any place in particular to go. The waitress assured us that we could stay as long as we wanted. She topped off my coffee cup every time she passed the table with a pot.

A young cowboy came in for a late breakfast and put money in the Jukebox. We were treated with a good dose of Hank Williams and Lefty Frizzell for the best part of the next hour.

It was 10:30 when the mechanic drove the car out of the repair bay. We were overjoyed to pay the garage just 28 bucks. With a new distributor cap and rotor, we drove out the east side of town, past Smith Farm Equipment Company.

"Do you think that $28 was supposed to pay for the towing and the repair?"

"I don't know. It doesn't seem like enough, but I don't want to turn around and go back and ask."

It was insufferably hot all day. Highway 40 ran straight through Abilene, Kansas, and I venture that we stopped for a stop-sign or signal at every intersection. A thermometer on the courthouse registered 108 degrees. We drove with all windows open.

The car radio kept us informed on the Dow Jones Average and the price of every commodity, from soybeans to pork bellies. Every town had a little AM station with a signal that would reach halfway to the next town.

It was just past 4 PM when we approached the outskirts of Kansas City. Elaina said, "What is that godawful smell?" A stench had filled our car through our open windows.

Elaina said, "What is that? I can hardly breathe." I knew. I had

———

73

smelled the same odor near Saticoy, California, when I worked in that area. I drove past an abattoir and meat market daily while going to and from my work in Simi Valley.

I told her, "It is a feedlot, dairy, or a slaughterhouse. I suspect a slaughterhouse." It turned out that it was the Kansas City stockyards, and surely enough, we soon saw the big "Swifts" meat trucks pulling away from the <u>abattoir</u>, hauling fresh meat to Kansas City's grocery stores and famous barbeques.

Neither Elaina nor I will ever forget the malodorous stench of Kansas City, Kansas. It was more than cattle manure. As a cattleman when I lived in Texas, I hauled hundreds, perhaps thousands, of cattle and hosed out the cattle trailers hundreds of times. No, the stink of Kansas City was more than cattle manure. It was that but mixed with the putrid smell of rotting flesh. That horrible stench stayed with us completely through Kansas City until we were cruising through the open farmland of Jackson County, Missouri.

Away from Kansas City, Missouri was a breath of fresh air. Hot, but not the stifling hot of Kansas. Darkness caught up with us as we worked our way through St Louis.

Travel was uneventful through Louisville and on to Lexington. It was after midnight and so hot we could hardly breathe. At a gas station, I asked a man why it was so hot. He simply said, "This is the stickiest night we have had." "Stickiest!" I have never forgotten the word.

Traveling south from Abingdon, we plunged into the Smoky Mountains along with a violent thunderstorm. It was driving rain, constant lightning, and crashing thunder on the sinuous mountain roads, the worst driving conditions imaginable. There was no other traffic on the road other than Roadway freight trucks. My brother-in-law told me later that there were at least three other routes that I could have taken, and any one of them would be better than the one that I took.

Relief came at daybreak when we emerged from the storm in Mt. Airy, NC. It was pleasant driving the rest of the way.

As we entered Winston Salem, a familiar aroma filled the air. Tobacco! It was the same earthy aroma that one would smell after opening a new can of Prince Albert. I remembered the aroma from my visits back in the 1950s when I was in the service. It was a sweet smell, nothing like the smell of tobacco smoke.

I inquired at a mom-and-pop gas station, and a helpful couple directed me to the side of town where I could find 1701 Queen Street.

My sister, Donna Dean, was a stickler for everything being spotless, proper, and perfect. She was furious when I knocked on the door. She had been upstairs vacuuming the floor wearing a house dress. By Elaina and I not having spent a night in a hotel on the trip, we arrived a day earlier than expected. Elaina and I were both too naïve at that time to know how gauche an unanticipated early arrival could be.

We ate, rested, visited, and roasted in the heat and humidity. Donna Dean served us Coca Colas on ice to cool us down. They were deliciously refreshing. Donna and Rocky's home was in a pleasant, uncrowded part of town. The rear of their house, which boasted a pleasant shaded screened-in porch, faced a wooded canyon that Rocky had bought the previous year. He had four acres of parklike paradise inside the city.

The following day was Independence Day in 1961, so Rocky had the day off to do what he loved to do. That was to act as a tour guide and show us the city that he loved, the city of his birth. We saw the Reynolds Tobacco Company factory where if the chopper on the Camel machine were shut off, the un-chopped cigarette would stretch for several miles.

He took us to Old Salem, the birthplace of modern Winston Salem, where Moravians first settled in 1766. He guided us on a tour of the beautiful Wake Forest campus and explained how, back in the 1940s, the RJ Reynolds family donated $100 million and 330 acres to convince university leaders to move Wake Forest University from Wake Forest, NC, to an all-new campus in Winston Salem.

Then he drove us to the Dairi-O out on Kernersville Road for their famous milkshakes. Rocky and Donna Dean were perfect hosts, and Rocky always said, "Your money is no good in Winston-Salem." Of all my visits, he never let me spend a dime.

We were to leave the following morning for the long drive to Arkansas, so we told Donna Dean not to get up, that we wished to leave before daybreak. What did she do? When we got up, she already had a breakfast feast cooked for us and a picnic basket full of goodies to eat on our trip.

The scenery was beautiful across the Blue Ridge in the Smoky Mountains bordering North Carolina and Tennessee; still one of my favorite drives. Further west, we enjoyed the Cumberland Mountains and rolling hills all the way to Memphis on the Mississippi River.

The Delta land of East Arkansas was covered as far as the eye could see with cotton and soybeans, from West Memphis to the Ozark foothills.

It was late evening when we reached Maynard and turned east on Richardson's Ferry Road. The gravel road, true to its name, led to the old Richardson's Ferry on Current River, near the little cotton-gin town of Reyno.

Maynard was a lively town when I was growing up. Farmers took their families to town on Saturday to do their shopping and socialize with friends whom they hadn't seen since the previous week.

Young people congregated in the cafes and pool halls on Saturday nights. A lot of juvenile courting took place in the booths of Maynard's cafes.

We spent two nights in my mother's home. This is on the home place that my parents bought in 1938 when I was still in a cradle. We spent our time visiting with my mother as well as some of my friends who came to visit with us. It was the first time I had visited my homeplace in five years.

The next day was Friday, July 7th. We headed south and west to cross into Oklahoma at Fort Smith, Arkansas. At Oklahoma City, we got on Historic Route 66. It wasn't historic then. It was just the highway to California.

I had driven Route 66 four years earlier on my trip to California after I got out of the army. I loved seeing familiar billboards and the roadside Burma-Shave serial poems.

At Gallup, New Mexico, we rented a motel room to spend the

night, the only rented room on the trip. At least, that's what we thought at the time.

Travel was good the following day through Holbrook and across the mountains at Flagstaff. At Kingman, the Arizona heat was boiling. It increased by the mile as we descended into the Colorado River lowlands. At Oatman, we decided to make it to Needles and stop and rent an air-conditioned hotel room. It was early afternoon, and the heat was unbearable. Our car radiator was boiling over every time we stopped and shut off the engine.

We rented a motel room, intending to stay under the air conditioning until after dark when the temperature would cool down. Darkness came, and the temperature didn't cool. It was still in the high 90s when we finally pulled out just before midnight.

We had intended to visit only my sister's family and my mother on the trip, but my mother leaned on us to visit her other son, my brother, Gene Outlaw, who lived in Lakewood, California, just south of Los Angeles.

It was near noon on Sunday, and my brother was off work so we visited about three hours with Gene, Joyce, and their two sons, Darrell and Mike. We were eager to get on the road again. Our trip was now over 5,000 miles, and we still had over a thousand miles to go.

We had faced a lot of highways and situations in the nearly fortnight of travel, but nothing was quite like the Grapevine. The Grapevine gained notoriety even before we drove it. It is a treacherous winding route down out of the Tehachapi Mountains to the valley floor of the San Joaquin. Somewhere between Tejon Pass and the bottom of Grapevine Canyon, overheated brake shoes give up, and giant trucks go careening down through the canyon. A lot of truckers and others have lost their lives on "The Grapevine."

I was asleep in the back seat when Elaina yelled at me to wake up. Freight trucks were on both sides of us, and one was about to either knock us off the road or blast us off with his air horn. Elaina found a place to pull off, and we sat for a bit to gather our wits before getting out among them again.

We crossed the Golden Gate Bridge into Northern California and continued driving all night. Before noon the following day, we were sitting in our driveway. We had driven over 6,500 miles in ten days and saw people and sights that we would never see again. If we had it to do over? Yes, but in a cooler season.

CLATSOP

Abysmal: extremely bad; appalling

A couple of years ago, I drove up the West Coast from central California to the northwest shoulder of Washington's Olympic Peninsula. A primary goal, and a reason for me to follow that route, was my desire to visit Fort Clatsop.

The present Fort Clatsop is a reconstruction of a fort that was built in 1805 by the men of the Lewis and Clark Corps of Discovery when they found they would have to spend the winter on that coast. In his diaries, Meriwether Lewis described the location as stricken with the most <u>abysmal</u> weather that one can imagine. His description is correct. Captain James Cook had mapped the coastline seventeen years earlier, and he named his landing spot Cape Foulweather. The name stuck. It remains that today. And by the way, it was raining the day that I visited.

An excellent account of Lewis and Clark's voyage to the Northwest and their dire situation causing them to winter on the West Coast can be found in Undaunted Courage, written by Stephen E. Ambrose. His material was based on the diaries of Meriwether Lewis. It remains one of my favorite books that I have ever read.

RICKLES

Acerbic: sharply or bitingly critical, sarcastic, or ironic in temper, mood, or tone but witty

The lounge shows were some of my greatest memories of attending the Las Vegas Strip back in 1963. In those days, one could walk into a lounge show in any of the large hotels, sit down, and order a cocktail. For the price of one drink, one could sit as long as he wished and watch great entertainment on the stage. It was a wonderful time. If he needed to go to the restroom, he would simply place his cigarette package (nearly everybody smoked in those days) on top of the drink glass, and the scantily clad cocktail waitress would see that it was still there when he returned.

One lounge act that stands out in my memory was the Don Rickles show in the Sahara Hotel Lounge. His <u>acerbic</u> humor was incredibly funny. One didn't dare to sit at the bar. That was too close to Rickles. The yokel at the bar would become the butt of Rickles's humor.

I miss Don Rickles. There have been a lot of great comedians, but Rickles was in a class by himself. Those were the days!

THE WINDY CITY

**Harbinger: A person or thing that announces
or signals the approach of another**

It had been a hot day in August when I started work in Illinois.
Now, it was late September, and the air was already brisk, which I
found surprising. I had spent the last two winters in the Panama
Canal Zone, a geopolitical region that no longer exists. With that all
behind me, I found myself living and working in Des Plaines, Illinois.
I had not expected to see frost in what should still be summertime.
It was a <u>harbinger</u> of things to come if I were to spend the winter
in that far north part of the country. That is why I responded with
such alacrity when JC suggested that we leave Illinois and go to
California. It seemed a no-brainer. It made sense in the fall of 1956,
and it still makes sense today. We didn't waste time. We started work
on a new job on October 9th, 1956, in Los Altos, California. It was
my 19th birthday. I never looked back at Des Plaines again. That was
an early phase of what I have written about as my "Vagabond Years."

THE PARSON

**Akimbo: with hands on the hips
and elbows turned outward**

Brother Connor, as we knew him, was an interesting pastor of our small hometown church. He would adroitly deliver his well-versed sermon while searching the eyes in the congregation. When it came time for the invitation, Brother Connor knew who his primary target was. He would lock eyes with the supposed sinner and stand <u>akimbo</u> after challenging the alleged miscreant with, "Are you ready to change your ways before it's too late?"

Brother Connor has seen many a Sunday morning attendee slide down in his pew, hoping not to become the recipient of the Pastor's stare. And that has included me.

THE REALTOR

Adroit: Clever or skillful in using the hands or mind

After working side by side with Elaina Blake on several property-related issues, I have developed an appreciation for her <u>adroit</u> approach to problem-solving. Elaina recently received an award for 55 years as a member of the Greater Las Vegas Association of Realtors. With that experience she has the ability to evaluate a problem and seek and enact alternative methods of solution. Among her contemporaries, there are few who can compare.

WISE DECISION

Acumen: the ability to make good judgments and quick decisions, typically in a particular domain

It was 1954 when I volunteered for immediate induction into the army. Following basic training, I was fortunate that Uncle Sam saw fit to send me to radar school in Fort Bliss, Texas. I, along with some 60 classmates, learned the skills of tracking everything from airplanes to artillery and heavy mortar rounds. The knowledge served me well during my assignment to military units in the Panama Canal Zone.

After completing my army enlistment, I worked on military bases in Washington. At Fort Lewis and McCord Air Force Base, I met a high-level officer in charge of the local air traffic controllers. Between my radar operation experience and the fact that I had some flying experience, I found that I was qualified to be hired as an air traffic controller. For any number of reasons, I turned down the opportunity. I questioned the decision for several years but eventually came to know that it was the right decision.

Air traffic controllers operate in a high-stress environment. They must have the <u>acumen</u> to make lightning-fast decisions and always with excellent judgment. I don't have a problem with the requirement for good judgment. I am confident that I can routinely make wise decisions. But to me, they have to be thoughtful, reasoned decisions, not hasty. No, I wouldn't want to be an air traffic controller. I leave that to the quick thinkers.

A PLATFORM FOR POLITICAL VIEWPOINTS?

Acrimonious: anger and bitterness: harsh or biting sharpness especially of words, manner, or feelings.

Several years ago, I got into the custom of using Facebook to express my conservative political viewpoints. I soon learned that vast multitudes of other social media users were doing the same things. There was an enormous amount of misinformation that adversely influenced many uninformed and misinformed people. When I tried to straighten out the misinformation, hordes of other misinformed yokels were on me like white on rice.

I finally had to swear off writing political opinions. I got tired of the <u>acrimonious</u> accusations that my postings precipitated. Don't get me wrong. I still have those opinions and still feel as strongly as I ever did. But I will desist. I don't need to see the hostility and animosity on my Facebook postings.

Fifteen Minutes
of Fame

**Acquiesce: Accept something
reluctantly but without protest.**

Some people just live to be offended. A lot of it came with the
BLM movement a few years ago. College students said they were
offended because they had to walk by a statue of Robert E. Lee. So,
the statue gets yanked down. University administrators acquiesce
to the demands of those who love to be offended. In the aftermath,
NFL teams had to change their names. The Washington Redskins
and the Cleveland Indians offended Native Americans. So, they had
to change their names. No more Redskins or Indians. Mercy me,
we don't want to offend anyone. There have been hundreds, if not
thousands, of similar incidents across the country.

Harrison Butker, a placekicker for the Kansas City Chiefs,
shared his conservative views with graduating students and guests
at Benedictine College, a small private Catholic school of around
2,200 students in Atchison, Kansas. His commencement speech
drew a standing ovation.

He spoke of his faith and belief in strong family values, which
align with Catholic teaching. Everybody loved it except a handful
of girls who said they were offended. So, they stirred up folks on

social media and then got coverage on national television. That was their fifteen minutes of fame. Now, Harrison Butker is a pariah in the eyes of those who just love to be offended. A Christian man now ranks right down there with the Boston Strangler in social media just because a handful of people didn't like what he said. I liked that he is a Christian man and is willing to let his faith show. Of course, I like Tim Tebow, too, and you know how he was treated.

The enemy is us

Obdurate: unmoved by persuasion, pity, or tender feelings; stubborn; unyielding

We have all heard the old axiom, "We have met the enemy, and they are us." That misquote, which has been lying around since the War of 1812, could be altered further and applied to most of us when politics are in play. We look at the people with views counter to our own, and we are convinced that they are the poster boys for Obduracy – that they will be unmoved by the truth, pity, or tender feelings. Their minds are made up. And, of course, they are wrong. We, however, have a better insight. We say that we have open minds, but we know that in the end, we will still believe the same thing and will be just as unyielding as the other side. We have met the obdurate, and they are us.

"Aw Shucks"

Paillasse: A straw mattress

Have you ever slept on a straw mattress? Throughout most of recorded history, people bedded down on straw. When the straw got too old, dirty, or too infested with bugs, simply throw it out and bring in some fresh straw.

Thankfully, our beds have evolved, so you can talk to them and have them adjust to suit your comfort. It hasn't always been that way. When I was a child, up in the clay hills of North Arkansas, we didn't have plushy mattresses. Our beds had a set of bedsprings and a cotton-filled mattress. It was a mark of affluence to have an innerspring mattress. When I would do a sleepover at a friend's house, I would never know what to expect. Sometimes, it would be a pallet on a hard floor.

Some of our neighbors had straw mattresses. They were made by filling a "tick," a bed-sized cloth bag, much like two sheets sewn together with a flap to keep the stuffing contained. Such a mattress is called a paillasse or a pallet. Once, when I stayed overnight with a friend, I bedded down on such a mattress that was noisy. I found that it was filled with corn husks.

A couple of decades ago, folks got into a waterbed craze. I am glad that has passed. Water weighs 8.5 pounds per gallon, and a big mattress could hold nearly 250 gallons. People collapsed upstairs floors just getting the mattress watered up.

Shady Deal

**Rectitude: Rectitude typically refers
to moral integrity—to "straightness"
or "rightness" of character.**

I have always considered myself a good person, a trustworthy individual, and an honest man. But how honest is honest? I recall the time that I was not completely honest with a car salesman in Jefferson City, Missouri. I got to him on a car deal and was pretty proud of myself. I had never trusted a used car salesman to deal with me honestly and uprightly. When I told my wife, she was shocked. She was upset with me and wanted me to go back to the car dealer and make amends. Then I was shocked. I had never faced that level of <u>rectitude</u> before. I had thought that I was a good, honest person. I learned, rather quickly, that my level of honesty was inferior to that of my wife. It was a lesson that I have never forgotten. Be that as it may, I still don't trust used car salesmen.

Homecoming to Arkansas

Riparian: relating to wetlands adjacent to rivers and streams

Several years ago, my project in Jackson, Mississippi, was nearing completion. My boss, Bob Tillery, over in Columbus, Georgia, notified me that the company had picked up a highway interchange project in North Little Rock, Arkansas. He encouraged me to make plans for Arkansas as soon as I could get loose in Mississippi.

I looked forward to the new location. I would be living in my home state for the first time in decades. The old hack is true that there is "no place like home." No matter how long one has been away, there will always be something missing in his life that can only be satisfied by looking at places that were familiar sights to him when he was a child.

The new project included a flyover connecting southbound U.S. Highway 67 to eastbound Interstate Highway 40. In order to connect, the flyover circled out over a small, slow-moving stream. Foundations and columns had to be built, which destroyed the natural flow of the creek. Our contract stipulated that we provide mitigation for the wetlands lost. That meant we had to build a wetland. And we did. We rechanneled the little creek, put in a series of small dikes and dams, and seeded the area with feed plants like wild rice and oats. It became a model <u>riparian</u> wetland far beyond our expectations.

It is rewarding to drive that flyover, look down upon our constructed wetland, and see various wading birds feeding and nesting in the reeds and wild rice.

I didn't realize the importance of wetlands until I lived near a swamp that was flooded every winter. I found it an excellent place for hunting wild ducks, fishing, and trapping fur-bearing creatures. I had a whole new appreciation for wetlands.

No Good Answer

Acquiescence: the reluctant acceptance of something without protest.

It was in the early summer of 1954. I was at odds with myself, so to speak. I had quit high school at the midterm of the 11th grade. I had thought that I would embark immediately into a country music career and achieve fame and fortune. That was not developing, and now my friends had joined the army. And I was broke. It didn't matter that my friends were older than I was. If they could go to the army, then so should I.

I posed the idea to my mother, reciting a laundry list of pre-imagined reasons why she should agree and allow me to sign up. Her thoughtful <u>acquiescence</u> surprised me. Looking back, I think she was worried about which road my idleness might take me. The discipline of military life might be just the thing to straighten me out.

So, that is how I wound up in the army at the age of 16 years. I was sworn into the United States Army on July 22nd, 1954, in Little Rock, Arkansas. (I was sworn at more often than I like to recall in basic training in Georgia. The non-commissioned officers were not gentlemen.) Two years later, I was honorably discharged at Fort Chaffee, Arkansas, and my military obligation was behind me.

Thousands of times, I have pondered the question about the wisdom, or lack thereof, of my leaving school and going into the army so young. There is no good answer. I missed out on the fun of high school years and graduation. However, I did a lot of growing up from the ages of 16 to 18, and it was the start of an adult life that, looking back, I wouldn't trade for anything else in the world.

YES, ELVIS TOO!

Abstention: The practice of restraining oneself from indulging in something; abstinence.

It is fortunate for my generation that, during our formative years, we were not faced with the insidious temptations that young people face today. The worst thing that a kid could get into was smoking tobacco. And, of course, I and most of my friends did it. Nowadays, there is a lot of far worse stuff floating around our schools. I am amazed at how many people that I hear of are hooked on drugs. Drug use is rampant in the entertainment industry. We can easily think of several personalities who have died from accidental overdoses. Matthew Perry's television career was still going strong when he died of a ketamine overdose. Michael Jackson was a superstar when he died of Propofol intoxication. The pop singer/songwriter Prince died of a fentanyl overdose. Tom Petty died from an overdose of fentanyl, oxycodone, and others. River Phoenix died of a heroin and cocaine overdose. Elvis Presley had methaqualone, codeine, barbiturates, and cocaine in his system when he died.

I had reached some level of maturity by the time street drugs became omnipresent. I count my blessings. Abstention was not my strong point with regard to tobacco. It might have been the same with the more dangerous temptations.

GRAMMAR SCHOOL FOR ENGINEERS

Abstruse: difficult to understand; obscure

There was a time, several years ago, that I had the pleasure – or challenge would probably be the better word – to supervise a group of engineers while building a nuclear power plant in Missouri. A great benefit for me was that when I faced an engineering or mathematical problem beyond my knowledge, I could rely on my good fortune that at least one of my engineers could solve it for me. The problem with engineers was that most of them could hardly spell their own names, and their daily reports were so <u>abstruse</u> that they had to be rewritten, sometimes a second time. During staff meetings, I told them that "concision" should be the goal when writing a report. Be concise and use the correct terms.

Brockman, my young engineer from a prominent family in Spartanburg, said, "They didn't worry us with that stuff at Clemson – just as long as we solved the engineering problems." I told him I didn't have time to teach him everything Clemson failed to teach. I wanted to talk to him about grammar school but decided I had said enough.

The engineers were young. I hope they gained some traits and practices that would benefit them in their careers when I was no longer there to guide them.

SUMMER OF '58 – EPISODE 1

Bazooka: The Bazooka was a taping machine used in drywall construction; so named because it resembled a 3.5-millimeter rocket launcher that we used in the army. It was commonly called a bazooka.

My story starts in Tacoma, Washington, in the spring of 1958. I was 20 years old, still not quite old enough to vote or buy a beer legally. That's funny because I had served two years in the army and had been discharged for nearly two years. Hey! I was a military veteran. Cut me some slack. I had gotten disenchanted with high school back in Arkansas, dropped out, and joined the army at the age of 16. So, I had gotten a head start on adulthood at the expense of what should have been the most memorable years of high school.

Following discharge from the army at Fort Chaffee, Arkansas, I squandered a couple of months of productive time, enjoying the sweetness of freedom and worrying about not a thing in the world. However, the exigencies of food and shelter said that I must get a job and start paying for my existence.

With no job opportunities in my hometown of North Arkansas, I extended my horizons. Memphis was not inviting, so I would have to look toward the north. It seemed that everyone from my hometown went "up north" to get jobs, so I skipped St. Louis. I had met people from St. Louis, and they looked down on us Arkies as some subculture. I committed Saint Louisans to the lower regions and went farther north.

Chicago should have more to offer. Surely enough, I struck pay dirt in Des Plaines, Illinois. I got a job taping drywall joints for $1.50 per hour. It wasn't a lot of money, but it was more than what the army had been paying me. But the Windy City couldn't hold me. It was too cold. The next six months found me peddling my newfound skills all over California and up into the Great Northwest.

During the following spring in the Evergreen State, I was living (sleeping at least) at a boarding house in South Tacoma, Washington. I had worked through the winter taping gypsum wallboard on a project at Fort Lewis. I had learned to tape with a "bazooka" in California before moving to Washington. My experience and skill with the bazooka (new in Washington) garnered me a premium hourly wage about 10% above the union scale that my fellow workers, most of them twice my age, were getting paid. I'll admit. I was probably a little overly cocky.

Following the completion of the Fort Lewis project, my friends, sheet-rockers, and finishers—boomers, we were called—scattered to other projects around the country. I decided to quit "booming" and stay in one place. I was happy. I had a good job and a pretty girlfriend that I had gotten quite serious about.

One afternoon, after I had finished my day's work for a local contractor in Tacoma, I was delivered a telegram. This was new. I had never received a telegram before in my young life. The telegram said, "Call Bill Elsholz in Plattsburgh, New York." And it gave a number. People didn't waste words on telegrams. Each word cost money.

Bill was a drywall hanger, or sheetrocker, as they were called. I showed the telegram to my girlfriend. I suspected that Bill wanted to tell me about opportunities for me to ply my trade and make some good money on a project in Plattsburgh. I was happy in Tacoma, so I tossed the telegram.

SUMMER OF '58 –
EPISODE 2

Injudicious: Showing very poor judgment; unwise

We were boomers in those days. I was so new to the culture that I didn't even know the term. I had met and made friends with a number of workers on that first housing project at Fort Lewis. They were highly skilled in their crafts and had worked on similar projects from Ohio to San Diego and points in between. Several of them routinely gathered in taverns on Old Highway 99 after work, and as the beer flowed, they reminisced about projects far and wide. I learned a lot just listening to these seasoned boomers.

When our project at Fort Lewis was completed, two of those friends, Bill Elsholz and Chuck Preston, and a couple of other sheetrock hangers had split to Plattsburgh, New York, where a big housing project was in progress at Plattsburg AFB. They were boomers, going where the most money could be made.

About a week or two after I had received the telegram from Bill Elsholz, Chuck Preston showed up back in Tacoma. His father was ill, so he came back to see him. While in Tacoma, Chuck got in touch with our friend, Jack Gillette, and me and told us of all the wonderful opportunities to make big money hanging and finishing drywall at the project at Plattsburgh Air Force Base. At Chuck's insistence, I reluctantly called the superintendent in New York and talked to him about it. Chic Chiccarelli painted the same rosy picture that Chuck did. That's when I thought, maybe I should consider it. I asked Chuck, "How would we get there?" Jack spoke up and said, "I have an airplane." I thought, oh my gosh, how exciting that would be. I had only ridden in one plane before, which had been a troop carrier in the army. I had never ridden in a small plane.

I couldn't possibly have imagined what an <u>injudicious</u> thing I was about to agree to, to fly all the way across the country in an old airplane that couldn't even fly as high as some of the mountains that we would have to cross, flown by our friend who had never flown east of the Cascade Mountain Range in Western Washington.

SUMMER OF '58 – EPISODE 3

Befogged: Made indistinct due to fog in the air.

Jack's airplane was a little 1947 Piper Super Cruiser. It looked pretty good to be 11 years old. Jack had paid $1,300 for it the previous year. The problem was, we could only take a couple of changes of clothes with us. Jack said that with three people in it and full gas tanks, it was already overloaded.

I was excited. I called my boss, Myron Heiberg and told him I was quitting my job to go to New York. Myron was unhappy, to say the least. I had quit him the previous year to go to a project in Denver. My girlfriend was sad too. It would be the second summer in a row that I had left her to work elsewhere. I must admit. My life at that age was about adventure and fun. Such things as maturity and responsibility were far from paramount.

We intended to take off on May 27th, but when the three of us met at South Tacoma Airpark, it was befogged and raining. A storm had blown in off the Pacific, and the Cascades were completely socked in.

The Cascades Range extends from southern British Columbia southward across Washington and Oregon and into northern California. It is significant with peaks such as Mount Rainier, at more than 14,000 feet, as well as Mounts Baker, Hood, Adams, and Shasta. To fly east from the Pacific, a plane must either fly over the range or fly through the Columbia River Gorge, the only break in the range.

We met again the following morning, May 28th, 1958. The weather was still bad. The sky was overcast, and there was a cold drizzle. We were determined to go. Jack said, "We'll go up and take a look at Stampede Pass, and if we can't get through, we'll fly down to Portland and go up the Columbia River."

I got my little bags out of my car and kissed my girlfriend goodbye. Jack saw my bags and shook his head. I had some books for a correspondence class that I was taking from the U. of Washington. My bags were too much for the little Piper. The books would have to stay. Elaina would keep them for me until I returned in the fall.

With our plan in place, Chuck and I shoehorned ourselves into the tiny back seat; Jack climbed in, and with the control stick between his knees, we took off—three sojourners aflight, heading off into a murky future.

Summer of '58 – Episode 4

Trepidation: A feeling of fear or agitation about something that may happen.

"I think we can make it," Jack said. I think I could detect a tinge of <u>trepidation</u> in his voice. I didn't say anything. I didn't like the sound of "think." It was raining hard, and the solid clouds looked to be just above the little Piper's cabin. I could just make out the mountains through the rain clouds. Suddenly, they seemed to surround us, sticking up on both sides of the plane.

Jack didn't seem scared. I tried to stay calm. I couldn't believe the mountains that towered above us seemed so close. Within minutes, the clouds seemed to simply disappear, and we were in the sunshine. We had crossed the crest of the Cascades and were looking downward at the "dry side" of the mountains.

US Highway 90 lay just ahead of us. We followed it, flying above Ellensburg and Cle Elum's apple and cherry orchards. We continued east to the Vantage Bridge on the Columbia River.

We turned north and followed Highway 283 through Ephrata and Soap Lake to Coulee City. There, we reached our goal: US Highway 2. We would follow it nearly two thousand miles across five states to Sault St. Marie, Michigan.

Just a word about the little plane that we were trusting for our lives. The Piper Super Cruiser was just like an early Piper Cub. The "stick" was just that, a control stick sticking up between Jack's knees. There was nothing like a steering wheel. Jack sat in the single seat in the middle of the front next to the controls. Chuck and I were wedged and strapped into the back seat. The plane had no electronics. Jack said it would go nearly a hundred miles per hour, maybe more if we had a tailwind. How did we know if we had a tailwind? We looked at the smoke coming out of the chimneys of the houses. If it was going the same way we were, then maybe we were going over a hundred.

Two miles east of Coulee City, we found a little airport. It primarily served crop-dusters that, in turn, served the dryland farmers of the area. Areas between Moses Lake and Soap Lake are pretty much desert-like. After gasoline, restrooms, and candy bars, we were back in the air and continuing east.

At Spokane, we turned north and continued following Highway 2. The outline of the Rockies loomed to our right. They looked menacing to us in our tiny plane. These mountains were 10,000 feet high, many of them higher than our little plane could fly. We had been flying just 1,500 feet above the ground most of the time.

SUMMER OF '58 — EPISODE 5

Ceiling: The maximum altitude that a particular aircraft can reach.

In the bottom of the Kootenai Valley of northern Idaho, the Bitterroot Range of the Rockies looks like it reaches to the heavens. We found a little airport near Sandpoint that based some crop dusters that served the valley farms. It was an old abandoned WWII airfield manned by one old salt who looked like he might have flown in that war.

Jack taxied to a gas pump, and we piled out and headed for the restroom. Jack engaged the old fellow in conversation and inquired about how to get through the mountains. That's when the seasoned fellow asked, "What's your <u>ceiling</u>?"

Jack answered, "About ten."

"You'll need ten five," the old fellow advised. Jack told him then that he'd better just fill the tanks half full.

The old fellow pointed to an entrance to a canyon and told us to get our altitude before going in "because it gets high fast."

"After entering the main canyon," he said, "the canyon splits three ways. Take the hard left. Don't take the first left because it is a dead end, and you won't have room to turn around." I had to think about that to grasp the full meaning of not having room to turn around.

We were soon refueled and refreshed and back in the air. Utmost in my mind was the old attendant's warning not to take the wrong canyon. "--- dead end, and you won't have room to turn around" kept going through my mind.

It seemed that it took forever just circling and climbing. The little 108 HP 4-cylinder Lycoming engine strained as hard as it might but finally would go no higher. We followed the old fellow's instructions, sphincter muscles as tight as fiddle strings. We discussed later how the canyon kept narrowing, and we wondered if we were in the wrong canyon. Surely enough, there was no room to turn around.

I searched Jack's face for a sign of solicitude but could not detect it. He flew us through the rugged mountains with an unruffled equanimity that bolstered my confidence for the rest of the trip. If he was anywhere near as apprehensive as I was, he didn't show it. He should have been a poker player.

My seatmate, Chuck, seldom at a loss for words, said, "I'll swear, I could see the color of the marmots' eyes on both sides of the plane."

For the next 250 miles, the terrain remained mountainous but beautiful. We enjoyed the scenery of the Kootenai National Forest, Kalispel, and Flathead Lake.

Columbia Falls provided a stop for us for gas, restrooms, and hamburgers. It takes a while to shake the kinks out of your hips and knees after a few hours in that tiny seat. The butt-cheeks take a beating. It would have been wonderful for both of us if Chuck and I could have switched places mid-flight. No chance of that.

Jack had a cousin in Shelby, Montana, just beyond the Blackfeet Indian Reservation. He had contacted her ahead of time and asked if she and her husband could put us up for the night. We still had 150 miles to go but arrived there with a couple of hours of daylight left. Ellen and her husband, Ray, picked us up at the little airstrip. They had a nice home on their wheat ranch, so they had plenty of room for us to spend the night.

What a day! It was undeniably one of the most memorable days of my life.

SUMMER OF '58 – EPISODE 6

Quandary: a state of perplexity or uncertainty over what to do in a difficult situation.

Our second day should be less eventful, and it was. No mountain ranges.

Ellen and Ray prepared us a sumptuous ranch-style breakfast. They were fascinated that we were on such an adventurous excursion. They were somewhere between upper Midwest and Eastern Slope folks and apparently had not traveled more extensively than a honeymoon trip to Disneyland.

There was nary a cloud to be seen as Ellen and Ray drove us out to the little airstrip. Shelby was 3,297 feet above sea level. The morning air was brisk, but at the end of May, it was summertime. It would be a hot day. We three in our tiny Piper were soon climbing into Montana's Big Sky.

We set our sights on the town of Glasgow, 260 miles straight east, just to the north of the giant Fort Peck Reservoir on the Missouri River. A couple of our friends from the Fort Lewis job had gone to a military housing project at Glasgow AFB. One of them had bought a car from Jack and had not paid for it.

The little airport at Glasgow was right at the edge of town. We needed a car to get out to the AFB. There were no car rental places in town, but the owner of a service station agreed to rent us his old 54 Ford station wagon for a few hours.

We enjoyed visiting with our old friends, Allan Thacker and George McCulley, for an hour or so. I don't know if Jack ever got the money that he said he had coming. It didn't seem terribly important. The visit was the main thing.

Back at the airport, we found that we were in a developing quandary that was worsening by the hour. During the day, the bright sun heated Glasgow to above a hundred degrees, maybe 105. Jack had filled the tanks full before he realized that the airport was over 2,000 feet high. Temperatures over 100 degrees make for just plain "bad air" for taking off; couple that with the thin air of 2,000 feet high, and it would be all the little airplane could do to get off the runway. Oh well, the whole trip was as temerous as anything we had ever done. Let's climb aboard and see if we can get airborne. It is a good thing we had a very long runway. We used it all.

The rest of the day was relatively uneventful across North Dakota and Minnesota. The only hiccup was somewhere over North Dakota the battery went dead. It was running on its magneto when Jack landed it on an abandoned field. Jack opened the cowling, used a rock, tapped on the side of the voltage regulator, and unstuck the contact points. With the battery completely dead, Jack propped the engine by hand, and we were soon in the air again, headed for Michigan's Upper Peninsula.

Darkness was just setting in when we got on the ground at Sault Ste. Marie, Michigan. Sault Ste. Marie is known as "Soo" by the "Yoopers," as denizens of the Upper Peninsula are known. It had been a long day. We ate burgers at a mom-and-pop café just before they closed. The nondescript motel next door was showing its age but was good enough and cheap. We were soon fast asleep in our rooms.

Summer of '58 – Episode 7

Muskeg: Approximately synonymous with bog or peatland and is a standard term in Canada and Alaska.

Our navigation method was primarily Chuck and me looking at charts and telling Jack which road to follow while Jack flew the plane. VFR (Visual Flight Rules) are for people flying where they know where they are going. We couldn't use IFR (Instrument Flight Rules) because the little plane didn't have instrumentation. Our charts were like a road map. They also showed prominent landmarks like racetracks, tall water tanks, drive-in theaters, etc. These were easy to spot from the air. We generally followed highways but would follow power-line rights-of-way or railroads when they provided good shortcuts.

Our difficulty developed in Sault Ste. Marie, "Soo" as it is locally known. We had arrived late in the evening after having flown all the way from Shelby, Montana. To fly straight east from Soo would all be over Canada. We could not stop in Canada without clearing Customs and Immigration in Soo. The problem is, it was Friday evening when we landed there, and the Customs people had all gone home for the Memorial Day weekend. It would cost more money than the three of us had to hire them to come back and clear us. The only alternative was filing a flight plan, which Jack had not done before. So, he filed a flight plan from Sault Ste. Marie, Michigan, to Plattsburgh, New York. Essentially, we could fly over Canada but could not stop.

Chuck and I trusted Jack's knowledge and competence to get us to our destination. Had he not safely flown us over two difficult mountain ranges? To fly straight east from Soo would be to enter Canadian air space immediately, something Jack was apparently hesitant to do, although he didn't confer with Chuck or me or anyone else about it. He decided to fly southeast over Manitoulin Island, skirting the eastern shore of Lake Huron, and then fly around the southern end of Georgian Bay and then head east. Apparently, Jack hadn't flown across large expanses of water and, without instrumentation, was not comfortable about it.

We had been in the air more than two hours and were due north of Toronto when we made the turn to the east. Maybe Jack already knew we might be in trouble, but he didn't say anything.

East of Georgian bay, it was all lowland, a lot of <u>muskeg</u> swamps, and no landmarks. There were no major highways for us to follow. I kept seeing lakes, or bodies of water, that looked like those on the map, but then the next one looked totally different. Soon, we didn't know where we were. We were <u>l</u>ost. Jack set a compass heading for due east, and we just hoped we could find the St. Lawrence Seaway before we ran out of gas.

Summer of '58 –
Episode 8

Incautiousness: a lack of caution, or carelessness

The little Piper Cruiser, with full tanks of gas, was known to have five hours of safe flying time, five and a half hours, maximum. We knew we had burned too much fuel by following the islands and coastlines rather than flying directly toward our destination. Too late to think about that now. And to make matters worse, we didn't know exactly where we were. Chuck and I studied the charts constantly for the next couple of hours. Every time we would spot a lake or stream that looked like one on the map, the next view would be something totally different. The lakes and catchments seemed to have changed after the charts were made. It became hopeless to keep searching the charts. As we approached five hours in the air, we could see that Jack, usually unflappable, was showing the signs of worry that Chuck and I had been feeling for three hours.

We actually started looking for a level field where we could set the plane down, but the terrain was all either covered with water or timber. After five hours had passed, Jack mentioned that he could cut off the gas from one tank, and if we flew 10 minutes before running out of fuel in that tank, we should have another 10 minutes of fuel in the other tank.

I remembered some of the teaching from private pilot ground school. If you lose power and have to make a forced landing, try to fly between two trees. Let the two trees shear the wings off. That will slow the forward momentum. There's also the option (not a good one) of trying to flare into the top branches of a tree, which hopefully will somewhat cushion the landing. Landing in the water, even if it is shallow, is not an option. Usually, as soon as the wheels hit the water, the plane flips upside down. I don't remember us talking about it, but it was predominant in my mind. Jack had been through the same ground school that I had attended, so I had a pretty good idea of what he was probably thinking.

All of these things were heavy on our minds when we spotted the St. Lawrence Seaway in the distance. It is the wide St. Lawrence River that separates Canada from the United States.

Across the river, on the American side we could see level row-crop agriculture. We relaxed a bit. We were not going to die. We determined quickly where we were and turned downstream into the nearby town of Ogdensburg, New York. Were we running on fumes? Who knows? I suspect so.

The airport operator asked where we had come from. We told him. Michigan! "Michigan?" "In this?" "Without stopping?" He was astounded. I still am.

With our crisis over, we decided to eat lunch in the little airport café before heading out for any more adventures. We didn't realize or remember it at the time. Jack had totally forgotten about his flight plan.

As I put this story to print, some 66 years have passed since that perilous experience over southern Ontario. We didn't die that day, as is quite obvious. Just how close was it? We'll never know. If we had run out of fuel after crossing over the St. Lawrence Seaway, we could have landed safely in one of the flat grain fields. However, if we had gone down in one of the many swamps or wetlands we flew over, the outcome would have been too grim for me to even think about. Looking back, the whole trip was incredibly foolhardy, but the <u>incautiousness</u> of trying to fly from Sault Ste. Marie, Michigan, to Plattsburgh, New York was beyond comprehension. It was 150 miles beyond the capability of the little airplane.

But stay with us, folks. The Summer of '58 is just getting started.

Summer of '58 –
Episode 9

Admonishment: To reprove harshly

We could fly straight over the Adirondack Mountains to Plattsburgh. That would have been easy enough. However, our pilot was understandably unnerved by the scare we had just experienced. He said, "I don't need any more mountains." We would fly down the St. Lawrence Valley and follow US Highway 11 right into Plattsburgh. It was only 120 miles. The attendant at Ogdensburg looked like he wanted to choke someone when Jack told him just to put $2 worth of gas in each tank.

We had not considered what was awaiting us in Plattsburgh. Our friend, Bill Elsholz, a nervous sort of fellow anyway, had gone to the airport to meet us. This is the same Bill Elsholz who had sent me the telegram a few weeks earlier, asking me to call him.

Bill had been waiting for us for hours, and as we were told, "He had been pacing the runway." Someone advised him to go to the CAA office and find out if there was a flight plan. That touched off a furor. The CAA, Civil Aeronautics Authority, was a predecessor and parent to the FAA, Federal Aviation Administration, established just three months later, on August 23rd, 1958.

The CAA found that Jack had filed the flight plan more than

eight hours earlier in Sault Ste. Michigan in a little plane that couldn't fly that far in a single leg. Moreover, it was over three hours past the time when it would have run out of gas.

I am not privy to their discussions, but Bill told Jack he had better go settle those folks down before they send out search parties. Jack could have, and should have, called in a cancellation to the CAA when we stopped in Ogdensburg, but it had not occurred to him at the time. The fact that he had not done so incurred the severest of <u>admonishment</u>. They mentioned that they could suspend his pilot's license for such an infraction.

Our trip was complete. That evening, we spent with our friends, shook off our anxieties, had a couple of beers, and recounted our trip all the way across the country. It seemed like it had been two weeks. It had only taken three days.

Summer of '58 – Episode 10

Misapprehension: A mistaken belief about or interpretation of something

Plattsburgh was beautiful. It was pleasant. I rented a little cabin right on the bank of Lake Champlain. It was the Memorial Day weekend. One of our friends had a big old car so we loaded up and paid a visit to Ausable Chasm. What a place! The 150-foot-deep sandstorm gorge is known as the "Grand Canyon of the Adirondacks." The Ausable River runs through the chasm and empties in Lake Champlain. The 91' Rainbow Falls floods into the chasm at the Southern end. This sandstone gorge is two miles long and is one of the northeast's oldest attractions. This popular tourist attraction in the Adirondacks has been operating since 1870. The visit to Ausable Chasm was one of the few treats I enjoyed during my short stay at Plattsburgh.

My time in northern New York was cut short. I had accepted the job and made the trip to New York under the misapprehension that a Yankee contractor's word was of some value – that if one quit a job on one coast of the United States and traveled a couple thousand miles to the other coast to work for him there, that the arrangement would at least somewhat comply with the terms of the agreement that was reached on the phone before the trip.

The evidence of this misapprehension was made clear on the first morning when I reported for work. Chiccarelli was at his home office in Pittsfield, Massachusetts. His foreman told me that his project had been inundated with French Canadian workers from Quebec. French Canadians are actually Indians from several northern tribes who had gotten their French names from the French missionaries. At the same time, the French trappers gave them several strains of venereal diseases.

These people supposedly were happy to work for $25.00 per day doing the drywall taping and finishing by hand. The result of this was that the contractor would not be utilizing the machines that were the tools of my trade. He most graciously offered me the same arrangement that the Canucks had. It was almost like an insult. I was making more money back in Washington than I would be making here. However, I was here, about three thousand miles from Washington, and I did not have enough money to get back there. Chuck wanted to kill somebody right on the spot. In fact, he said he would tear him into small pieces and let God sort them out.

I got Chuck settled down and told him, "To hell with this project. We'll let Chiccarelli and his aborigines do it. We'll find something better." Of course, I didn't know what or where. I thought about it for less than a day but had to do something soon.

I remembered that Ed Hall, a fellow I had worked with at McCord AFB, was working around Buffalo. I managed to find his number and called him. He was glad to hear from me, and I was glad to hear his voice—one without a New York accent.

There was a giant power plant construction project in progress in Niagara Falls, so there was a lot of activity in the area. Ed gave me a couple of company names, and I started making phone calls. I finally negotiated a deal with Angelo Lucano Contracting for Chuck and me.

We talked another friend into going with us to Niagara Falls.

Pee-Wee Gibbons had a Ford station wagon. That's why we needed him. He had transportation.

It was a warm summer day, perfect for travel, and the three of us were excited about the prospects of a new beginning in Niagara Falls. The first half of our nearly 400-mile trip was through the scenic Adirondack Mountains. I was surprised at the beauty of rural upstate New York. The rest of the trip was through the rolling hills of western New York. It was the land of family farms and villages. We passed numerous roadside stands where homemakers were selling fruits and vegetables, produce from their farms.

We found some cabins for rent behind a bar on Pine Boulevard, and I called my new employer. He was ready to put the three of us to work on a new project near the falls and the power project.

We were excited. It was the new beginning that we had hoped for.

Summer of '58 – Episode 11

Suicide Clutch: A foot-operated clutch that works much like the clutch in a manual-shift car.

I spent the summer of 1958 working for Angelo Lucano Contracting, a local prime contractor and sub-contractor on the Niagara Power Plant. It was a good job. Lucano was my boss but not one of my drinking buddies. I demanded to be paid $5.00 per hour. That was nearly a dollar over the union scale. It pained him greatly to pay me that rate, but he knew I was making him money. He referred to me as the "Hot Shot California Kid." I ate it up.

I soon found that I needed some kind of transportation. I had never been without a car since high school, except for the two years that I was in the army. My car was at my girlfriend's house back in Tacoma.

Then I had the eureka moment. I'll buy a motorcycle. Motorcycles have always fascinated me, so it made sense. I found a 1950 Harley Davidson advertised for $450 by an airman out at Niagara AFB. I agreed to buy it and told the fellow that I would pick it up as soon as I got my next paycheck.

I had never ridden a motorcycle before. My friend, Ralph Kipp, had a Harley that was very similar, so he took me to a big empty parking lot. It was at a mall, but it was on a Sunday, so all the shops were closed. Ralph showed me how to stop and start it and how the controls worked, especially the <u>suicide clutch</u> and the gears. The gearshift was an awkward thing mounted on the left side of the gas tank and operated by hand. Ralph sat in the shade sipping a cold beer for a half hour while I learned to ride his bike. That was the extent of my driving school in preparation for riding my new one back into Niagara from the Air Force base.

My new 1950 Harly Davidson Hydra-Glide was eight years old and had an ugly green paint job, so I took it to the Harley shop in town for a bright red paint job and some dress-up chrome. It was a wonderful feeling, motoring around western NY for the rest of the summer.

As with all early Harleys, it had a hand-operated shift and a foot-operated clutch, known as Harley's infamous "Suicide Clutch." It was so-called because to shift gears, the rider has to clutch it with his left foot and then remove his hand from the handlebar to operate the shift lever. This is where it gets worse. When you stop at a stop sign or signal, you cannot put your left foot on the ground. It must stay on the clutch. You have to balance the bike with your right foot. If it tips to the left and you take your foot off the clutch, that is bad news. You just shot forward into traffic. Suicide Clutch!

My old Harley was beautiful, though. Upstate New York is an excellent place for motorcycling in the summertime. The weather was good, and there were many small roads and villages to check out. I made friends with several other bikers, and we went to rallies, hill climbs, dirt dig-outs, and scrambles. I bought the garb, the motorcycle boots, the Harley cap, and a leather jacket. It was a blast.

I decided that I wanted to keep the bike, so I planned to ride it back to the West Coast when the season was over. People with sane minds recommended against it, but it just sounded like a new adventure to me. I would not be dissuaded.

SUMMER OF '58 – EPISODE 12

Depositions: Formal, usually written, and recorded statements to be used as evidence in a trial

It was late September and "too damned cold for this time of the year," I muttered as I scraped the frost off the seat of my bike. "I am glad to be getting out of here." I stomped the kickstarter a half dozen times and felt the old Harley come alive. Soon, the city of Niagara Falls was sinking into the distance behind me.

I had come down from Plattsburgh a couple of months earlier to work on the big Niagara Power Project, which was said to be the largest construction project in the free world at that time. But the good season was over. Spray and mist from the Falls were freezing on the overlook handrails on cold nights. I had also gotten crosswise with some powerful bad guys and had begun to fear for my health. Time to move on.

The bad guys I mentioned is a story in itself. I'll try to be brief. One evening in late summer, I was sitting in Frank Rotundo's bar in front of the trailer park with a couple of ladies from the trailer park. Late in the evening, two young ladies that we knew drove in and parked in front of the bar. Their husbands were following on their motorcycles. Frank was standing outside smoking a cigarette. Apparently, the ladies parked their car too close to Frank's Thunderbird. I don't know if they bumped it with a door or not. Anyway, Frank was berating them when their husbands rode up. There were words between Frank and the young men. A fight started and between Frank and his big bouncer/bartender, who was using a club; they beat the young men up so badly that they were hauled out in an ambulance.

Many of the patrons in the bar were from the trailer court and, thus, Frank's tenants. I, along with my lady friends, had seen nearly the whole thing, and we could see that the police and news people were getting a distorted story about what had happened. I determined to set the record straight and sought out the older policeman who seemed to be in charge, and we told our version of the story. I had yet to learn that the patrons, mostly my trailer park neighbors, were afraid to go up against Rotundo. Among other things, he was their landlord.

Lawsuits and countersuits were filed, and over the next few weeks, I gave depositions of what I would testify in court against Frank Rotundo. I was then told that the Rotundos were Mafiosos and Frank was a cousin to Peter Magaddino, son of Don Stefano Magaddino, head of the Buffalo/Niagara Falls crime family, later known as La Cosa Nostra. The Godfather, Don Stefano's nephew, was Joseph Bonanno, one of the five family heads in New York City. The two Mafia bosses were from the same Sicilian town of Castellammare del Golfo. The Commission decided in 1931 that Stefano Magaddino and his Buffalo family would control Buffalo and Ontario, Canada, and the Bonanno family would control Quebec.

I was told that to testify against a "Family" member" could be very dangerous, deadly even. I didn't sleep well the last couple of weeks in Niagara Falls. I envisioned being machinegunned off my Harley. I didn't leave a forwarding address.

I felt good to be on the road, free from any worries behind me. My old 1950 Harley Davidson had a new paint job, new chrome, and a Buco windshield. It was a used windshield that I had bought at the Harley shop. It had a couple of girlie decals and a couple of reflectors in it. I had my little Harley cap and my leather jacket, and I was King of the Road. I was on my way to celebrate my 21st birthday with my mother and my friends in Arkansas then motor on out to the West Coast. That all sounded pleasant and easy. There was no way I could have predicted the travails that would befall me during the next few weeks.

SUMMER OF '58 – EPISODE 13

Harbinger: A person or thing that announces or signals the approach of another

It was a cold morning when I motored out of Niagara Falls on my old Harley. Actually, the 1950 model was only eight years old. It seems like an antique when I look back several decades later. The sky was clear, so it would warm up pretty soon. I motored south through Tonawanda and the Wurlitzer jukebox factory. I always wanted to tour the place.

Jukeboxes were always pretty and fascinating for a country boy. Just the thought brings back memories from my early years. I was about 15 years old. I, and Leo Cox, my good friend who taught me my first chords on my guitar, would sit near the shiny Wurlitzer jukebox in Burl's café in Maynard, Arkansas, hoping someone would put some money in and play one of our favorite songs. Radio and the jukebox were our only way of learning songs. The jukebox was the best because we might wait a week or a month to hear a favorite song again on the radio.

Twenty miles south was Buffalo. It brought back memories also. A few weeks earlier, a helper and I taped and finished the drywall in Buffalo's new National Guard Armory building. Looking back from some six decades later, I wonder if my building is still in use. In our country, we have a despicable culture where if a building is no longer big enough or new enough, we blow it down and build a bigger one.

South of Buffalo, I got on US Highway 90, known as the New York throughway. I felt good motoring west on the throughway. The scenery was good. The entire route was along the shore of Lake Erie, which had many views of the water. The roads were good. I was feeling that wonderful freedom that only a motorcyclist can feel out on the open highway.

I was excited to be heading toward my hometown in Arkansas. I would see my mother, whom I hadn't seen in two years. I would laugh and create hilarity with my childhood friends. I anticipated showing off my pretty red and white Harley. The anticipation was exhilarating.

I would have smiled, but as we know, a smiling motorcyclist gets bugs in his teeth.

Soon I crossed over into Pennsylvania. Travel continued easy and pleasant. The midday sun melted away the chill that I had felt leaving Niagara Falls. Pennsylvania didn't last long, and I was in Ohio. This was thrilling because these were places totally new to me.

My first problem of the trip, a harbinger of things to come, but I didn't realize it, was just west of Cleveland. My front chain on the bike was loose and needed attention. It shouldn't be a big problem. I backtracked into downtown Cleveland and managed to find the Harley shop. I needed a new chain. The good folks at the shop learned that I was on the road, so they hustled and got me a new chain installed, and I was back on the road again.

The detour back into Cleveland had cost me a lot of time. I don't remember much about the city except what an incredibly long way it was from the outskirts through the suburban towns to the center of the city. Naturally, this diversion knocked a hole in my day. It was rush-hour traffic getting out of Cleveland. It was all city streets and traffic signals. There were no interstate highways in those days.

I still had some daylight left, but after a couple of hours, the sun dipped behind a cloud bank just above the horizon, and the air became chilly. I started looking for a motel. I was in no particular hurry, and I was sightseeing. This part of the country was new to me, and I might never see it again.

I rode into the Village of Mount Gilead, Ohio, and found an A&W, which was good for a hamburger and a root beer float. Just across the street was an aging motel. The rooms cost eight dollars. My first day on the road was history.

Tomorrow would be a day that I would be happy to forget.

SUMMER OF '58 –
EPISODE 14

Stash: a store or supply of something.

It was a frosty morning in Mount Gilead. I grabbed a quick breakfast at a diner next to the motel and hit the road. I was determined to knock down some real mileage today and maybe make it all the way to Arkansas. My garb was my leather jacket, Levis, and leather gloves. It was cold.

I headed out of Mount Gilead on US Highway 42 with my sights set on Springfield on Highway 40.

I was not more than 15 miles out of town when I caught up with an 18-wheeler. It was a two-lane road and there was a lot of morning traffic. I waited an insufferable length of time for a chance to get around him. Finally, I could see a chance, but I would have to hustle to get back in my lane ahead of oncoming traffic. I downshifted and cranked the throttle wide open. I kept it open and shifted into fourth. I didn't look at the speedometer, but it was probably hitting around 80 when I pulled into the right lane, still wide open because the oncoming traffic was another 18-wheeler, and he was coming on strong.

When the big truck went by me, with both of us moving fast, the wind blast from the truck hit. It wobbled my bike and snapped the top half of my windshield clean off. The big shard of windshield nearly knocked me off my bike when it hit me in the face. I felt like it had broken my frozen nose. I touched my nose with my glove and saw no blood, so I felt relieved.

However, I needed to replace my broken windshield.

I stopped at a gas station in the next little town and told the man to fill it up. A family was in a station wagon on the other side of the pump, and the lady and kids looked at me like I was some sort of monster. I thought, "Didn't you ever see a motorcyclist before?" I went into the restroom, and when I looked in the mirror, I could hardly believe my eyes. The flying windshield had cut my cheek near my right temple. I had dried blood all back across my ear. I had been so cold that I had not even felt the cut or the blood—no wonder the folks in the car looked at me like I was from outer space.

I washed the blood off as best I could, paid the attendant for two gallons of gas, and was back on the road again. I continued on Highway 42 to the town of Delaware, then turned south on U.S. 23 and rode into the city of Columbus. I felt downright silly as I rode past and among the Ohio State University students with half of a windshield. Instead of looking cool on my Harley, I felt like a spectacle.

Columbus had a population of nearly 400,000 in those days. I think that included 17,000 students. They have 66,000 students now, and the city has grown to nearly a million.

After about three stops to ask for directions, I found the Harley-Davidson shop and soon had a new windshield installed.

A new chain in Cleveland and a new windshield in Columbus were chipping away at my <u>stash</u> of travel funds.

Back on the road, I turned west on Highway 40. My mishap had cost me both time and money. Maybe I could still make it to St. Louis before dark. I pushed the old Harley pretty hard on a good straight Highway and soon crossed into Indiana.

I had just ridden through the town of Greenfield, Indiana, and was back on the open road. I was running at highway speed for a couple of miles, then caught up with some slower traffic. When I saw the opportunity, I downshifted for passing gear, cranked open the throttle, and passed two vehicles. I was hardly back in my lane when my engine made a sound, much like a dynamite blast, and started rattling and shaking the whole motorcycle. I managed to get off the road onto the shoulder and checked my engine. Obviously, a piston rod had broken. My engine was totally destroyed. I was about 25 miles short of Indianapolis, Indiana, and afoot. What in the world am I to do now?

SUMMER OF '58 – EPISODE 15

Disobliging: Deliberately unhelpful; uncooperative

It is a helpless feeling to be standing at the side of a two-lane road somewhere out in the eastern Indiana countryside with a broken-down motorcycle.

The only sign of civilization was an isolated farmhouse I had passed about a quarter mile back. I hoped there was someone at home and that they didn't have a vicious yard dog. I left the Harley just off the shoulder of the road and started walking.

The farmstead had an attractive layout, surrounded by lush green cornfields. The two-story white house sat behind a complementary white picket fence. The brilliant green sward of grass surrounding the house and hay barn suggested that farmer Brown once had livestock, but that had been in years past. The only outbuilding that was in regular use was the equipment shed. Like many in the Midwest farm belt, farmer Brown had given up on subsistence farming and became a corn farmer.

I opened the front gate, walked to the door on the side porch, and knocked on the screen door. Presently, a lady opened the wooden door a few inches. She looked every bit the character of a middle-aged farmer's wife. Her husband was probably out plowing corn, and she was probably wishing she had a gun in her hand.

I explained my plight through the screen door and told her I would pay for a long-distance call if she let me use her phone. The farmer's wife, as I appraised her, was naturally cautious. Her Christian raising, however, would not allow her to be <u>disobliging</u> to a wayfarer in need. And I was in need.

Her countenance softened as she could see that I wasn't too threatening. I found the Harley dealer's address in the Indianapolis phone book and called. I had the lady of the house explain where we were, about 25 miles east of Indianapolis on Highway 40. The Harley shop said they wouldn't have time to work on it that day, but they would send a pickup and trailer to haul me in. I thanked the lady and, gave her a couple of dollars for the long-distance charge, and headed back to my bike.

After a long half-hour of sitting by my broken motorcycle, Carl, one of the mechanics, showed up, and we loaded the bike on his trailer. Carl was about 50 years old and a friendly sort of fellow. We visited in his pickup on the way back to Indianapolis. He asked me where I was from and where I was going. He had a little trouble sorting out how this young fellow, barely out of his teens, was from Arkansas but now in Indiana riding a motorcycle from New York to Washington State on the West Coast. He was a little fuzzy about where Washington was. He had never been "out west". He said what I was doing was the kind of thing he wished he had done before getting married and starting a family.

We got the bike unloaded at the Harley shop and pushed it into the garage. He said, "Let's hear it." I thought, "Oh, please don't!" He kicked the starter a couple of times, and it fired up, knocking, rattling, and smoking. He turned it off in just a moment and said, "Well, son, she sounds like she is about used up." I have never forgotten his words.

It was closing time at the shop. They will start on it tomorrow. They locked up the shop and I set out walking to find a hotel for a night or two.

SUMMER OF '58 – EPISODE 16

Photostat/Photostatic: A copy of a document made by using a photostat machine

It was the evening of September 30th. I should have been in Arkansas by now, or at least in St. Louis. Instead, I was stuck in Indianapolis for some indeterminate length of time while my motorcycle was being repaired.

I had found a motel and café three or four blocks from the Harley shop. I had a plate-lunch dinner at the Minnie's Diner, then checked in at the motel. There were still three hours of daylight left, and I had nothing to look at but four drab walls in the motel room. I didn't know a soul in four hundred miles. It would have been nice if the room had had a television.

Looking for a way to spend my evening, I found a bar a few blocks away. It was a nice cocktail lounge with a fellow in a sequined jacket playing and singing at a piano bar.

For clarification purposes, even though I was only 20, my ID said I was 21. The birth date on my driver's license indicated that I was born in 1936 rather than 1937, ever since I had "doctored" my <u>photostatic</u> birth certificate and joined the army when I was

16. Photostatic documents were black with white lettering. My alteration of the date was sloppy, but nobody caught it.

I noticed that there were several women sitting at the piano bar but not even one at the bar. In the course of the evening, I chatted with a local fellow, and he explained that women were not allowed to sit at a bar in Indiana. They also couldn't stand up with a drink. They had to be seated at a table or the piano bar, which was considered a table. That was the law. I later learned that Washington had the same law. Those laws stayed on the books for decades and were finally repealed in 1969.

The following day, October 1st, I walked back to the Harley shop to check on the progress on my bike. Carl and his helpers had torn down the engine, salvaged pistons and a crank pin from another bike, and were putting mine back together. It was a complete overhaul, and they would have it done in the early afternoon.

I was glad to be back on the road. My poke that I had accumulated during the summer was a lot lighter now. As I rode, I reflected on the recent events that had accelerated my exit from Niagara Falls.

The two ladies that I witnessed the brawl with in Rotundo's bar were Rosemary Zink and Eleanor Kipp, wives of Lisle Zink and Ralph Kipp. Lisle and Ralph had been out of town at a motorcycle rally that evening. Rosemary and Eleanor had both given recorded depositions to a lawyer, the same as I had. When I started hearing, down at the motorcycle shop, who I was set to be witnessing against in court, and the connection to prominent Mafia people, I started not to sleep well. I met with Lisle and Ralph and their wives. They were more familiar with Niagara's crime scene than I was, and they took it seriously. Lisle hooked up his house trailer and left for Kansas. I never heard of them again. Ralph hooked up his house trailer and pulled out for Montana. I was the only one left to testify against Frank Rotundo. I left, too.

Again, happy to be free from those worries, I motored halfway across Illinois before stopping for the night. I planned to forget about the past and have fun with some of my old friends in Arkansas.

Summer of '58 – Episode 17

Trill: a quavering or vibratory sound

A day with no mishaps is a good day when one is riding an old Harley.

That's what I had on October 2nd. The weather was good, and the bike felt good under me. I continued west across Illinois, crossed the Mississippi River into Missouri, and turned south on Highway 67. I was excited now. I was in familiar territory.

An hour later, I was in Farmington, where my mother was working as a housemother at Presbyterian Children's Home, riding herd on a bunch of unruly boys. I hadn't seen my mother since I had headed west to California two years earlier when I was 18 years old. We had a wonderful visit for a couple of hours, and then I headed on down toward Arkansas. My mother would ride down on a bus in a couple of days to spend my birthday with me.

Maynard had fewer than 300 residents in 1958. It was not too many folks short of that when I was a kid some 15 years earlier, though. It was still a lively town on Saturdays and especially on Saturday evenings.

I remember the war years. I was a small child. On Saturday, my step-father, Aden, would harness up the mules, load up the wagon with what eggs we could sell, and cream from our dozen Guernsey cows. He would throw some loose hay in the wagon bed for me and my sister to sit on. It was still a dusty and bumpy ride in a steel-rimmed wagon on three miles of gravel road.

Saturday was shopping day. Virtually everybody from the surrounding area went into town to buy groceries, get haircuts, and visit with neighbors, some of whom we saw weekly, either in town on Saturdays or in church on Sundays—others we might not have seen for a month or two. Saturdays were always exciting.

As I got a little older, I was allowed to stay in town after my parents went home. There were three cafes, two pool halls, and a movie theater. It was exciting, and if I had a quarter, I could go to the movie and see cowboy stars like Tex Ritter, Rex Allen, and Sunset Carson. There was always a gory Batman serial that gave us something to have bad dreams about.

There was a remnant of that left in '58. Weekend evenings were still lively. Television was pretty new. There was hardly a speck of affluence in Maynard in those days, so very few people had television. Older people sat on their front porches and visited. Younger folks hung around town sipping sodas and visiting with their friends.

I felt like a king motoring in on the only main street in town with both straight pipes blaring the unique Harley Davidson sound. The first person I met on the street was my childhood friend, Levon Cox. I parked my bike right in front of the café, and we went inside. There were others from my high school days. I had much to share about my experiences over the last couple of years. Friends gathered around to hear my stories.

Finally, it was time to say goodnight to my friends and motor three miles out of town on Richardson's Ferry (gravel) Road to my mother's house. I found a key and turned on some lights. All was familiar. My bed was as it were when I had last seen it.

I had forgotten how quiet the night was out in the country. There are the night sounds from the trees and gardens. When I heard the trilling calls and answers by the whippoorwills, I realized that I had not listened to the <u>trill</u> of whippoorwills in years. I pulled up a lawn chair in the carport and soaked it in for over an hour.

I was at home.

Summer of '58 – Episode 18

Inebriated: Drunk, Intoxicated, Snockered

What a feeling: It was nostalgically exhilarating to ride my Harley around all the old roads that had been familiar to me for all of my childhood years. None of the roads were paved, and some were quite primitive. The only exception was Highway 115, which ran from the Missouri state line down through Maynard and on south to Pocahontas, the county seat of Randolph County.

In the early afternoon, I crossed the Current River on the old ferry to pay a visit to Reyno and see some friends who were picking cotton in the river bottoms. I rode out into the cotton field to smell the cotton and say hello to my friends, the Cox family. Earlene, a younger sister of my pals, was fascinated with my bike, so I gave her a ride. I had known Earlene since she was a tyke.

Reyno is a little town on the east bank of Current River, just trying to stay alive after the highway bypassed the town. Reyno is pronounced like Reno, Nevada, by the locals, but the name has a different origin. Reyno is a shortened version of Reynolds, named for Dennis Wells Reynolds, who opened the first store and built a house there in 1857.

Earlene said she didn't want to pick any more cotton that day and asked me to take her home on my motorcycle. I told her that I intended to ride back up across the state line and visit some of the honky-tonks where I used to play music. She said she wanted to go with me.

We still had a few hours of daylight left, so we headed for Doniphan, Missouri. We visited a couple of the old clubs where I used to play. It was fun reminiscing about some of the old days. Earlene was well-known in the Doniphan honky-tonks, although she was likely not more than 16 years old, 17 at the most. I was 20. Earlene had an easy laugh. She was a great dancer and a lot of fun. She then told me that she had married James Rudd just before he joined the army. He was in basic training at Fort Chaffee. At least on this day, Earlene was not even remotely concerned about James. I figured that if she wasn't concerned about being married to James, why should I be?

In an hour or so, things were getting a little sideways, and I could see that Earlene had too much to drink. We got on the bike and headed toward home. I thought taking the gravel road down through Minorca and Supply was prudent to avoid going through Maynard, where everyone would recognize us. I soon realized that Earlene had had way too much to drink. Pretty soon, she was not even holding on to me. She was waving both arms in the air, singing, and I was riding my bike with my right hand on the throttle and my left arm trying to hold her to keep her from falling off the motorcycle onto the gravel road.

We approached the Glaze Creek bridge, and I stopped. If need be, I would throw her in the creek to sober her up. I walked the <u>inebriated</u> teen down the bank to the gravel bar. We sat down and washed our faces in the cold, clear water. After a half hour, she started to sober a bit. I felt better, too.

As we started back up the bank, a pickup stopped next to my bike, and a young man asked if we needed any help. I thanked him and told him we were fine. As he drove away, Earlene said, "That was James's cousin."

SUMMER OF '58 –
EPISODE 19

Impaired: Weakened or damaged

It was great to be on familiar ground. It was nostalgic. I had left my hometown when I was 16 and went to the army. Two years later, following my discharge, I saw that I was going to have to go to work, so I hitch-hiked to Chicago and got a job. Before the year was over, I was in California. So, in a nutshell, in 1958, between the time I was 16 and 20, I had spent very little time in my hometown. I was enjoying it, but I had little time to catch up because I needed to be on the road headed west.

October 4th was Saturday. Saturday was always an exciting day in the '40s and '50s. It was shopping day. Farm families came to town to buy groceries, staple needs, feed, etc., and even clothes, as I recall. Saturday evenings were lively. The cafés and pool halls were full. There might be a fight or two, usually around one of the pool halls, but everyone else had fun.

My friend Levon and I decided to go to Reyno, a little cotton-gin town in the Current River bottoms. Even when I was in high school, young guys liked to get out of town and go to a neighboring town. Why did the girls seem to be prettier in the other towns? I still can't answer that. It seemed more exciting, though.

US Highway 67 ran smack through the middle of Reyno. It was a busy highway carrying all the traffic from Dallas and Little Rock north to St. Louis. We were in front of the café right on the corner in Reyno when Levon thought he wanted to ride my Harley. Levon had had a few drinks. I can't say about myself, but in retrospect, my judgment was obviously <u>impaired to some degree</u>.

Anyway, I cranked up the bike and offered it to Levon. As he took hold of the handlebars and I had released them, his right hand cranked the throttle wide open. Before he could get on the bike, the racing engine caused the suicide clutch to vibrate forward and engage. As the bike started moving forward, Levon was trying to hold it back or get on. Out across Highway 67 they went. It would have been a hilarious spectacle if it weren't so dangerous. Anyway, thank heavens, no traffic was coming along at that second. The bike crashed into a ditch on its side with Levon on top of it. The engine was racing, and Levon was trying to find a way to shut it off. Levon was unhurt, but guess what? There was a post there, and it broke the new windshield that I had bought just a few days earlier in Columbus, Ohio.

SUMMER OF '58 – EPISODE 20

Curtailed: Reduced in extent or quantity

It was Sunday. I was my mother's little boy again. And it was a pleasant feeling. She had arrived on an early bus from Farmington. There was time for us to make the 11 o'clock church service. She was proud to take me to church at the Maynard Methodist Church.

Over the years, the little stone church has often struggled to have enough attendance to pay the pastor. I remember its heyday when people packed in the sanctuary like canned herrings during revival meetings. Those crowds are no more. The faces change. The first names are new, but the family names never change. They are the faithful: the Martins, the Sullivans, the Lincolns, Carrolls, and Templetons.

We ate lunch at the downtown café, and there was more of the after-church crowd, both from the Methodist and Baptist churches, for us to visit with. I spent the rest of the afternoon with her. It was a great visit.

My mother, Donna Lois (Wilson) Cates, was likely the most extraordinary woman I have ever known. Donna Wilson was the daughter of Isaac Thomas Wilson and Clemmie (Perkins) Wilson. She was born in the wilderness of Columbia County, in northwest Oregon. Her father was a logger in the mountainous forest near their home. Due to Donna's mother's health, the Wilson family moved to Missouri when Donna was only six years old.

Donna's mother, Clemmie, never regained her health. Donna was just 12 years old when Clemmie died, but she had learned a lot in her young life. Clemmie knew that her life would be prematurely <u>curtailed</u>, so she tried to teach Donna everything she needed to know to get along in the challenging world she would have to face.

Donna could prepare meals for her father and brothers. She could sew their clothes, and she could play the piano. She raised lambs and turkeys and trapped rabbits for their fur and for meat. She wanted to be a teacher, but her local school only had basic elementary classes. So she went to Linn Creek, Missouri, where she kept house and cooked for a family in exchange for room and board during school years.

Don't go looking to see what Linn Creek looked like in 1912. Following the completion of Bagnall Dam on the Osage River in 1931, the Original Linn Creek lays submerged in the bottom of Lake of the Ozarks.

Donna worked her way through school and became a railroad telegrapher at the age of 17. She was on her own. Her mother was gone, and her father had sold the Ozarks home place and moved to Texas. Her work took her west at a time when the West was a rough place for anyone. It was the "Wild West."

She had to carry a gun to protect herself while working in railroad depots in the mining towns on the frontier of Oklahoma, Kansas, New Mexico, and Colorado. Years later, during the Great Depression and afterward, in Alabama and then Arkansas, she raised four children virtually alone after the death of her husband. She faced all obstacles with self-confidence that she could overcome. One of those difficulties was breast cancer, which hit her hard when she was 56 years old. She overcame that obstacle, too, and lived to the age of 91. She was an amazing woman, a hard-working saint of a lady.

That long-ago Sunday that I spent with my mother reigns supreme among my treasured memories.

Summer of '58 –
Episode 21

Somber: Sad, depressed

It was Monday, October 6th. I look silly riding a motorcycle with half of a windshield, and soon, I will be headed for the West Coast. It would be ludicrous to try to ride 2,000 miles without a windshield.

The nearest Harley Davidson shop was in Jonesboro, nearly halfway to Memphis on US Highway 63. Folks at the Harley shop didn't ask questions about why my obviously new windshield was missing its top half. I didn't try to explain it.

Back at my mother's house in the early afternoon, it would soon be time to take her to the bus station in Pocahontas. We enjoyed a late lunch and put things away. I would be leaving in a few days, and she might not return for several weeks or months. I used her 1950 Ford to drive her to Pocahontas. We were both somber and teary-eyed as we said goodbye. She climbed aboard the big Trailways bus and was headed back to the rowdy boys at Presbyterian Children's Home in Farmington, Missouri. We didn't know when we would ever see each other again.

The next evening, October 7th, I visited Pocahontas with friends. I left there at around 8 PM, motoring back to Maynard. By that time, it was dark. The route has always been a winding, hilly road. Parts of it were closed on both sides by the wooded hills.

About five miles out of Pocahontas on Highway 115, I was motoring steadily, probably around 60 miles per hour. Suddenly, like a flash, I saw a brown blur from the left side of the road. Then, Bang! A big bird came through the top half of the plastic windshield and hit me right in the throat.

I struggled to maintain control of the bike and stopped in the road. I didn't know what had hit me, but I could do nothing about it. I broke the rest of the windshield off and rode back to Maynard. Of course, when I told people about it, I could see that they thought I had made up the story. "Yeah, how many drinks have you had?"

The next day, I was lucky that the Harley shop in Jonesboro had one more windshield. When I told the folks at the Harley shop what had happened, they were not surprised. They said it was a hoot owl, not an uncommon occurrence. Apparently, something about the sound of a Harley's exhaust attracts hoot owls. I had the new one installed along with a new rear chain, which was needed.

It was about this time that I realized I was not likely to have enough money to get back to Washington.

I stayed in Arkansas long enough to spend my 21st birthday, on October 9th, with friends. The next day, it was time to hit the road. I was not excited to be back on the road this time. It was cold and cloudy, and I didn't know how far I could get before my money was totally depleted. The old Harley needs gas. And it's not like a car. You cannot just lie over and go to sleep in it.

I got a late start and rode up through northwest Arkansas and southwest Missouri into Kansas. The sun had gone down, and a cold wind was blowing when I reached Hays on Highway 40. Most of Highway 40, all the way across Kansas, was a two-lane road with stop signs and signals in every town. I gassed up at the edge of town and inquired where to find the cheapest motel. It was only a couple blocks away, a little roadside court, and the rooms cost $8 for the night. That's what I needed.

During my second morning on the road, I could hear my drive-chain on the motorcycle rattling. I'd been told it would happen, and I would have to tighten it. It had gotten worse by the afternoon.

I rode into the little town of Powder River, Wyoming. At a local gas station, I requested and got permission to work on my bike there.

I put the bike up on its jack, got out my wrenches, and adjusted the rear wheel by moving it farther to the back, which tightened the chain, just like on a bicycle. I was proud of my work. I'd never done it before on the motorcycle. I thanked the man at the station, straddled my bike again, and took off feeling good. I had not gotten out of town when a car pulled out from a side street. I stomped on my brake. I heard a screech like a wounded hyena, then a metallic clank, clank, and my rear wheel brake didn't work anymore, ever.

I avoided hitting the car and pulled to the side of the road to see what had happened. The sad news was evident. When I had adjusted the wheel, I neglected to adjust the brake rod that operated the rear brake. Without being adjusted, it was, in effect, too short. When I stomped the pedal, I wrenched it clear out of the brake drum. There was an ugly hole in the brake drum, where the brake arm used to be, and the brake rod, arm, shrapnel, and all were dragging the ground.

I gathered up the debris, threw it in a ditch, and crawled back on my bike. I would have to learn to ride it with just a front-wheel brake.

I rode on north to the town of Thermopolis. There was only one stop sign in the whole 100 miles between Powder River and Thermopolis. I was getting along with just a front-wheel brake. What choice did I have?

At Thermopolis, I found a truck stop and ordered a roast beef sandwich plate and water for dinner. I think it cost 85 cents. I was feeling panicky about running out of money. I inquired about the cheapest hotel in town. The guy at the truck stop said, "That would have to be The Antlers. It is pretty rustic." I had a pretty good idea of what he meant by "pretty rustic," and I wasn't wrong. Ten dollars!

I sat on the bed in my "pretty rustic" room and tallied my shekels. I knew that my friends, Ralph and Eleanor Kipp, lived somewhere around Helena, Montana. Helena was nearly 400 miles on up the road. If I didn't have more trouble, I had enough money for gas to get there. But that was it. I would be broke. After making a few calls, I got Ralph on the phone. He told me how to find his trailer and said I could bed down there.

Summer of '58 –
Episode 22

**Combine: A large farming machine that
cuts, separates, and cleans grain**

It was a brisk autumn morning when I checked out of the Antlers
Hotel, gassed up at the truck stop, and headed north. The sky was
clear. Hopefully, it would be a good day, a day without bike troubles.
It seemed that I had been plagued with motorcycle problems nearly
every day since I had left New York two weeks earlier.

When I talked with Ralph Kipp on the phone the evening
before, he said he had his trailer parked on his mother's ranch out
on the Great Falls Highway. He told me to stop at the Eller's Corner
store and inquire about the directions to the Kipp Ranch.

Ralph and Eleanor Kipp had been my friends in Niagara Falls.
Eleanor was one of the ladies I was with when we saw the fight that
eventually caused us all to flee Niagara.

Ralph and Eleanor (Little Red as she was known) were lifesavers.
They provided me with a place at their table and a <u>sofa to bed down</u>
on. Ralph was working for a drywall and painting contractor in
Helena. I went with him to work the following day and met his
boss. Upon Ralph's recommendation, he agreed to put me to work
immediately.

Ralph's mother had remarried in the last year or so and consequently had acquired a 16-year-old stepdaughter. Her daughter, Shelly, was also 16 years old. These two very pretty girls were both seniors in high school. I looked forward to their getting off the school bus in the late afternoon and would sometimes give them rides back to the ranch house on my motorcycle.

Helena, Montana, was an exciting place. It was the kind of place most folks probably thought never existed, or at least not within a century or two. It was a "wide open" town. The main street downtown was lined, on both sides, with bars and brothels. The street's name was Last Chance Gulch, which was the city's original name. It was a wild place.

One afternoon, Ralph and I were going to go for a ride on our motorcycles. The girls wanted to go with us. So, Ralph took his sister, and I took his step-sister on my bike. I think her name might have been Christi. We rode around mainly on the turn rows of a couple of large wheat fields. The wheat had been combined a few weeks earlier, so the fields were covered with short, dry stubble.

At one point, Ralph turned or waved at me, signaling it was time to return to the ranch. I swung a large circle into the wheat field to get turned around. Unbeknownst to me, there were parallel drainage ditches across the wheat fields. They were small, only a couple of feet wide and about that deep. When combining the wheat, they had let the headers of their combines extend over the ditches so they were virtually impossible to see from a distance.

Yeah, you guessed it. About two-thirds around my circle, the drainage ditch appeared before me. I couldn't avoid it. I hit my front wheel brake, the only brake I had. The front wheel slid out from under me and laid me down. We slid on the stubble until my front wheel hit the other side of the ditch. Christi flew over my head. I was concerned that Christi was hurt. She was only concerned for me. I was embarrassed. Thank God neither of us was hurt. My adrenalin was really pumping. I yanked that 600-pound bike out of the ditch and upright and didn't even realize I had done it.

Following that little incident, I had road rash on my right leg up to my hip. Now, it matched my other leg. I had road rash on it from when a woman pulled out in front of me from a side street in Ohio. I had laid the bike down and bounced off her rear tire.

I worked for the Helena contractor for two weeks, and it was time to hit the road. It was late October and cold in the mountains. Helena is in the rugged Rocky Mountains, and local folks told me that it could get 60 degrees below zero.

SUMMER OF '58 – EPISODE 23

Avow: Assert or confess openly

It was the coldest I have ever been, 66 years ago. You would think memory would fade in 66 years, but I can still <u>avow</u> that it was the coldest that I have ever been.

I had been on the road for a month since that frosty morning when I left Niagara Falls on the old Harley. Mishaps along the way had drained my wallet. I had spent a week in Arkansas visiting my mother and celebrating my 21st birthday. I stopped and worked a couple of weeks in Helena, Montana, to get enough money in my pocket to make it across the mountains to Tacoma, Washington. But the problem was, it was way after freeze-up in Montana's high country.

I tried to crank the old Harley. It was so stiff the crankcase oil seemed frozen. We hooked a rope from the fork of my bike to Little Red's car, and she pulled me out across a wheat field until the engine fired and started running.

The Kipp Ranch, where I had been staying, out on the Great Falls highway, is at about 4,000 feet elevation, but I had to get over MacDonald Pass just west of town and it was 6,312 feet high. It started snowing hard before I got to Missoula, and from there, through the Bitterroots and Coeur d'Alene Mountains, much of the highway was completely covered with frozen snow and ice.

My problems were twofold. I only had a front-wheel brake. As you might recall, my rear wheel brake had been destroyed by a mishap in Wyoming. The other problem was that this was in the days before goose-down clothing. My protection from the cold was a leather jacket and some cotton long-john underwear. Not nearly enough. I would stop for a couple of gallons of gas every hour and go inside the gas station for warmth. My knees were so frozen that my legs wouldn't straighten. If I warmed up any at all in the gas station, I would start shivering uncontrollably. That would continue for about five minutes after I got on the road again, and then numbness, I suppose, quieted the shivers.

I recall that ascending Lookout Pass on the Montana/Idaho border, the two-lane highway was in the sunshine and covered with melting snow. When I reached the crest and started down the western side, the roadway was shaded, and the rutted snow was frozen hard. I rode with both boots down on the ice all the way into Kellogg, Idaho. The slush that had soaked my Levis's lower legs earlier was frozen hard.

The pavement in Spokane was wet with patches of snow. The first dry pavement was west of Cheney. I breathed a sigh of relief. It was the first dry pavement in over 300 miles. And it didn't last long. Near Ritzville, it was getting dark and had started snowing again. I found a cheap hotel and covered up with every blanket that I could find.

Summer of '58 – Episode 24

Villainous: guilty of wicked or criminal behavior

I ate a hot breakfast at Denney's, not in a hurry to face the elements again. I hit the road at about 9 o'clock. Travel was easy. Overnight traffic had beaten most of the snow off the roadway. I crossed the Columbia River at Vantage by noon. It was time to face those same Cascade Mountains that Jack, Chuck, and I had flown through back in May. By now, I had gotten used to having only a front-wheel brake.

The highway over Snoqualmie Pass was half-covered with snow but not nearly as bad as the Rockies and Bitterroots. I followed a snowplow up the incline. It pulled off the road at the summit. From there on, it was a piece of cake. A happy piece of cake. I was so glad to be getting home to be with my girlfriend. I would be warm again.

It had been the most memorable summer of my life, with experiences stretched from coast to coast, an almost historic voyage in an old, very primitive airplane, and a motorcycle trip that lasted nearly two months. A villainous employer made broken promises in Plattsburgh, and there was a Mafioso threat in Niagara Falls. I have marveled at the multitude of people and experiences. Some now say I am lucky to be alive. I suspect that's true.

It was late afternoon when I motored to my girlfriend's sister's house where she was staying. It was October 31st, Halloween, 1958, when I climbed off my bike in Tacoma, Washington. I felt <u>ten years older</u> than when I had left in the little airplane just five months earlier.

These 24 episodes tell the story of my experiences in the Summer of 1958.

Additional Note:

One day in late 1963, as I was sitting in a South Tacoma barber shop, I picked up a Life magazine and found an article about Joe Valachi. He was the first Mafia mobster to break the code of silence, the Omertà, and turn the state's evidence. He named the twelve family heads, the "Dons" of La Cosa Nostra. The article pictured Stefano Magaddino as the original Buffalo Area Boss and told about Magaddino's funeral home in Niagara Falls. After reading that article, I started counting my blessings all over again. I was reminded of the wisdom and luck that I had gotten out of Niagara Falls when I did.

VERONA

Agri: Agri is the plural form of 'ager,' which means 'field' or 'land.' It is the standard abbreviation for agriculture.

It was in the early summer of 2011, and it was the first day of my venture to drive from southern France all the way to Eastern Europe. We drove the highway that looked down on the Cote d'azur. The Mediterranean was seldom out of sight as we crossed the Alpes near where they simply fall into the sea.

After crossing into Italy, we skirted around Genoa and turned north to the Veneto Region. It was late afternoon when we reached our Agriturismo le Case di Campagna.

The agriturismo is part of a program that encourages farmers to branch out and provide facilities intended for tourists. This provides additional income for involved farmers and abets the local economy. The term is shortened to Agri.

Our Le Case di Campagna was, in fact, a kiwifruit farm. The kiwifruit grows on vines similar to wine grapes but much higher. The poles and wires supporting the vines were at least eight feet above the ground. It reminded me of the hop vineyards in Yakima Valley. That made it all the more interesting. The farm had been in the hands of the Pasquetto family for generations, and several members of the family were on the scene. Frederico and Simonetta, our hosts, were a delight. They introduced us to their family members and explained their farming operation.

In our small-town high school in the 1950s, the girls took classes in home economics, or commercial, which consisted of typing and shorthand. We boys, without exception, were assigned to agriculture classes. We called it "Agri." Our classrooms were in the Agri Building. We seldom used the full term agriculture. It was simply "Agri."

The following morning, we said our goodbyes to Frederico and Simonetta and loaded up our little Peugeot for the next leg of our journey.

The <u>Agriturismo</u> plan is attractive. I suspect there are a myriad of mom-and-pop farms in the United States where such a program would benefit both small farms and tourists.

IBERIA

Aguardiente: Is a type of distilled alcoholic spirit that contains between 29% and 60%

There is a lot to love in the Iberian Peninsula of Europe. The Peninsula encompasses the nations of Spain and Portugal. In Portugal, the language, as one would expect, is Portuguese. However, most of the population, especially the younger folks and those working in the hospitality industry, also speak English. Spain, on the other hand, is more challenging for English-speaking tourists such as we Americans. There are several languages, or regional dialects, spoken in the country. The official language is Spanish, or Castilian Spanish, from the autonomous region of Castile. In Barcelona and the surrounding Catalonia, the language is Catalan. Basque is spoken in the Basque country, which borders the western Spanish/French border.

In Spain and Portugal, like in nearly all European countries, the people drink a lot of wine and a great variety of distilled spirits. You will have the opportunity to sample aguardiente, as it is spelled in Spanish. It is a distilled alcohol spirit that contains between 29% and 60% alcohol. Be careful. It will incapacitate you before you know it.

I became interested in the Iberian Peninsula years ago when our cruise ship itineraries provided us with visits to Vigo, Malaga, Almeria, Valencia, Barcelona, Spain, and Lisbon in Portugal. All of these were seaports. I wanted to see the real Iberian Peninsula, such as the Spanish cities of Zaragoza, Salamanca, Seville, and Granada, and the Portugues cities like Lagos, Porto, Coimbra, and Sintra, and the villages and countryside in between. There was one answer. Fly to Barcelona, buy a car, and spend six weeks touring the whole interior of both countries.

It was a good plan, but the challenges encountered in driving in a foreign country can best be classified as "lessons learned" and "adventures." I will never forget when we crossed the bridge over the Guadiana River that separates southern Spain from the Algarve Region of Portugal. As soon as we crossed the bridge and saw the overhead sign that said, "Welcome to the Algarve," my nav system started screaming at me to take the next exit. "Navadean," as I called my nav system lady, knew more than I did. I was on a toll road that required a windshield sticker and was monitored by cameras. I had seen the signs but couldn't read them in Portuguese. And what would I do if I took the next exit? I didn't know where to go to get a permit.

I finally turned Navadean off to shut her up and drove on to Lagos.

If I ever go back to Portugal again, I hope they don't throw me into the bottom of a Lisbon dungeon.

Panama

**Ambrosial: Extremely pleasing to
the taste; sweet and fragrant.**

It was the first week of January 1955. I was agog with excitement. I had just spent a week on a navy troop carrier from cold, wintery New York and had landed in the Panama Canal Zone, where I would spend the next 18 months in Uncle Sam's Army.

We boarded the trans-isthmus train that would take us from Cristóbal, on the Caribbean side of the isthmus, some 50 miles to Balboa, on the Pacific side. The windows of the train cars were open as the temperatures were comfortable. Before the train started moving, and at various stops along the way, native women walked alongside the train, selling tropical fruits and pastries through the windows to the soldiers. As we said goodbye to Cristobal and to the gaily-clad native women and our train started moving forward, I sat back and relaxed, just wondering what this new phase of my life would be like. As we moved into the jungle, the wonderful <u>ambrosial</u> aromas wafted through the open windows and presented me with a sentiment that I still recall.

At Balboa, we disembarked the train and climbed onto a bus that, likewise, was open and airy. When we entered the gate at Fort Kobbe, I beheld the most beautiful sight. The buildings, whether barracks, administration buildings, or officers' homes, were all of cream-colored stucco with roofs and overhangs of bright red Spanish tile. The palm trees were trimmed perfectly, and the lush green grass looked like a California stylist had groomed it. No view had ever graced this country boy's eyes such as I beheld. I felt like I had arrived in heaven.

I was soon to learn who would keep the place looking perfect. I can avow that when I left Panama 18 months later, the grass looked just as good as when I found it. Thanks to my buddies and me, who spent many days swinging machetes to keep Fort Kobbe looking beautiful for the captain's approval.

I have returned to Panama several times in recent years, and that same feeling reawakens each time. I love the tropics.

GIRL FROM IPANEMA

Amplitude: Amplitude is a measurement of the amount of energy transferred by a wave.

I can never forget the day that I decided to take a dip in the Atlantic Ocean. I have never been an ocean swimmer, or even a beach person, for that matter, but here I was at the famous Copacabana and Ipanema Beaches with the melody of "Girl from Ipanema" pulsing through my brain, and I just had to give it a try. I think the pulse and energy of Rio de Janeiro do that to a person.

I had not thought about the <u>amplitude</u> of the waves that had crossed the breadth of the southern Atlantic Ocean all the way from Africa's Cape of Good Hope. If they can lift a 200,000-ton cruise ship and make it rock and sway, what can they do to a novice swimmer? I was about to find out.

When the force of that first wave hit me, it flipped me over like I was a twig. When I regained my footing, I knew that I had had enough. I trudged back up the beach to my wife, snorting sand and seawater with every step. That was my solitary experience of trying to swim at Rio's famous Ipanema Beach.

GOLDEN YEARS

Analogy: a comparison between two things, typically for the purpose of explanation or clarification

Aging is a reality that I and my contemporaries are aware of each morning when we get up to face a new day. We don't have the vigor that we used to have. As it has been said, if we have to get down on the floor to pick up something, we look around to see if there is something else that needs to be done while we are down there. Somehow, we learn that bottles are more challenging to open than they used to be. Jar lids are on tighter. Like the belt, the socks are tighter. The bulk that we once had in our biceps and shoulders has settled in our torsos.

We hear a lot of axioms about aging; "Getting old is not for sissies!" "Youthful vigor is wasted on the young!" There are plenty more, and sadly, they are all true. But the sobering <u>analogy</u> is that our golden years, to which we all looked forward, are also said to be the autumn of our lives.

"THE TIMES THEY ARE a-CHANGIN'

Androgynous: Partly male and partly female in appearance; of indeterminate sex

A troubling trend that surfaced in the late 20th century is even more in vogue today. It is the apparent proliferation of androgyny in our population, especially among the younger age groups. The increase in <u>androgynous</u> people has mirrored, or is collateral with, the public growth of the LGBT movement. We watch TV and see individuals whose sex cannot easily be determined. And it is no accident. We were just coming to grips with LGBT, which stands for Lesbian, Gay, Bisexual, and Transgender. Now the group has expanded to LGBTQIA, which stands for Lesbian, Gay, Bisexual, Transgender, Queer, Intersex, and Asexual/Aromantic/Agender.

We laugh when we see characters on TV who fit the description in the Jerry Reed song: They are "just boys who look like girls who look like boys who look like Cher."

The changing with the times is not new. Bob Dylan's "The Times They Are a-Changin'," in 1964, was seen as a capture of the spirit of the 1960s. Six decades later, the words ring as true as they did when Dylan penned the folk song.

YOU DIDN'T WANT
TO KNOW THIS

Anthropophagy: The eating of
human flesh by human beings.

It's not something that we like to talk about, but cannibalism has existed in many places around the world throughout history. We might tend to think it had to have been in some remote tribes on isolated islands. Not necessarily so! It happened right here in the Americas. The Aztecs and the Maya in Mexico practiced it. But did it happen here in our country?

The 1913 Handbook of Indians of Canada (reprinting 1907 material from the Bureau of American Ethnology) claims that North American natives practicing anthropophagy included the Montagnais and some of the tribes of Maine; the Algonkin, Armouchiquois, Iroquois, and Micmac; and farther west, the Assiniboine and Cree, Foxes, Chippewa, Miami, Ottowa, Kickapoo, Sioux, and Winnebago; in the south the people who built the mounds in Florida, and the Tonkawa, the Attacapa, Karankawa, the Caddo, and Comanche; in the northwest and west, portions of the continent, the Thlingchadinneh and other Athapascan tribes, the Tlingit, Heiltsuk, Kwakiutl, Tsimshian, Nootka, Siksika, some of the Californian tribes, and the Ute. There is also a tradition of practice among the Hopi, and there are mentions of the custom among other tribes of New Mexico and Arizona. The Mohawk, Attacapa, Tonkawa, and other Texas tribes were known to their neighbors as 'man-eaters.'

Texas history stories tell about the fierce hatred between the Comanche and the Karankawa, whereas when they captured an enemy warrior, he would be lashed to a stake and burned alive, then eaten.

Maybe you didn't want to know this, but it is part of American History, albeit the history that nobody likes to talk about.

LIFE AT SEA

Antiscorbutic: A drug or food that prevents or cures scurvy.

Those of us who have traveled extensively have naturally spent a good deal of time on cruise ships. We realize that cruising is not for everybody. However, there are folks out there – I call them contrarians – who are adamantly opposed to leaving an American port on a cruise ship. Many of them, I suspect, have a deep-seated antipathy toward anything that they haven't done. They ask questions like, "How can you stand to be away from home that long?" Others think anything longer than a three-day cruise to Cozumel is too long. When I tell some of those about a grand world voyage, they are aghast. They surely think that I must be taking an <u>antiscorbutic</u> drug or constantly sucking on limes to keep from getting scurvy.

Not so. An increasing number of senior citizens have eschewed onshore retirement communities to live at sea. The food is beyond compare, the onboard temperatures are controlled, there is entertainment every evening, and there is always a doctor and some nurses on board.

We heard of a fellow named Mario Salcedo, who got on a cruise ship 23 years ago and never got off. All in all, Salcedo has spent over 9,000 nights on board luxury cruise ships. A lady on our Grand World Cruise on Holland America's Amsterdam in 2008 had spent some 1,600 nights aboard Holland America cruise ships. When questioned about how she chose her cruises, she said that her choices were based on the destinations shown on the itinerary. When asked about her favorite destinations, she said, "Oh, I don't know. I never get off the ship."

Whose dictionary?

Anxious: Experiencing worry, unease, or nervousness, typically about an imminent event

I have been called a "word person" because I like words. In fact, my writing these short essays and anecdotes and the hope of putting them in a book are a result of that interest.

I detest the fact that people can misuse a word so long that the dictionary writers, whoever they are, change the dictionaries to make incorrect words acceptable.

An example is the word "forte," which means a person's strong point. It comes from the word, fort, which implies strength. So, people use it correctly, except they pronounce it incorrectly as "for-tay." The "for-tay pronunciation has always been proper for "forte," the musical term. Now, the big Webster's book says that pronunciation is acceptable in all cases.

Another common example is the misuse of the word "anxious." Anxious has always indicated anxiety, which is generally pretty negative. The correct word is "eager" if one eagerly anticipates a coming event. One might be eager for Aunt Ava's visit but anxious about Unkle Fred coming with her since he is such an irascible old codger.

So, it depends somewhat on what dictionary one uses. We will embarrass ourselves if we say something is wrong when someone can produce a different dictionary that says it is right.

I'M PEDALING AS
FAST AS I CAN

**Apace: at the same speed or rate
as, for a comparison.**

Back in the 1970s, we were moving to computers to conduct our office work on construction projects. We used them first for word processing, and then we found that we could use them for cost accounting. Then we had to learn Microsoft. We learned dos. (Disk Operating System) Then dos became old hat, and we had to learn Windows. We used Word Perfect and WordStar. In the 1980s, we started using dbase for massive databases in power plant construction. Then, we had to learn Lotus 123. That wasn't good enough, so we had to use Excel.

By the 90s, I was using Primavera, a powerful and expensive scheduling program. I was at the top of my game using Primavera and PowerPoint for workshops at national conventions in places like Fort Lauderdale and New Orleans. By the late 1990s, my knowledge of Primavera for planning, scheduling, and logistics resourcing won me a position at the University of Texas System in Austin.

I was so involved in preparing construction schedules for projects in U.T. System's 15 components around the state and enforcing the requirements for prime and subcontractors to plan their operations properly that by the time I retired, the software I was using was the only thing I knew.

From that point on, every computer that I bought had to be set up by an IT person, who went through the steps of loading software so fast that I didn't know what he did, only that he did it.

I didn't know it was happening when it was happening, and I have found that technology was moving way too fast for the old country boy. Even young men have difficulty staying apace with the advancement of technology. How in creation can an old person hope to keep his head clear?

I recently read a book about Elon Musk, the creator of Tesla cars, Space X, and a few dozen other ventures. He hires only engineers. All of the people that he hires to work with him have to be proficient at writing code for computers. Who even knows what "code" is? I think it has something to do with his spaceships, rockets, thrusters, and stuff that he builds. The advancement of technology has left me in the dust like a fuel dragster would leave a 1929 Madel A Ford.

SINGING DUNES

Aridity: a deficiency of moisture (especially when resulting from a permanent absence of rainfall)

There's more to the desert than serpents and cacti. There is music. I realize most folks will laugh if I try to tell you that the sands of the desert actually sing. But it happens right here in the Mojave Desert.

Singing sand dunes, an example of the phenomenon of singing sand, produce a sound described as roaring, booming, squeaking, or the "Song of Dunes." This natural sound phenomenon, which can reach up to 105 decibels and last several minutes, occurs in about 35 desert locations around the world.

A popular place to hear the singing sand in California is at Kelso Dunes, near Baker in San Bernardino County. But singing sand can be found right here in Nevada at Sand Mountain, a singing dune 20 miles east of Fallon.

Sand Mountain is a 6-story mountain of sand and one of only a handful of singing sand dunes in the world. Who would've thought something that seems straight out of the Sahara is right in the middle of Nevada?

The aridity of the sand has much to do with the volume and clarity of the sounds. The Mojave Desert of California and Nevada

175

is the driest desert in the United States, slightly more arid than the Sonoran Desert of Arizona and Mexico.

Now that you know that deserts can sing, you will be curious about a river in Mississippi that is widely known to be a singer.

No Combat
Engineers for me

Befallen: To happen, especially by fate

I cannot begin to sum up the blessings that have <u>befallen</u> me in my long and somewhat tumultuous life. An early benison that came out of nowhere befell me when I joined the army at 16 years of age. In the days before I actually signed up, Jackie Spencer, a friend of my family, gave me some sensible advice. He advised me to apply to be assigned to the Army Combat Engineers. As he said, the combat engineer soldiers learned how to build things such as bridges and temporary airports, anything that needed to be built. The guys learned how to operate construction equipment like bulldozers, motor graders, and even construction cranes. That way, they could get a job when they got out of the army. That sounded like good advice. I was excited.

I went to the draft board in Pocahontas, Arkansas, and volunteered for immediate induction. That meant I was able to be part of the county draft allotment and go in for a two-year term. When I asked about being trained as a combat engineer, I was told, "You'll take basic training first, then you'll have to talk to them about that."

In just a couple of months in the army, I realized that what he told me was a bunch of malarkey—a draftee, the status that I was classified, doesn't request anything. A person has to be a three-year enlistee in order to request anything.

Time passed, and when I finished eight weeks of basic training in the summer sun of Camp Gordon, Georgia, I received my orders to report to Fort Bliss, Texas, for radar school. I was the only one out of 180 trainees to receive that assignment.

At Fort Bliss, much of our training was classroom instruction. We learned to operate early surveillance aircraft radar, as well as field artillery radar that could track heavy mortar and artillery rounds. It was interesting and enjoyable.

Upon graduation from radar school, I received orders to be assigned to Fort Kobbe in the Panama Canal Zone. My classmates and I were flown to Camp Kilmer, New Jersey, for overseas placement. My friends were assigned to various locations in Europe and in the Far East, which included places such as Korea, Vietnam, and Cambodia. I was the only one from our class who was assigned to the Panama Canal Zone.

While at Camp Kilmer for a couple of weeks, waiting for our ship, we ran across several of our buddies from basic training. They had, like me, completed eight weeks of advanced training and were being assigned, like my fellow classmates, to locations in Europe and Asia. Some of them had just finished combat engineering training in Fort Leonard Wood, Missouri. They told me how miserable they were in training. They were out building roads and bridges when everything was covered with either mud or snow and ice. And now they were headed for Germany, which was just as cold as Missouri. And besides, it was December 23rd, and they were going from freezing Missouri to an even colder Germany without being allowed to go home for Christmas.

How did it happen that I was so lucky to spend my 18-month assignment as a radar operator in a tropical paradise?

Nobody Hurt
But the Pig

**Arbitrator: An independent person or body
officially appointed to settle a dispute**

Here's a war that the United States was involved in that many
of you have never heard of. It became known as "The Pig War." It
happened in June 1859, 165 years ago.

There had been ongoing border disputes between the United
Kingdom (Yeah, it's those Brits again!) and the United States
regarding the border between Canada's Vancouver Island and our
Oregon Territory. Then, a pig got shot.

Lyman Cutlar, an American, had moved to San Juan Island
and started farming. It seems that Charles Griffin, a Canadian
shepherd for the Hudson's Bay Company, had a herd of pigs that ran
wild. One big black pig got into Cutlar's garden and was rooting up
his potatoes, so Cutlar shot it dead. Griffin got upset about it and
wanted Cutlar to pay him $100 for killing his pig. Cutler said the
pig was a Canadian trespasser on his American property and refused
to pay. The British Navy threatened to intervene.

The US sent the 9th Infantry, under the command of Captain
George Pickett, to San Juan with orders to prevent the British from
landing on American soil. The British sent three warships under

the command of Captain Geoffrey Hornby. Pickett built a redoubt and sited his cannons on high ground overlooking Griffin Bay and the Strait of Juan de Fuca. (The redoubts still exist and can be easily visited and toured.)

By August 10th, 1859, 461 American soldiers and 14 cannons were opposed by five British warships, mounting 70 guns and 2,140 men. No shots had been fired.

Commanding Officers on both sides had been given essentially the same orders: defend yourselves, but absolutely don't fire the first shot. For several days, the British and American soldiers exchanged insults, each side trying to goad the other side into firing first.

When news of the crisis reached Washington and London, cooler heads got involved. President James Buchanan sent General Winfield Scott to negotiate with Governor Douglas. Unable to come to a final agreement, the military de-escalated, and two camps were established: a British camp on the north side of San Juan and an American camp on the south side. This situation went on for another twelve years. Finally, the dispute was referred to International Arbitration with German Emperor Wilhelm I as the arbitrator. After more than another year, the arbitration commission chose the American boundary, and the crisis was finally resolved. No shots were fired, and nobody was hurt but the pig.

I wrote about the Pig War several years ago. Then I learned that my wife used to own a home on San Juan Island, so we decided to visit. The big MS Kaleetan ferried us from Anacortes to the island for a nice visit and a tour of the famous "battleground."

NICOTINE

Bereft: deprived or robbed of the possession or use of something

Back in 1982, I found myself divorced for a second time. It is not something for a person to be proud of, but it happens to some folks. Although it is not considered to be of paramount importance in the grand scheme of a divorce, I found myself <u>bereft</u> of any reason to continue smoking cigarettes. I had wanted to quit smoking for years, but my wife smoked, and I blamed her as the reason that I could not quit.

It wasn't easy, but I could no longer place blame on anyone but myself for my addiction to nicotine. I probably made my kids miserable for a month or so, but the cold turkey approach worked.

Nicotine is a terribly addictive substance. Our mamas told us, from as far back as we can remember, not to smoke. Yet, when we were old enough and thought we were smart enough to make our own decisions, we started smoking. By the time we become senior citizens, afflicted with COPT and at least a half dozen other maladies, we realize how adolescent those early decisions were. We now encourage people, young and old, not to acquiesce to the temptations to use tobacco.

Some people, when they get a divorce, start drinking. With me, I got a divorce and quit smoking.

"THIS IS YOUR CAPTAIN SPEAKING."

Bight: A curve or recess in a coastline, river, or other geographical feature

We were crossing the Great Australian <u>Bight</u>, just off the south coast of Australia and offshore from the Great Victoria Desert Nature Reserve. (Australians love the adjective, "Great.") We were sleeping soundly, as only one can when being lulled by the gentle rocking of a giant ship. At 1:50 am, we heard the alarm bell sound over our in-room speaker. That sound will awaken you, I suspect, even if you are dead. Then the voice came on: "This is your Captain speaking." By now, we were sitting up in our bed. Something is serious. The captain quickly assured us that we were in no danger, and then he went on to say that he had a request. He said that if we have a passenger aboard who has AB or O-Negative blood type and has a current donor card, there is a person in the Medical Center on Deck 1 who "critically" needs a transfusion. "So, please go to the Medical Center if you have that blood type." He repeated his request twice to express the importance clearly.

Neither my wife nor I had donor cards, and I have no idea what my blood type is. With nothing we could do to help, we said a little prayer and went back to sleep. We learned later that eleven people showed up at the Medical Center prepared to donate the required blood. That is fantastic. Eleven people climbed out of bed at 2 am, dressed, and hurried to the place where they were needed.

We learned later that the patient was stabilized and removed to a local hospital after we landed in Melbourne.

A BITTER WIND BLOWS

Blue Norther: A cold wind from the north that brings rapidly falling temperatures to the Kansas, Oklahoma, and Texas regions.

My Texas friends know full well what a blue norther is. They have lived with them throughout their lives. I had never heard of a blue norther until I moved to San Antonio back in the 1980s. I learned quickly.

I was surveying on a construction project that would build the "Stockyards Bridge." It was a combination interstate highway and bridge project on the south side of San Antonio to build elevated lanes over the San Pedro Creek and the San Antonio Stockyards.

I was advised and learned quickly to take a jacket with me. The cold front can move southward at the speed of a Lamborghini, causing the temperature to plummet like an untethered weight. One of my earliest experiences occurred while surveying frontage lanes on the northbound side of IH-35. My rodman was about a thousand yards up the road from me, and we were communicating on CB radios. At one point, he said, "The blue norther just hit. You will feel it in less than a minute." Surely enough, it hit like a sledgehammer.

Blue northers are climatic features on the high plains and the southern plains. I now live in the Mojave, so I will never experience a blue norther again. Believe it or not, I kind of miss them.

THE ATLANTIC AND
THE MEDITERRANEAN

**Boreal: Of, relating to, or located in
northern regions. boreal waters**

It was the perfect trip. The brochure spoke of several countries
that we would visit. We would frolic with the natives and tour the
caves in the Azores Islands. We would visit the Spanish Canary
Islands. We would explore the caves of Hercules in Morocco and tour
the subterraneous fortifications in Gibraltar. We would sit atop the
famous rock and watch the ships as they approached Tangiers, just
across the Strait. We would visit Valencia, drink local wine, and eat
paella, the national food of Spain. Rome, Naples, and Messina would
share their Italian delights. Athens and Corfu would teach us to
speak Greek. It would be a 55-day round trip from Fort Lauderdale.
Could any excursion be more irresistible?

Our first port was San Juan, Puerto Rico. The highlight was a
visit to the 400-year-old Castillo San Felipe del Morro, which is old
but still impregnable. After two days and nights and a day trip to
Sint Maarten, we set out across the breezy Atlantic.

Our fellow excursionists were a pretty savvy lot. Seasoned
travelers are so different from the seven-day Carnival cruisers from
Galveston – people who might show up in jean cutoffs with their

---

gimmy caps on backward on a formal evening. Of course, there are always a couple of oddballs. Shamus was from Ireland and brought an old melodeon that he thought we wanted to hear. I have heard melodeons before, but Shamus's ragged old instrument sounded like it had a chronic case of asthma.

After a full week battling the pitiless <u>boreal</u> sea, we came in sight of the first of the Azores Islands. Excited cruisers raced to the outer decks with their binoculars to get a first view. I joined them.

The entrance to the harbor at Ponta Delgado was narrow and exposed to the foul weather, so we had to hang loose until a tempest abated. The snow-white houses of the town nestle cozily in a sea of fresh green vegetation. They have no yards. The land surrounding their houses is planted with strawberries, grapes, corn, and bananas. Not a foot of soil is left idle.

Our supposedly savvy fellow excursionists might know all the intricate details about Paris or Istanbul, but they, like me, knew nothing about the Azores. The tiny archipelago lies in the center of the North Atlantic Ocean, equidistant from St. John's, Newfoundland, and Casablanca, Morocco.

After two days of pleasant sailing, we entered the Strait of Gibraltar and made fast to the dock in the British Territory of Gibraltar. We would explore the subterranean guns and tunnels inside the famous Rock, then set our course for the eastern Mediterranean.

I will cover more of the cruise in another chapter.

Mergers and Struggles

**Bower: a pleasant shady place under trees
or climbing plants in a garden or wood**

The little stone church in Maynard, Arkansas, like so many
across the country, could tell a lot of tales of the thousands of people
who have come and gone in the last century.

In the early 20th century, Maynard, Arkansas, as a town, was in its
fledgling stage, but devout Methodists vowed to replace their humble
frame church with a stone edifice that would withstand the ravages
of time. They completed construction in 1925 and christened it
Maynard M.E. Church. Its denomination was Methodist Episcopal.

The Methodist Episcopal Church (MEC) traces its origins
to the First Great Awakening when Methodism emerged as an
evangelical revival movement within the Church of England.
Methodism had spread to the Thirteen Colonies, and Methodist
societies were formed under the oversight of John Wesley. As in
England, American Methodists remained affiliated with the Church
of England.

The history of Protestantism in the United States is rife with
strife, resulting in splits and fragmentations. The MEC experienced
this on numerous occasions.

In 1939, the Methodist Episcopal Church, the Methodist Episcopal Church, South, and the Methodist Protestant Church, which had separated earlier, reunited and formed the "Methodist Church."

In 1946, the Evangelical Church and the Church of the United Brethren in Christ merged to form the Evangelical United Brethren. In 1968, the Evangelical United Brethren and the Methodist Church finally formally recognized the similarities of their polity and theology when they merged to form the United Methodist Church.

The UMC church in Maynard has struggled through the changes and keeps holding on for the few faithful who gather every Sunday. When I was growing up in the area, in addition to services every Sunday morning and Sunday and Wednesday evenings, there were active meetings of the United Methodist Women and Methodist Youth Fellowship. Revivals would fill every pew. There was a pleasant <u>bower</u> under the oak and elm trees where men set up tables on sawhorses, and the women loaded them with their personal delicacies. A lot of wonderful memories were made there.

The pleasant bower is gone now. I revisited recently to find that the giant chinkapin oak that graced the front churchyard is gone, and the area has been paved over for parking spaces. Time marches on, and the little stone church that has withstood all changes for a century will hopefully serve the faithful in Maynard in the centuries to come.

FRIED SQUIRREL
FOR BREAKFAST

**Bucolic: Relating to the pleasant aspects
of the countryside and country life**

There can be no greater blessing for a young boy than growing up in the country. My grade school sat on a hill in the small town of Maynard, nestled in the heart of the North Arkansas hills. I venture that of some 40 students in my grade, only two lived in town. And even then, with a population of only 250 in the town, it was still closely akin to country living.

My country life was not unique, although it was special to me. There are rural areas in all fifty states that provide the kind of freedom that I enjoyed in my young years. I had the freedom to roam every inch of the 140 acres that I grew up on. If I wanted to follow the creek past the watergates onto the neighboring farms, I was free to do so. The neighboring farmers were family friends. My constant companion was my dog, Jack, who protected me from venomous snakes. My biggest responsibility was to be at home before dark for supper.

When I was a little older, my closest friends, whom I visited hundreds of times, lived a half-mile off the gravel road in the delta where two small clear-running creeks converge. These were the creeks where one could fly fish for bluegills and sunfish. There was the swimming hole where we skinny-dipped every day of the hot summer. There were the creek-bottom copses of hardwood trees where Mr. Cox would harvest a half-dozen young squirrels, and Effie Cox would have fresh squirrel and gravy cooking when we awoke. It was also the home where Leo Cox taught me my first three chords on a guitar and started me on a lifetime of music as an avocation.

Even now, several decades later and a thousand miles from my childhood home, I cannot think of a more <u>bucolic</u> setting than my friends' creekside home.

When in Naples, do as the Napolitanos do

Canaille: The common people, the masses.

As a popular song says, "I'm a common man, drive a common van. My dog ain't got a pedigree." John Connally pretty accurately describes my nature in that song.

As I have traveled the world, I have done so in the company of a myriad of people. We are all different. Many of my companions eagerly head to the museums to see the great masterpieces. Some of those are beautiful. Some are thought-provoking. And there are some created by some deranged person that will leave you dumbfounded trying to figure out what you are looking at.

I am different. In a foreign country, it is my nature to mix with the ordinary folks of the population. That is where I find the real character of the people. A good example is when I visit Naples. I head for the market and buy a pizza from a streetside cart. I grab a glass of wine at a plaza café and watch the local people hurry to and fro to their jobs. These are the true <u>canaille</u>, the Napolitanos. Pretenses are not part of their way of life. My sophisticated friends frown on it. My family members say I am risking my life, a peril that seems to be more paramount to them than it does to me.

Getting high in the Andes

Coca Tea: Also called mate de coca, is a herbal tea (infusion) made using the raw or dried leaves of the coca plant, which is native to South America.

We had landed and spent a night in Lima. Our goal was a visit to the remains of the ancient city, Machu Picchu. Machu Picchu is a 15th-century Inca citadel located in the Eastern Cordillera of southern Peru. In order to visit Machu Picchu, high in Peru's Andes Mountains, one has to fly to the 11,000-foot-high city of Cusco and acclimate to the altitude before traveling on to Machu Picchu. Not that Machu Picchu is higher. It isn't. But touring Machu Picchu is physically demanding. One needs to be prepared.

This is where our guide, Ruben, came in. He met us at the Cusco Airport and told us he would prepare us for the visit to Machu Picchu. He told us that we would visit several sites in the Sacred Valley of the Incas for a couple of days and that we must listen to him and follow his instructions. We are to walk slowly, drink lots of water, and drink <u>coca tea</u>. For the next two days, we carried coca tea with us and drank from it frequently. Did we get high? At 11,000 feet, we were already high.

A visit to Machu Picchu is a once-in-a-lifetime event for most people who set aside a week to make the trip. Within our group, an excursion of 24 people, one couple from Wichita was stricken with altitude sickness in Cusco and never made it to Machu Picchu. How heartbreaking it must have been!

We never forgot our guide, Ruben, nor our getting high in the Andes. Could we take any of the coca leaves home with us to America? No! We would be arrested.

IT PAID WELL

Cognoscenti: People who are considered to be especially well-informed about a particular subject

At the turn of the 21st century, I was working as a scheduler/planner at the University of Texas System in Austin. Our group, the Office of Facilities, Planning, and Construction (OFPC), was responsible for building facilities at all 15 of the System's components.

Out of the blue, I received a call from a Midland attorney who was representing a large construction company that I had worked with in the past. The company that he represented was embroiled in a contract dispute in which the contractor's construction activities had been unduly delayed by change orders generated by the owner/client. He wanted me to review all aspects of the construction schedule and appear at the mediation hearing as an "Expert."

I was taken aback. I had been called a lot of things in my time but had never been called an "expert" in the legal sense.

I questioned, "Why did you choose me?" He responded, "You are the scheduling guru for the UT System. We need a <u>cognoscenti</u> with credentials beyond challenge. In your position with UT System, you have those credentials."

The attorney, his clerk, and the contractor, came to Austin and scheduled the deposition on a Saturday in order for me to be available without interfering with my job at UT. I had been called a scheduling guru many times, but <u>cognoscenti</u> was a new word to me. I liked it. It paid well.

FOLLOW THE RIVER

Commemorate: Celebrate (an event, a person, or a situation) by doing or building something.

Here's that old question again. "Have you read any good books lately?" Permit me to suggest one.

"Follow the River" is a story about a young pioneer woman in the Virginia Mountains. Mary Draper Ingles was twenty-three, married, and pregnant when Shawnee Indians invaded her peaceful Virginia settlement, killed men and women, and then took her captive. They killed babies by bashing their heads against the log walls, and then they burned the settlement.

You are saying, 'This book is too sad.' Well, it is sad, but it is gripping, and you won't want to put it down.

The savages took their captives, including Mary and her two little boys, across the country to the river, then took them downstream nearly a thousand miles to a camp in the region that became Kentucky.

For months, she lived with the Indians, unbroken, until she escaped. She escaped from their camp near present-day Big Bone, Kentucky, and started walking back up the river. Winter came, and Mary trudged on. Her clothes and shoes became shreds. Eventually, they were gone, torn by the briars and bushes. She followed the river, having to swim across the near-frozen tributaries when she encountered them.

Mary followed a nearly thousand-mile trail to freedom, an extraordinary story of a pioneer woman who risked her life to return to her people. The story was made into a movie in 1995 starring Sheryl Lee and Ellen Burstyn. Historically the event is known as Draper's Meadow Massacre. The attack occurred July 8th, 1755, near present-day Blacksburg, Virginia. (Some records and a monument say it happened on July 30th.)

A plaque near Engle's Ferry reads: Mary Draper Engles "was the first white bride married west of the Allegheny Mountains. Captured by Indians in 1755 at Draper's Meadows, now Blacksburg, Virginia, and carried to Ohio; escaping from her captors, she made her way home, in winter, alone, some 800 miles through a trackless wilderness, guided only by streams and subsisting on nuts and roots for 40 days."

No greater exhibition of female heroism, courage, and endurance are recorded in the annals of frontier history. To commemorate her noble character and wonderful heroism, a monument was erected of the stones from the chimney of the cabin in which she lived and died after her return from captivity."

Readers have wondered what happened to Mary's two little boys. The youngest one died in captivity, and the older one was ransomed from the Indians and returned to Virginia when he was in his teens.

My roots are deep in the Allegheny Mountains, from my Perkins, Bourne, and Thomas families in Grayson County, Virginia, and to my Outlaw family east of there on the seaboard. I love to visit there and travel up the "hollers," where my forebears forged clearings and raised their families.

"Follow the River," by James Alexander Thom, is an amazing story. I recommend it.

Happiness before Enlightenment

Concubine: A woman who lives with a man but has a lower status than his wife or wives

My, how times have changed. When I was coming onto the world scene, upwards of four-score years ago, it was generally assumed that the fairer sex retained their virginity until they married; whether they did so or not remained a guarded secret. However, they typically chose a white wedding dress for the wedding occasion. The tradition was well-established. The practice likely traces back over 2,000 years, with roots in the Roman Republic when brides wore a white tunic. White represented purity, symbolizing a woman's chastity and transition to a married Roman matron.

Maybe we are a more honest population now. Progressives would use the word enlightened. Being enlightened is not something I had ever striven for; frankly, I think I was happy enough before this age of enlightenment.

It is not for me to say whether one way or another is morally correct, but if a young woman chooses to live with a man and not become a blushing bride, then it will be left to her to accept that she is, in fact, a <u>concubine</u>.

WHAT GOES AROUND COMES AROUND

Curmudgeon: a bad-tempered person, especially an old one

The little town had a hotel on the corner at the single intersection that identified the village's downtown. We wondered about the hotel. The façade was of stone and emblazoned in the upper portion, the contrasting mortar spelled out, "Hotel, 1925." I don't recall it ever operating as a hotel. Nobody had come through town and stayed there for a night or fortnight in my memory.

I never knew who owned the building, but an elderly couple moved in and made it their residence. I don't know where John and Bird Caldwell came from, but they seemed to have some family connections in the area. Caldwell was a common surname in the county.

Likewise, I am not sure that John and Bird had any friends, and I have some doubts as to whether they might have wanted any. To say that John was a curmudgeon is more complimentary than derogatory. And Bird, an insufferable old soul, was, if possible, even more crotchety than John. They were constantly in conflict with the rest of the population. They obviously hated children.

John figured the sidewalk in front of his "hotel" was his property.

He sat on a rocking chair on the narrow sidewalk when it was shady and we boys couldn't ride past him. John would kick the front wheel off his sidewalk, resulting in a nasty spill for the rider. When conflicts escalated, Bird was reputed to come out, flashing her butcher knife.

It is little wonder that as we boys grew older, I confess, we persecuted the old misanthropes with late-night firecrackers and the squealing of tires in the wee hours.

When I was sixteen and decided to join the army, I found that I needed to have my signature and birth certificate notarized, and guess what! John Caldwell was the only notary in town. Sometimes, our deeds come back and haunt us.

As strange as
a velocipede

Denigrate: To criticize unfairly, disparage

Leaving the comforts of home to join the army presents a shocking change for a young man. It is especially shocking if that young man is just 16 years old, came from the hills of north Arkansas, has not finished high school, and has not traveled extensively like many young folks today. This was some 70 years ago, in the middle of the 1950s. My contemporaries will understand. To the younger generations, conditions in that period will be as strange to them as a velocipede.

One of my early revelations, and one that has puzzled me ever since, was how people from other regions <u>denigrated</u> Arkansas as a place where people, regardless of age or gender, went barefooted, smoked a cob pipe, and likely were bereft of most of their teeth.

Much of the ignorance of those days has faded with the passage of years. People from across the country have learned to love visiting the Ozark and Ouachita Mountains, fishing and floating the pristine streams that flow out of those highlands, and just touring some of the prettiest country in America.

I think the movies had a lot to do with it. There were the old Ma and Pa Kettle movies and the Judy Canova films. And, of course, there was Deliverance. What a fecal pile that was! Even True Grit and Lonesome Dove had portions that perpetuated the stereotype.

Hollywood moviemakers should spend a week in the beautiful Ozark Mountains and learn what the real hill folk are like.

EVANGELINE

**Diaspora: A group of people who live outside
the area in which they had lived for a long
time or in which their ancestors lived**

In 1755, the British began the forced expulsion of Acadians from
their homeland in Acadia, which is now Nova Scotia, and nearby
areas. This event, known as Le Grand Dérangement or "the Great
Disturbance," was a state-sponsored action that involved rounding
up Acadian men on a Sunday morning, burning their homes and
crops, and threatening families with bayonets. These were British
Loyalists persecuting French Catholics because they wouldn't swear
allegiance to the Queen of England and convert to the Anglican
Church of England.

Many of the Acadians were imprisoned and forced to board
British ships for unknown destinations. The deportation was
inhumane and unnecessary on military grounds, and it resulted in
the deaths of about half of the Acadian population from disease,
starvation, and violence.

Some Acadians were sent to the Colonies, some to France, and
some to the Caribbean. The 13 American Colonies were British.
They didn't welcome the French-speaking refugees, so they moved
them down the coast. They didn't find a friendly welcome anywhere
on the Atlantic coast, so they rounded the Florida Peninsula into

the Gulf of Mexico. After days of traveling westward, they found welcome and solace among the French Catholics of South Louisiana. In the late 1700s, some 3,000 Acadians settled along the coastal waterways and bayous of Louisiana, where their descendants live today. They have become known as Cajuns, a corruption of the words Acadiens or Acadians.

Henry Wadsworth Longfellow immortalized the tragedy of the Acadian exile from Nova Scotia in his famous poem, Evangeline. Evangeline is an epic poem about the Acadian lovers Evangeline and Gabriel, who are separated during the Great Expulsion from Nova Scotia. Evangeline spends years traveling in search of Gabriel.

A giant live oak on the bank of Bayou Teche, near St. Martinsville, Louisiana, marks the legendary meeting place of Emmeline Labiche and Louis Arceneaux, the counterparts of Evangeline and Gabriel. Longfellow himself never got to visit the place that he immortalized in his poem. The Evangeline Oak has its own little park and museum on the bank of Bayou Teche in St. Martin Parish, South Louisiana.

I fell in love with South Louisiana and its Cajun Country culture the first time I visited it in the 1980s. I love the culture and the music, and I just love hearing the old Cajuns talk with their South Louisiana Cajun accent.

I have returned to Bayou Teche and the Evangeline Oak many times and have repeatedly felt the serenity of the place, which means so much to the descendants of that terrible diaspora 350 years ago.

CAPTIONS AND CUTLINES

**Didactically: In a way that is intended
to teach, especially in a way that is
fixed and unwilling to change.**

For several years, maybe fifteen or so, I have been writing morning greetings on Facebook. I have usually posted a travel-related photograph and an associated comment that I refer to as a caption or cutline. Actually, the photograph is intended to simply capture my readers' attention. It is not necessarily intended to stand alone. My comments are <u>didactically</u> constructed to provide information about instances and locations around the world that my readers will never see otherwise.

Ducks lay fried eggs

Gelid: Icy, extremely cold

We had been at sea for two weeks. It was midwinter, and there was a gelid bone-chilling breeze as we cast off from the dock in Port Everglades. Ten days later, it was springtime, and we were in the Cook Islands, and shortly after that, we wound up in Australia in the hottest part of the summer, all within a fortnight.

The bus driver, like many bus drivers do, to make conversation, asked if I was enjoying the weather. I said it was mighty hot. He said it is not hot here. Go up around Darwin if you want to know what hot is. The ducks up there lay fried eggs.

Sydney should have about the same climate as Little Rock, Arkansas, since they are at similar distances from the equator, although in opposite seasons. Not so! Sydney's temperatures are modified by its adjacency to the Tasman Sea. Little Rock, by comparison, has freezing winters, boiling hot summers, and tornadoes.

Australia's good climate is restricted to its various coasts, of which it has an abundance, being surrounded by the waters of the Pacific Ocean, Indian Ocean, Southern Ocean, and Tasman Sea. That's why all of Australia's cities are on the coast. Almost no one lives in the interior. There are no cities in the interior larger than a good-sized cow camp. They call them stations here.

We had to train our ears, as well as our brains, to understand and process words and terms that should otherwise be easy to understand. Our guides would routinely pronounce words like paper as pyper, and table as tyble. We would learn that an umbrella was a brolly and sunglasses were sunnies. It was a language that I would call Crocodile Dundeeish.

The Royal Botanic Garden is a not-to-miss attraction in Sydney. We booked early to make the most of it. The 74-acre garden is located at Farm Cove on the eastern fringe of downtown. Opened in 1816, it is the oldest scientific institution in Australia and one of the most important historic botanical institutions in the world.

Captain Cook discovered Australia in 1770 and claimed it for England. England saw it as an excellent place to send convicted criminals. England eventually sent over 80,000 convicts to Australia. Of course, in England, a person could be convicted and imprisoned for the most minute infraction. This is the same country that would torture a person to death just because he wouldn't convert to the king's church. They executed some 70,000 Christians that way under King Henry XIII. Many of the current residents of South Australia can trace their lineage to some of those early British prisoners.

Several countries found it expedient to get rid of their wrongdoers by sending them to some remote location. France did it with French Guiana off the coast of South America and sent right at 80,000 prisoners to the Devil's Island prison system. Maybe you have seen the movie Papillon, starring Steve McQueen.

Having had the pleasure of two cruises to Australia, with excursions in all the major cities, I can highly recommend Australia for a visit. Allow plenty of time. It is an immense country. It is a six-hour flight from Sydney to Perth. Take it! By road, it is nearly 3,000 miles. I am not sure anyone has ever driven all the way.

Big River

Floe: Floe is a noun that specifically refers to a mass of floating ice. It can be a solid sheet or rafted broken ice.

It was early 1977, and I was working on the Mississippi River, on the Arkansas side, just across from Greenville, Mississippi. My office trailer sat right on the bank of the river and much of our project was actually in the river under the surface.

We were building a water intake system for a paper mill that was under construction near Arkansas City, Arkansas.

Arkansas City is a town of fewer than 400 folks in Desha County, on the protected side of the Army Corps of Engineering Mississippi River levee. Over the last century and a half, the town has experienced growth, crippling natural disasters, downfall, and infamy.

Arkansas City was an important commercial and cultural center and one of the most important ports on the Mississippi River. It grew to become an important riverport in the late 19th century with steamboats offloading goods from St. Louis and New Orleans and on-loading cotton to haul to the mills in the northern cities, and lumber that helped build Memphis and Natchez. It had a natural harbor for steamboats and two railways, as well as fourteen saloons and three sawmills. An opera house was moved to Arkansas City in

1891. River trade continued to grow, and the town prospered. That was until the disastrous flood that occurred in 1927.

The Flood of 1927 was the most destructive and costly flood in Arkansas history and one of the worst in the history of the nation. It afflicted Arkansas with a greater amount of devastation, both human and monetary, than the other affected states in the Mississippi River Valley.

The town of Arkansas City lay beneath the muddy water of the Mississippi and Arkansas rivers from April through August 1927. The Red Cross cared for the entire population of 1,500 people while the town was being rebuilt.

The flood inundated the farmland as far west as the town of McGehee, ten miles away, and almost two stories high in Arkansas City proper. When the water finally went down, local residents found that the river had formed a new channel over a mile east of the port.

With the city no longer situated on the river, the steamboats had nowhere to land, and the railroads no longer had a reason to stop. The thriving port town, whose population some estimates say peaked at more than 10,000, began to fade into the Delta dirt.

Some 15 years later, the United States was embroiled in a do-or-die war in the Pacific against Japan. Due to fear that the large population of Japanese Americans might form a security risk during the war, the United States established a government agency named the War Relocation Authority.

During the war, the United States forcibly relocated and incarcerated about 120,000 people of Japanese descent in ten concentration camps across the country. One of those camps was just across the levee from our jobsite. The Rohwer War Relocation Center, a 10,161-acre facility, held as many as 8,475 Japanese Americans from September 18th, 1942 to November 30th, 1945.

I drove past the Rower War Relocation Center site each day between my home in McGehee and my office.

The winter of 1976-1977 had been particularly cold. Patches of ice were flowing past our project. We had Coast Guard radios that kept us apprised of conditions and happenings up and down the river. This was important since we regularly received barge loads of equipment and materials delivered by tugboats to our site: stone and riprap from quarries on the Ohio River and structural steel from the mills in Pittsburg.

On January 16th, 1977, Coast Guard radio reported that two ice dams, estimated to be 10 feet high, had formed on the Mississippi River just north of Cairo, Illinois, spanning the river. The river remained closed to shipping for several weeks. It was quiet on the river at our location during this time.

It was March 1st when it was announced that the ice dams had broken and the ice was flowing downstream. We were 450 river miles downstream from Cairo, so we mistakenly assumed that we might not be affected by the flow. Flowing at about two miles per hour, we would have a couple of weeks before it reached us.

The Coast Guard then reported that the flow of heavy ice was ripping out all the navigational buoys and destroying docks and wharves at all the ports.

We scrambled to get all of our barge-mounted equipment off the barges and on high ground. We then hired a tug boat out of Greenville to push our barges up onto the bank.

When the ice <u>floe</u> reached us, it wiped out everything we had in the river, including our crane dock. It twisted heavy steel pilings like corkscrews. The ice floe, three or more feet thick, was made up of millions of chunks of ice, also feet thick, covered the river, which was a mile wide at that point, from bank to bank, and still covered 90% of it just downstream at Vicksburg.

We should have known to expect the possibility of such a weather event. During our idle time, pre-thaw, we learned that in 1899, an ice flow such as this carried ice past New Orleans and into the Gulf of Mexico.

Like all weather events, if it has happened once, sooner or later, it will happen again.

A SEAFARING CUSTOM
KNOWS NO DEATH

**Asea: Asea is an adverb that means
"toward the sea" or "at sea".**

I have cruised on more than one troop ship and at least a couple
dozen cruise ships. I cannot count myself as a "sailor." I have never
hoisted a topsail, reefed a jib, or (thank God) never been keel-hauled.

My brother-in-law, Bob Clydesdale, was a modern-day sailor.
He spent a whole career in the USN. (Uncle Sam's Navy). Bob said
he was seasick from the time he stepped on a ship until the day he
stepped off it, and that was the case throughout his Navy career—
strange words from a career sailor.

On my various voyages, I did learn one immutable fact about
ships: that any time a ship is <u>asea</u>, it has to be painted. This goes
back to the time of Noah, and at sea, a custom knows no death. It
will stay solidly in place until the sea goes dry.

I sailed on troop ships back in the 1950s. The Navy owns and
operates the ship, and the dog-faced soldiers, such as I was at the
time when in transport, spend all of what should be leisure hours
painting the blasted ship. I suspect that when the paint is so thick
that it is about to sink the ship, they chip off the old paint and start
over again.

211

Many of my readers will make cruises on cruise ships. You won't have to paint the ship but will be aware that just outside your staterooms, someone will be chipping off paint from the rusty spots and retouching it with white or marine gray. The custom will never end.

Too soon old, too late smart

Discontentment: To be dissatisfied or unhappy about something

Alfred was an easygoing chap. He had been married once before but it somehow didn't work out. In looking back later, he wasn't quite sure why it had ended. But then he met Amie. Amie was some eight years younger than Alfred. Amie was not married, but she had a small boy from a previous relationship. Alfred, at nearly 30 years of age, felt that it was time that he should get settled down. Taking on a wife and child shouldn't be too much of a challenge.

Life was full of fun for a little while. Alfred and Amie produced a darling baby girl. Alfred was a construction worker, and Amie became a housewife. It was hard making ends meet on one paycheck, especially in the building trades, which were somewhat seasonal. Alfred tried different lines of work, even in a factory at one point.

The biggest problem in the family was Amie's inability to settle down and be happy. She disliked the house that they had rented, so Alfred bought a new house in a nearby town. Soon, that home was as unhappy as the previous one. Everyday life, which was normal for others, was somehow stressful for Amie. The unhappiness she felt was like a contagion and affected the other members of the family.

213

When her everyday life overwhelmed her, her remedy was to leave and go stay with a friend or her sister in another state.

This went on for several years. Alfred could see no improvement. He tried to clamp down and put an end to the turmoil that her periodic departures caused. Amie didn't comprehend the level of Alfred's <u>discontentment</u> when he told her that if she left again, it was going to be the end of their marriage. She left again. Alfred was daunted by the responsibility of raising the two children, but he would do it, and this time it would be without Amie.

Alfred said his biggest problem was the old Pennsylvania Dutch adage, "Too soon old, too late smart."

He said he would be more circumspect before tying the knot again.

CONSTRUCTION WORKER

**Disingenuous: It describes someone who
pretends to be something they are not.**

It was a routine business trip to UTEP in El Paso. At the time,
I was making two round trips nearly every week from Austin to one
or more of the University of Texas campuses around the state. I was
doing a lot of flying on Southwest Airlines. In those days, it was a
practice of the airline to put nice new Southwest Airlines magazines
in the seatback pockets on the first of every month. The magazines
were all alike and stayed that way until a new issue came out at the
start of the following month. To fill my time, I routinely filled out
the crossword puzzle. I usually needed help using the answer page
the first time out, but by the return trip, with a clean puzzle, I could
usually finish it without a problem. On the next trip, a few days later,
I could complete the puzzle in just a few minutes.

On this particular morning, I sat next to a pleasant-looking,
well-dressed lady. She was about middle-aged and looked as if
she were headed to some educational system meeting as a school
administrator. I pulled out the airline magazine and was pleased to
find that the crossword puzzle had not been filled in. It was nice and
clean. I took the ink pen from my shirt pocket and started filling
in the blanks. In less than five minutes, the puzzle was completely

filled in in ink. I put the magazine back into the seatback pocket and stuck my pen back into my shirt pocket.

I was aware that the lady was watching me intently. When I put the magazine away, the lady commented, "That was impressive." I thanked her for the compliment, and then she asked, "What is your profession?"

"My profession?" I asked.

"Yes, what do you do for a living?"

"Oh," I said. "I am a construction worker." She was speechless. I closed my eyes as if ready to take a nap. But behind my closed eyelids, I was smiling.

Was I crassly <u>disingenuous</u>? Somewhat, I suppose. It is true, though. I worked in the construction industry throughout my entire career.

Hoppin' John

Cowpeas: a plant of the pea family native to the Old World tropics, black-eyed peas

Cowpeas, also known as field peas, played a significant role in the Civil War.

Brought to the Americas by enslaved Africans in the 1600s, black-eyed peas were considered animal feed by Union soldiers who raided Confederate food supplies during the war, so they passed them up. Consequently, southern families, who had their other foodstuffs stolen by Union foragers, survived the winter by eating the peas and salt pork and came to consider themselves lucky. Robert E. Lee even called them "the only unfailing friend the Confederacy ever had." Today, families across the South eat black-eyed peas on New Year. It is a sign of good luck.

In some areas, the traditional New Year's fare is called "Hoppin' John." It consists of black-eyed peas, cooked with fatback or sausage, served with collard greens and cornbread.

The name might have come from an invitation: "So hop in, John, and join us for a mess of peas. If we don't eat them up, we'll have them again tomorrow as Skippin' Jenny."

WE DON'T ALL AGREE

Dispel: Make a doubt, feeling, or belief disappear.

Recently, there has been at least one person hanging around the entrance to the post office, carrying a clipboard. That person, whoever it is, is often talking to one of the post office patrons, and I got an idea he – or she, at times it was a woman – was promoting something. On one occasion, I let him approach me, and he said he was collecting signatures on a petition to make abortion on demand a legal constitutional right. I cut him off shortly and said plainly, "I am pro-life!" He had an abashed look, but I wanted to firmly <u>dispel</u> any thoughts that he might have that everybody that he talked with would agree with his petition.

It's an Offal Day

Haggis: A Scottish dish consisting of a sheep's or calf's offal mixed with suet, oatmeal, and seasoning and boiled in a bag, traditionally one made from the animal's stomach.

"There are Kiwis, and there are kiwis."

New Zealand is a tough place to visit unless one has a surfeit of money for plane flights or plenty of time to go there on a cruise ship. The country is strung out a thousand miles from north to south. The cities are spread out on the two main islands. There are some 700 other islands that are mostly uninhabited.

I am often amused that most Americans have just a general idea of where New Zealand is. They figure it is somewhere way south, close to Australia, and that's about it. The fact is that New Zealand is some 1,200 miles across the Tasman Sea from Australia. It took us two nights and a day to travel between them on a relatively fast cruise ship.

It was on our 2008 World Cruise on Holland America's "Amsterdam." We had worked our way down through French Polynesia, then the South Seas Islands of Samoa, Tonga, New Caledonia, and a couple of others. We made port in Auckland on February 1st, Wellington on the third, Christchurch on the fourth, and Dunedin on the fifth.

Each place had its own charm, and the people were a little different. The indigenous Māori people came down from Polynesia nearly a thousand years ago and settled mostly in the northern part of the country. They are seen in abundance in Auckland and its surrounds.

New Zealanders are known as Kiwis. The name alludes to the kiwi, a flightless species of bird native only to New Zealand. The practice of calling New Zealanders Kiwis seems to date back to the First World War. New Zealand soldiers were called Kiwis, and the name stuck. Eventually, all New Zealanders became known as Kiwis, and they wear the moniker proudly.

When we landed in Dunedin, we immediately identified it as a suburb of Heaven. In fact, it is said in Dunedin that people stopped there on their way to heaven and thought they had arrived. Dunedin is a pure Scot town named after Dùn Èideann ("fort of Edin"), the Scottish Gaelic name for Edinburgh.

My wife emailed her sons back in Texas to "Sell the house and farm and send us the money. We're staying in New Zealand." She was not serious, but it indicated how impressed we were with the country.

We were privileged to visit Dunedin on Robert Burns's birthdate, January 25th. The poet is Scotland's favorite son, and Scots and Brits, the world over, celebrate it with Burns Night. To understand a Burns Night, one must understand the haggis. The haggis is a famous foodstuff in Scotland, mainly eaten at ceremonial events, especially honoring Robert Burns.

The "Address to the Haggis" is the most important part of Burns Night and traditionally the first item on the order of proceedings. The party's host carries the haggis into the room on a silver salver with a knife at ready. They then invite the party to pay respect to the haggis by reciting Burns' famous poem about the famous foodstuff.

Filled with imagery and metaphor, the poem is a passionate ode to a unique and symbolic part of Scottish culture. Don't hold back – channel your inner Rabbie and deliver the address with gusto!

I had experienced the haggis ceremony only once before in

Edinburgh, Scotland, a couple of years earlier. I suppose there might be Scottish enclaves where it is practiced in the USA, but I had never heard of it.

We had already visited Christchurch, which is every bit as English as Dunedin is Scotch. Christchurch even has an Avon River running through, and the adjacent expanse to the southwest of the city is the Canterbury Plains. Christchurch deserves its own story. I'll get to it later.

El Paso or Else

Duplicitous: Deceitful. "treacherous, duplicitous behavior."

It was a bitter cold January 1998 when I loaded up, hitched up, gassed up, and headed to Texas. I had been working on projects in the South for five years. My wife was in treatment for lymphoma. I had determined to move to Austin where there was a plethora of doctors and hospitals. My wife's medical needs should be in good hands.

One of my friends, who also finished work in Mississippi and moved to Austin, was working in the home office of the J.D. Abrams construction company. I contacted my friend, who said he believed the company needed a good planner/scheduler. He referred me to the engineering manager, and I gave him a call. He confirmed that they indeed needed a scheduler with my qualifications. That happened around the middle of December, and I told him that I could be available to start work in Austin in the middle of January.

My wife was receiving medical treatment in Kansas City while I was making the move to Austin. Once I was set up, I called the Abrams office. I was then told that they had filled the scheduler position from another department, but they needed a scheduler for their bridge projects in El Paso. I told the manager that I couldn't move to El Paso as we had just moved to Austin to be near my wife's daughter as well as the doctors and hospitals that Austin could provide. He said he was sorry, but El Paso was the only place that he had available. I was crushed.

I learned later that Abram had three major projects in El Paso and was behind schedule on all of them. The state threatened to shut their jobs down if they didn't get a qualified scheduler and new schedules to show how they could get back on track.

It was <u>duplicitous</u> for Abrams to tell me that the Austin position had been filled. It had not. They were in a bind in El Paso and were trying to force me to take the position and bail them out.

As upset as I was at the time, serendipity was to come, and I thank the good Lord above for it. Had the Abrams company fulfilled its promise and I had gone to work for them, I would have missed out on the opportunity to finish my career working for the University of Texas System, the greatest blessing of my entire career.

The Old Masters

Ecstasy: A state of extreme happiness, especially when feeling pleasure

I have drawn away from following the hordes of art lovers on excursions to European museums. I love the beauty but I just cannot gush with <u>ecstasy</u> at the viewing of works by the old masters, Raphael, da Vinci, Botticelli, etc. And to witness others doing so leaves me with a bit of nausea.

THE APACHE OF THE GREAT SOUTHWEST

Enmity: A feeling or condition of hostility; hatred, ill will; animosity, antagonism

In the far southeast corner of Arizona lies some of the most rugged country in America. It is Cochise County, named after the famous Chiricahua Apache leader. The Dragoon Mountains provide a ruggedness that will capture your imagination. During the years of enmity between the Apache and the U.S. Army, Cochise led his band of about a thousand – five hundred warriors and five hundred women and children into an area that is now known as Cochise Stronghold. Cochise's father-in-law, Chief Mangas Coloradas, and his Mimbreno band of Chiricahua already lived in the fortified canyon. After Mangas's murder in captivity by the U.S. Army, Cochise became the chief of the entire Chiricahua in the Dragoon Mountains.

Cochise is reputed to have been a master strategist and leader who was never conquered in battle. He died peacefully on the newly formed Chiricahua reservation in 1874. His son, Taza, succeeded him as chief. Upon his death, Cochise was secretly buried somewhere in or near his impregnable fortress. The exact location has never been revealed or determined.

We toured the Dragoons and visited the stronghold in the early summer of 2024. Cochise Stronghold is located west of Sunsites, Arizona, in the Dragoon Mountains at an elevation of 5,000 ft. This beautiful woodland area lies in a protective rampart of granite domes and sheer cliffs, once the refuge of the great Apache Chief, Cochise, and his people.

Don't look for a health certificate

Beanery: A restaurant or café, sometimes used as an informal term for a cheap or inferior restaurant

I asked Gordo, "Where did you get those tamales?"

He responded, "Oh, there's a little <u>beanery</u> down on Nogalitos Street." As his name implied, Gordo was more than a little bit "gordo." I suspect he had eaten a lot of tamales in his time. Gordo was one of our security guards at our construction project on the south side of San Antonio.

I had to ask. "What's a beanery?"

"Oh, it's a little café, kind of a taco joint. Don't look for a health certificate."

I checked it out. It's my kind of place. Over the next year, I ate a lot of lunches at the little jacalito. No, I didn't see their health certificate.

Jack was a Country Dog

Envenomation: The process of being injected with venom or toxin through the bite or sting of an animal.

Rattlesnakes were nothing new to Sandi. She had lived next to Canyon del Oro for ten years and had taken her dogs for walks down the trail daily during the cooler seasons. The 21-mile-long Cañada del Oro trail followed the wash alongside Catalina State Park in Pima County, Arizona. Catalina State Park occupies 5,500 acres of rocky foothills and canyons. It sports some 5,000 saguaro cacti and probably three times that many rattlesnakes.

Sandi had encountered several rattlesnakes in her driveway over the years and had grown to be pretty comfortable about them, albeit granting them a wide berth with due respect for their danger. This time, however, as she was walking out to her mailbox on the cul-de-sac, she was looking ahead where her dogs were running instead of looking down, and she stepped on the damned thing. Hearing the rattles buzz at her feet, she jumped sidewise, caught her heel on a rock, landed on her posterior, and jammed a couple of vertebrae in the lumbar area of her back. The rattlesnake slithered away post haste toward the rocks in the wash where he would be safe from being further tromped upon.

The snake was luckier than Sandi. She would need several weeks of treatment and therapy before she was completely recovered.

Sandi didn't wait until she was fully recovered. She called and made arrangements for rattlesnake avoidance training for her two dogs. Envenomation from a large rattlesnake can be fatal to humans as well as animals. In rattlesnake avoidance training, dogs are fitted with electric shock collars. Then, they are exposed to the sound, smell, and sight of rattlesnakes, and at each occurrence, they receive a small electrical shock. It teaches them that any encounter will produce discomfort. Rattlesnake avoidance training for dogs is a popular business in Tucson, Arizona.

When I was a kid, my trusty dog, Jack, a stalwart police dog, killed every snake that he saw, venomous or otherwise. It didn't matter to Jack. Of course, Jack was a country dog.

A MAN OF GOD

Gospeler: a person who zealously teaches or professes faith in the gospel, preacher, evangelist

American Protestantism is a cornucopia of beliefs. Their services can range from the liturgical churches with Anglican roots to the snake-handling Pentecostals of Appalachia and everything in between. I have attended a few of these churches where the so-called "holy rollers" danced down the aisles and had to be controlled by "handlers."

I grew up in the Methodist church, a middle-of-the-road denomination. Periodically, our Methodist Church, as well as the nearby Baptist Church, would have revivals, supposedly to revive the spirit of those whose faith might be flagging. Often, the gospeler invited to preach the revival would be a roving evangelist. Some were pretty good preachers, and some of them, I suspected, had never actually attended seminary.

A wonderful example of an excellent preacher, though, and an exemplary man, was Billy Graham. He was the most famous evangelist of our generation. I admired Billy Graham and never doubted that he was a man of God.

PISA IS A KNOCK-OFF

**Extant: (especially of a document)
still in existence; surviving**

Pisa is a puzzle. How can a building so tall and massive as the Leaning Tower of Pisa be safe?

We visited Pisa a few years ago. You know, that Italian city has a tall bell tower that is noticeably out of perpendicular. Some say it was built that way. Probably not, but who's to say? There are no <u>extant</u> surveyors' notes from construction days to shed light on the question.

The Leaning Tower of Pisa is not the only leaning tower, though. Halfway across the world, the giant Huzhu Pagoda near Shanghai leans in excess of 7 degrees, as opposed to the Pisa tower leaning just 4 degrees. Moreover, the Chinese tower was built in 1079, 294 years before the Pisa tower was completed. We visited the Huzhu Pagoda back in 2009. Our Han guide proudly quipped to us that the Pisa Tower was a "knock-off."

The Biggest Nut

**Ferrocement: Ferrocement is a type
of thin-wall reinforced concrete.**

What do you do when you're driving down the road and suddenly appears in front of you, the world's biggest nut? Well, you do what I did. Check it out and spend the night. It has to be an interesting place.

The <u>ferrocement</u> pistachio nut sculpture is unique, even among America's diverse roster of roadside titans. Visible from a mile in either direction along US 54, the 30-foot-high Pistachio is an alien-looking monolith rising from the Chihuahuan Desert, with a buff-colored shell and purple-and-green seed.

Tom McGinn started the pistachio farm back in 1980. Thinking big, as Tom was known to do, he increased his grove to 12,300 pistachio trees. Tom's son, Timothy, now runs the operation.

A bronze plaque at the base of the monolith dedicates it to Tom McGinn, closing with the sentiment that he "dreamed big, expected big, and accomplished big things. He would have said the monument is not big enough!"

STEAMBOATS PLIED
THE RIVER

Freshets: The flood of a river from
heavy rain or melted snow

There's never a shortage of subjects to precipitate a controversy. We are all familiar with the age-old mantra that you "don't talk about religion or politics." And it's true. But we have other controversial subjects. The Israel-Palestinian thing – boy, there are some harsh feelings there. And it is a problem. And then there are the issues of solar power, wind farms, and electric cars. You can even mention Daylight Saving Time and stage an argument. A good portion of what you hear or read on social media can, with a little serious research, be classified as misinformation.

And then there's the big one that has been with us for a while and will probably stay with us until the old planet turns into an apocalyptic fireball. It is global warming or climate change. Coincidental with climate change is the fact that our burgeoning population is outgrowing the availability of water. Acute droughts and local short-term dry spells affect varied areas regularly. It is the chronic or long-term drought that poses a severe problem. The effects are evident around the country.

Major lakes and reservoirs are far below capacity and shrinking daily. Even my favorite river when I was growing up has shrunken. In the 19th century, cargo steamboats plied the Current River almost to the Missouri state line. Now, a fisherman in a johnboat must carefully navigate drifts, logjams, and shallow shoals. The creek that ran by my childhood home had a good swimming hole and lots of fish. Now, it no longer runs at all during the dry months. When a local downpour occurs, my little creek turns into a raging <u>freshet</u> that will last for hours or a day, then it returns to its new normal, just scattered pools with no flow across the gravel shoals.

In Las Vegas, where we make our home, there is an area-wide move to replace water-thirsty lawns with artificial turf. The water company subsidizes the change, making it easier for us to absorb the cost. It benefits us by lowering our water bills each month.

IT STARTED ON SULLIVAN'S ISLAND

Fulcrum: A thing that plays a central or essential role in an activity, event, or situation.

As we motored across the confluence of the Ashley and Cooper Rivers to Sullivan's Island, I reflected on what life might have been like back in the middle of the 19th century and how this primitive, scantily populated state in economic decline could have become the <u>fulcrum</u> of the greatest tragedy ever to beset our fledgling nation – the American Civil War.

I had visited Fort Sumter a few decades earlier but apparently gave little thought to the gravity of events that unfolded there in the spring of 1861. Historical tragedies seem to weigh more heavily upon our consciences as we advance into our later years.

Tops of undersea mountains

Fumaroles: Vents or openings at the surface where volcanic gases and vapors are emitted.

We had been nine days without the sight of land, and the last two had been through a storm with 70 MPH winds blowing across our bow. We were still in the middle of the Atlantic Ocean. It is unusual to see islands so far from a continental shelf, but the Azores is one of those oddities, as is Bermuda.

The Azores is a volcanic archipelago. That means that the nine islands that make up the archipelago are the tops of volcanic undersea mountains, with just their tops jutting above the surface of the Atlantic.

It was May 10th, 2011, and Ponta Delgado was a welcome sight. The fog was lifting above the seaside buildings and the rest of the island was socked in. Ponta Delgada, on São Miguel Island, is the capital of the Azores archipelago of Portugal.

We went ashore and boarded an excursion bus for the Furnas Valley on the island's east end. The sun was trying to burn its way through the fog. The Furnas Valley is an enormous crater. We were allowed to walk among the <u>fumaroles</u> that were spouting steam and gases, unlike the geyser field in Yellowstone, where the geysers are fenced off for protection.

We steered a wide berth from the most active volcano-type vents as they were hissing and spouting sulfur dioxide and hydrogen sulfide in the air, poison, I assume.

There was an enormous amount of geothermal activity, including bubbling and steaming fumaroles alongside Furnas (caldera) Lake. Fumaroles are like mini volcanos that are dotted around the landscape.

Geothermal activity, such as we were exploring, doesn't all go to waste. The Azores harness the resource for 42% of the electrical power on San Miguel Island. Geothermal power accounts for 60% of the Azores' renewable energy, which in turn makes up 37% of the archipelago's total electricity.

We could do the same thing in the Geyser Basin in Yellowstone National Park, but we prefer to preserve the area for tourism.

The visit to Furnas Valley was one of those unforgettable experiences that bubble to the surface every time we hear news of a geothermal event like some hear of periodically in Yellowstone and Iceland.

BRAZIL

Funicular: A railroad car operating by cable with ascending and descending cars counterbalanced.

We had crossed the Atlantic from Cabo Verde, off Africa's Senegal coast, and were due to make port in Salvador de Bahia, Brazil.

When visiting a foreign city where resources are scarce, it is advisable to seek advice from someone who has been there before. I turned to Chris and Julita Michalski. Chris and Julita were both born in Poland, met in London and had settled in Toronto. They were the most traveled couple that I ever met. Chris related that, in Salvador de Bahia, there is a low town near where we dock and a high town where most of the city is. He said we would need to take the funicular to the high town to see the interesting sights. I immediately forgot about attractions and asked, "What's a funicular?" He gave me one of those "Where have you been?" looks and said, "It is an incline railroad that takes you up the steep hill to the city."

In the years hence, after seeing funiculars in nearly every hilly city in the world, I have wondered how I could have lived on this planet for more than 70 years before learning what everybody else already knew, that a funicular is one of those trainlike cars that haul passengers up and down steep inclines.

IT IS NOT COMPLICATED

Gluttonous: habitual greed or excess in eating

I don't subscribe to the thought that Americans are fat because of "habitual greed." We are fat because we are <u>gluttonous</u>. We have no control over our appetites. We are the fattest developed nation in the world. The only fatter populations are those in the South Pacific Islands, where big is considered beautiful.

It is not complicated. We simply eat too much. Restaurants serve too much food. My wife and I go to a restaurant and split an order. Often, we still carry part of it home. And we still feel like we have eaten too much.

TV commercials encourage it. I watch these Whataburger ads and see people taking bites that are bigger than a whole hamburger used to be. If I took a bite like that, I would wind up flopping around on the floor, hoping someone would know the Heimlich maneuver.

I sat in my pulmonologist's waiting room one morning recently and noted that every person in there was overweight, and half of them were grossly obese. I see a lot of people of what I call "working age," middle-aged and younger, who would be incapable of holding down a job. They are simply too fat.

Don't call it Sheetrock

Gypsum: A soft white or gray mineral consisting of hydrated calcium sulfate.

Rising from the heart of the Tularosa Basin is one of the world's great natural wonders - the glistening white sands of New Mexico. Great wave-like dunes of gypsum sand have engulfed 275 square miles of desert, creating the world's largest gypsum dune field. White Sands National Park preserves a major portion of this unique dune field and the plants and animals that live here.

For most of my life, I had wanted to visit White Sands National Park. It took me over 80 years, but I finally made it. I spent a baker's dozen years of my young adulthood working as a drywall finisher, taping the joints on gypsum wallboard. I didn't know, in those days, that the word gypsum could ever imply anything better than plain hard work.

There's not much to see at White Sands National Park except sand or gypsum. It is immense and impressive, though. I am glad I finally made it. I visited and photographed the dunes on May 29th,

2021. The photograph that I have archived requires an explanation. It just looks like me standing in a snowbank.

By the way, don't call gypsum wallboard "Sheetrock," because that is a registered trade name by the United States Gypsum Company.

Worn-out Tires
and Nut Trees

Happenstance: Chance or a chance situation, especially one producing a good result

It was a pleasant afternoon when Shameem and I landed at the San Francisco Airport in Oakland, the kind of day California describes in their travel brochures. We shuttled to the Avis rental office and picked up a beige-colored Toyota. Shameem and I were traveling light so that the Camry would be adequate. There were a couple of hours of daylight left, and Oakland is a great place not to be after dark. We set out across the hills to the Central Valley. We grabbed a bite to eat in Livermore at the edge of the Coast Range that separates the bay area from the San Juan Valley before continuing to our Hampton Inn in Stockton.

Shameen was a structural engineer who still spoke with an accent concomitant with that of the thousands of Indian engineers who have sought out the large engineering and construction firms of America that are eager to hire them. He, like I, had been working for the H.B. Zachry Company of San Antonio, Texas, for about three years. The big coal-fired power plant that we had been building in the eastern part of Bexar County was nearing completion. The Operations Manager of the Power Division had made it known that he planned to expand the division's footprint beyond the Texas region. Shameem and I were to check out some of the power generation facilities in California. Our group was experienced in building conventional power plants fueled by oil, coal, and lignite. We were to check out opportunities in plants that burned alternate fuels.

We targeted two small plants hidden back in canyons on the west side of the Valley. The first one was fueled by agricultural waste. Who knew that there could be a never-ending supply of bulldozed nut trees? California produces the vast majority of the world's almond supply. Almond orchards occupied 760,000 acres when we visited, and the number is well over a million acres today. As a grove ages, its production decreases. The grove is bulldozed and replanted. It is an endless cycle. California also has some 400,000 acres of bearing walnut trees. The fuel supply from those trees will be endless.

I suspect it would be a rare Californian who would turn on a lamp and consider that part of the electricity came from a walnut tree.

The next plant we visited was some 30 miles south in a similar canyon. It was fueled strictly by auto and truck tires. Truckloads and trainloads of tires were hauled in from as far away as San Diego. We were shown a side canyon with a stockpile of more than seven million tires. The plant was operating at full capacity when we visited. I expected a cloud of acrid black smoke to fill the sky in the canyon. Not so! The tires burn so hot and so quickly that they emit no black smoke whatsoever.

Shameem and I had satisfied the needs of our California visit and had volumes of information to take back to Texas. The second part of our assignment was to fly to Las Vegas and meet with representatives of Nevada Energy Company as they were planning a new power plant to be built in Moapa Valley just up the Salt Lake highway northeast of Las Vegas. We turned in the Avis rental and took the late afternoon flight to McCarren Field in Las Vegas.

The desk clerk at the Golden Nugget said, "I have a message for you, Mr. Cates." The message said, "Call Ben Alves in San Antonio."

What could Ben Alves, Construction Manager for the H.B. Zachry Company, want with me? I called and caught him still in the office. He said, "We just got awarded a combined cycle gas turbine power plant to build for Florida Power and Light. Get back down here. We have a preconstruction planning meeting Saturday morning."

"Good God, Ben, it is Memorial Day weekend." I didn't say it, but I wanted to.

"I want you to go to Indiantown, Florida, next week to start setting up the job."

Within the next few weeks, I had leased a home in Port St. Lucie. My wife and I moved in and became Florida residents for the next couple of years. That is just a little kink in the life of a construction man. His life doesn't follow a well-defined plan. The crooks and turns of his career are most likely governed by happenstance.

The Home team

**Inculcate: instill (an attitude, idea, or
habit) by persistent instruction**

It is a cultural standard that I have wrestled with for years. It is
not necessarily a bad practice; it simply gives one pause for thought.
We are taught from childhood that we are a good family. We
love each other and support each other. We are the home team.
When we go to high school, our basketball team is the good guys.
We cheer them on. We are taught to be patriotic. Our fruited plains
are better than those in other countries.

In school, we study our state history. I recall that in Arkansas
History, we are told that our state is distinctly unique from all the
others. It could stand alone on its own natural resources. It is good
that we are <u>inculcated</u> to always pull for the home team. Sometimes
we fail to remember that in the dozens of other countries around
the world, the people feel just as strongly about their countries as
we do ours.

THE CHICKEN
OR THE EGG

**Inflation: A general increase in prices and
a fall in the purchasing value of money.**

What came first, the chicken or the egg? It is one of those
questions that have been around forever, and there is no answer that
one can lean on and say this is true.

Politicians on the stump are always "going after the big
corporations" because they are the cause of inflation. Inflation hurts
the "little guys," so the politicians pander to the little guy's votes. It's
all a big whitewash, and here's why.

Laborers, represented by unions, are the little guys. Of course,
they are always wanting higher wages. And if they don't get increases
yearly, they will go on strike. Of course, the employer must raise the
prices of his products to pay the higher wages. It is an endless cycle.

Another example regards a well-known liberal politician, Gavin
Newsome, Governor of California. Last year, he signed into law a
requirement that large fast-food chains must pay their workers a
minimum of $20.00 per hour. With that in mind, can anyone think
that the price of their Big Mac won't be increased?

So, who's responsible for increased <u>inflation</u>? The corporations have no choice. Workers get paid more, so prices have to be increased. Think of this the next time you look at the price of your Big Mac.

What came first, the chicken or the egg?

You can't call them that

Insane: In a state of mind that prevents normal perception, behavior, or social interaction

Here's a word that you haven't seen in print lately. In fact, you haven't even heard it spoken in recent times. Pertaining to people, it is a dirty word. Politically correct folks will be on you like white on rice. I know. I have had it happen. It is a good word, though. Its definition accurately describes a condition. Apparently, no one is insane these days, though.

But get this: these days, in a murder trial, the number one defense is "Not guilty by reason of 'temporary insanity.'" So, we find that people will admit to being <u>insane</u> only if it will keep them from going to prison.

On the other hand, it is in vogue for people to struggle with mental illness but not insanity. It seems that half the personalities in Hollywood have mental issues. Everybody has his own "shrink." They talk publicly about it and write books about their struggles.

There are no more insane asylums, although there are a lot of "crazies" out there. You just can't call them that anymore.

A SELF-IMPOSED DISEASE

**Intemperance: Lack of moderation
or self-restraint. especially excessive
use of alcoholic beverages.**

We don't hear much about intemperance in our everyday lives, but it is around us every day. We all know someone who drinks too much. Maybe they are now addicted to alcohol, and we are inculcated to view the addiction as a sickness and not place blame on the addicted person. Be that as it may, if the addicted person had effectively practiced temperance from the start, he, or she would not have become addicted.

Somehow, our 21st-century culture looks at our addicted population as victims, whether it is alcohol or illicit drugs. We are not to place blame, but whether we like it or not, there is blame. In fact, in most cases, it is a self-imposed disease.

When it comes to illegal drugs, it goes deeper than that. The person who buys illegal drugs to feed his habit, or his <u>intemperance</u>, is committing a crime. If the punishment for criminal activity were severe enough, I suspect a lot of people would learn to be more temperate.

WHERE IS MEXICAN HAT?

Irrepressible: incapable of being repressed or restrained; uncontrollable:

There's something about the American West of the 19th century that piqued my interest from my days as a small boy. Surely, it affected my friends in much the same way. At school, we talked about our heroes, such as Red Rider, Roy Rogers, and Gene Autry, as well as their horses, Thunder and Trigger and, of course, Champion the Wonder Horse.

But with me, the allure went even deeper. I read what was known as "dime westerns," and they told me of places like Cheyenne, Laramie, and Dodge City. And the stories imbued within me an irrepressible desire to go and see those places for myself. Even as an adult, I put myself in harm's way, weather-wise, just to drive through Cheyenne, Shoshoni, Cody, and Red Lodge in the middle of a snowy and icy winter.

As the years have rolled by, I fulfilled many of those dreams. I have visited all those places, including Silver City, Virginia City,

Medicine Bow, and Rhyolite. Even as an octogenarian, I was thrilled to visit Monument Valley and Mexican Hat.

Has my Old West fascination been completely sated and laid to rest? Somehow, Carson Valley is on my mind. Maybe that will be my next goal. My friends are invited to join me.

THE PINEY WOODS

Lighter Knot: A hard piece of resin-filled fatwood from a decaying pine tree

We were finishing up our project on "The Stack," a series of interchange structures on the south side of Jackson. Helmer, my dirt foreman, came into my office all hot, sweaty, and frustrated. He said, "We've got to get rid of that Dempsey kid. His head is as hard as a lighter knot." Helmer was from the piney woods of eastern North Carolina and spoke with a heavy accent.

I told him, "Take him off the wheelbarrow if it's too complicated for him, and just give him a shovel." Then I asked, "What's a lighter knot?"

He said, "You know, it's what you start campfires with."

"No, I don't know. Tell me about it." I had never lived in the piney woods. It turns out that when a pine tree dies and decays, the sap, or resin, collects and hardens in the tree's heart. It is called fatwood. Full of resin, stick a match to it, and it is immediately aflame. The best part of fatwood is the resin-filled knots that have hardened while the rest of the tree decayed around it. It is known as a lighter knot and is about as heavy and hard as anthracite. However, it is perfect for starting a fire.

The Dempsey kid's head must have been pretty hard if it was as hard as a lighter knot. We took him off the wheelbarrow, and he did just fine.

252

GALILEO

List: When used as a verb, "list" (in the sense of tilt) means to lean or incline to one side

Our friends, Bob and Iris, met us as we walked ashore in Livorno. We had visited the port city of Civitavecchia the previous day. Livorno was a breath of fresh air. At Civitavecchia, everyone was scrambling to get on a train to Rome. At Livorno, by comparison, our fellow excursionists were happily anticipating a leisurely visit to nearby Pisa.

Following our Tuscan breakfast, accompanied by a delightful bottle of Chablis (We had already learned that wine is standard with every meal in Italy), we motored to the ageless city, always dominated by its tilted tower.

The Leaning Tower of Pisa never disappoints. The famous bell tower is now some 900 years old and has been listing to the Southeast since the day it was built. If one stares at it long enough, he eventually starts to doubt his own equilibrium. We wonder if Galileo Galilei was affected in the same way. If he was, he didn't say so. He did, however, have plenty to say about his fascination with the Tower and his experiences studying gravity.

Galileo, a professor of mathematics at the nearby University of Pisa, used the Tower to perform his experiments on gravity. He carried weights of different sizes to the top of the tower, then dropped them simultaneously and determined that they dropped at the same speed regardless of the size. As we labored up the interior stairways, we commented that the good professor surely didn't carry cannonballs to the top just to see them splat off the grass below.

When climbing the stairs, we observed that we always knew which side of the tower we were on because we naturally gravitated from one side to the other with the rise and dip of the tower. The stone steps are foot-worn on the ends, depending upon where they were in the tower.

The bell tower was not the only structure that fascinated Galileo. The nearby Duomo, or Cathedral, is one of the finest and most beautiful in Europe. Like the Tower, the Cathedral is nearly a thousand years old. The baptistry is where Galileo observed the swinging of the overhead lamp and recorded his description of the pendulum. Galileo was the first to examine its unique characteristics. He found that each pendulum has a constant period. The period is the time in which a pendulum completes a single oscillation, i.e., returns to the position it was in at the beginning of the period.

A visit to Pisa and a tour of the three edifices, the Bell Tower, the Cathedral, and the Baptistry, which also has a <u>list</u> of 0.6 degrees, is more than enough to tire even a fit man.

Highway 50

Loneliest: Abnormally lonely

Do you ever want to take a country drive just to get away from other people? Do you abhor crowds and traffic jams? I think it is part of my having grown up in the country where one never had to deal with such things.

I love people, but they don't all have to be on my road when I want it to myself. I have long sought such roads. I recall driving from Sanderson, Texas, to Ozona one Sunday morning, returning from a visit to Big Bend National Park. It was a stretch of near barren desert (actually ranchland) from Sanderson to IH-10, about 80 miles, and we only saw one other vehicle in that distance. But that Route 200 is not the <u>loneliest</u> road in America. No Siree!

If you want to get away from freight trucks and interchanges, I have just the drive for you. Hop onto U.S. Highway 50 somewhere around Fallon, Nevada, and point your hood ornament east. Between there and Ely, Nevada (a good place to stop for lunch), you won't be bothered by traffic.

U.S. Highway 50, all 408 miles of it across central Nevada, was dubbed "The Loneliest Road in America" by Life Magazine in July of 1986. Central Nevada is proud of that notoriety. Hotels and gas stations along that route – there aren't that many – proudly post notifications to that effect.

Nobody is overweight in Montevideo

Maté: Pronounced MAH-tay, also called Yerba Maté. It is made by soaking dried yerba maté leaves in hot water.

We had drunk coca tea, or coca de maté in the Andes Mountains in Peru. When our Uruguayan guide in Montevideo told us that everyone in Uruguay drank <u>maté</u>, we assumed it to be the same as the coca de maté that we drank in Peru. Not so. The coca tea that we drank in Peru was to deal with the high altitude in the Andes. And it was made with real coca leaves. Uruguay didn't have altitude problems. In fact, Montevideo sits at sea level on the Rio de la Plata. However, everybody seems to drink maté in Montevideo and always drink it through a bombilla or a silver straw. Even their bicycles are fitted with holders for their maté cups with their bombillas.

Our guide assured us that maté was what kept all Uruguayans slender. Maybe he was right. We never saw even one overweight person while we were in Uruguay.

Boston Cabbie

Maundered: talk in a rambling manner.

The Boston cabbie <u>maundered</u> on and on about how bad our president was, and how his administration was destroying this country, without a word about how bad politics and living conditions are in Nigeria, his home country. I have had cabbies in Barcelona that I would trust far beyond this African. I have never understood why cab drivers think they are so much smarter than their fares.

House parties in the 1950s

Merriment: Lighthearted gaiety or fun-making

When one reaches an age that is well on the south side of 80, he has to look deep into the murky past to remember the fun things he did as a teenager.

As I reflect upon those years and my friends, playmates, and classmates, I remember the evening house parties. We played the innocent little games that the more creative ones could come up with and a couple that were a bit more exciting for us teenagers. I cannot think of a better occasion of light-hearted <u>merriment</u> and fun.

I remember a party at the Lincoln house – the Lincolns had nearly 20 kids before they quit – where we blindly chose the hand of one of the girls and had the opportunity to walk with her up the gravel road, away from the light of the house. There was time for a couple of sweet kisses in the dark before we returned to the gaiety of the party.

On one occasion that evening, I had chosen the hand of Norma Jean Lincoln, a pretty girl who was only about a year my senior. She had just put on a heavy layer of lipstick. When we returned to the party, the kids looked at me, with my face lipsticked up like a Ringling Brothers clown. I was the object of derision, and I didn't know why. The reason for their great mirth was soon pointed out to me, and I was more careful from that time forward.

It is funny to look back at some of that silliness. I saw Norma Jean a few years ago. It had been some 60 years since the party. She and I had a good laugh about it. I didn't give her the opportunity to do it all over again.

THEY REPORTED TO
THEIR PROBATION
OFFICERS

**Icehouse: a cross between a convenience store,
a neighborhood bar, and an open-air gathering
place. "Icehouse" is now a colloquialism for
an open-air bar in many parts of Texas.**

As quitting time approached, the Cruz brothers, Hector and Isidro, invited me to stop by the <u>icehouse</u> and have a beer with them. I had to inquire, "Why go to an ice house to drink beer?"

It turns out that, in Texas, the icehouse is kind of a small open-air beer hall. I had much to learn about Texas terminology – such as ice houses, beaneries, and blue northers.

The Cruz brothers were laborers on our job, rebuilding U.S. Highway 90 across the south side of San Antonio. Hector and Isidro were likable little guys, both in their early or mid-20s, and probably neither of them weighed more than 130 pounds. They showed me the scars from their knife fights in the past. I had to give both of them time off every two weeks to report to their probation officers.

This was back in 1985, and my first project in Texas. Culture shock!

ADEN

**Misalignment: The incorrect
arrangement or position of something
in relation to something else**

My father died when I was three years old. A couple of years later, my mother married Aden Damascus Cates. I have often wondered how such an unspiritual man as Aden had a middle name with biblical roots. His mother must have had great hopes for him. Surely, she was disappointed. I never knew her. Anyway, it was through my mother's marriage to Aden that I got my last name, Cates.

Aden had one conspicuous imperfection by which he was known. It was a <u>misalignment</u> of one of his eyes. I don't know which one, but both of them didn't look in exactly the same direction at the same time. Some of the insensitive kids – I think we were all insensitive in those days – called him Old Cross-eyed Aden, not to his face, though.

Aden was not a jewel. (Bless his heart, as they say down south.) My mother put up with him for nearly ten years. The only thing left of Aden now is the name Cates, and I am stuck with it.

THE SOUTHERN CROSS

**Asterism: A prominent pattern or group
of stars, typically having a popular name
but smaller than a constellation.**

The old Irish proverb says, "You never miss the water until the well runs dry." A new American proverb (I wrote it this morning) says, "You never miss the Big Dipper until it is not in the sky."

We were a week out of Fort Amador, cruising southwest for the Marquesas Islands. The days were getting noticeably longer as our north latitude was headed for zero. We had been in the doldrums for a day and a night. It is good that we did not have to depend upon the wind in our sails to get us out of the "calms."

Although it was just the middle of January, summer was just beyond this imaginary hump in the globe. We would, within a matter of minutes, cross that imaginary line known as the equator. Try as we may, most of us will never feel the bump when we cross the line. Some will say they felt it. They are probably the same people who claim to feel earthquakes that do not show up on a Richter scale. I suspect they are the same people who would eat the desiccant package from their aspirin bottle.

Last night was our last opportunity to view the Big Dipper. It followed the North Star and slid out of sight below the northern horizon.

The Big Dipper is a uniquely American invention. It is part of the Great Bear or Ursa Major constellation. The southern half of the world can't see it because it is in the northern sky. Our neighbors across the pond in UK and Ireland are confused and call it a plough. The rest of the boreal countries are so wrapped up in the Great Bear that they pay no attention to the seven stars that make up the asterism that we love and call the Big Dipper. It is ours.

South of the Equator, we scanned the austral skies and search for the Southern Cross. We finally spotted it just above the southern horizon. I expected it to look like the shoulder patch on my uniform shirts when I served in the Southern Cross Division in Panama. Not so! It is a little hard even to identify it as a cross. It seems to be lying on its side, kind of lazy-like. However, it is real and we continued seeing it for the next few weeks. I hoped to see it straighten up as we got beneath it down around the southern region of Australasia, but it didn't happen.

Wichita didn't get it

Antemeridian: The antemeridian is a line of longitude at 180 degrees from the Prime Meridian

We talked about the Equator. Now, we will talk about a different line that is exactly perpendicular to the Equator.

We were way down in the South Pacific. I like the sound of that. It reminds me of the great movie starring Rossano Brazzi and Mitzi Gaynor. It had been 23 days since we had embarked on the big MS Amsterdam at Fort Lauderdale, Florida.

We were making our way toward the <u>Antemeridian</u>, that imaginary line that runs from the North Pole to the South Pole. It is 180 degrees East Longitude and 180 degrees West Longitude, exactly at the far extremity of the earth from the Prime Meridian in Greenwich, England.

Together, the Prime Meridian and its Antemeridian form a great circle. This great circle divides the Earth into two hemispheres: the Eastern Hemisphere and the Western Hemisphere. As we crossed it, we were crossing from the Western Hemisphere into the Eastern Hemisphere, although we were cruising west. If you think all of that is confusing and hard to understand, hold on!

Crossing the Antemeridian would be meaningless to us except for one thing. It was the International Date Line. It was Saturday, January 26th, when we approached it, and the instant that we crossed the line, it was Monday, January 28th. Sunday, January 27th did not exist; for us, and it would never exist.

Some of our dining room tablemates were all aflutter. "We just got screwed out of a day of our vacation."

I tried to calm them by explaining that we would get our day back an hour at a time as we continued around the globe. That calmed all of them except the couple from Wichita.

Harold said he would file a claim against Holland America for a portion of his fare. He was convinced that after we had cruised around the world and got back to Fort Lauderdale, it would be just 116 days instead of the 117 days as the cruise had been advertised. His wife, Emma, was no help. I suspect our Wichita friends would mistake the finger bowl for an aperitif and wonder why it tasted funny.

Dead Man's Hand

Muleteer: a person who drives mules.

You have heard about Calamity Jane. We all have, but few of us know more than a smidgeon of details about her.

Calamity Jane had a rough start in life. Martha Jane Canary was born May 1st, 1852, in Princeton, Missouri. The family was moving west by wagon train when her mother died. She was 13 years old. A year later, her father died, so here was Jane, at 14 years old, responsible for five younger siblings. She loaded them on a wagon and took them to Piedmont, Wyoming. There, Jane worked as a dishwasher, cook, waitress, dancehall girl, nurse, and <u>muleteer</u>.

When she was 20, she was scouting for the U.S. Cavalry near Goose Creek, Wyoming, when they came under attack by Indians. Her commander, Captain Egan, was shot and falling from his horse when Jane caught him, threw him on her horse, and they galloped to safety. From that incident, Captain Egan nicknamed her "Calamity Jane," and the name stuck.

The Anaconda (Montana) Standard wrote of Jane: "She was simply a notorious character, dissolute and devilish, but possessed a generous streak which made her popular."

Jane was guiding wagon trains across South Dakota when she met Wild Bill Hickok in Deadwood. Jane claimed she was married to Bill Hickok and that he was the father of her two daughters.

In 1881, Jane bought a ranch on the Yellowstone River, west of Mile City, and operated an inn there.

In 1893, she joined Buffalo Bill Cody's Wild West Show. She also participated in the 1901 Pan American Exposition World's Fair in Buffalo, New York.

In 1903, Jane returned to the Black Hills and went to work for her friend, Dora DuFran, owner of a bordello in Belle Fourche. She earned her keep there by cooking and doing laundry for Dora's "girls." Jane only lived a few more months and died on August 1st, 1903. She is buried next to Wild Bill Hickok at Mount Moriah Cemetery, Deadwood's Boot Hill. She had just about done it all.

There are lots of stories that have been handed down about Calamity Jane. Some say that she made up some of her history. She didn't need to do that. Her life was interesting enough.

Several years ago, my wife and I were on our way to Alberta, Canada, when we decided to stop and visit Deadwood's Boot Hill. Following our visit and appropriate homage at the graves of Bill and Jane, we drove back into downtown Deadwood for dinner.

We dined in the historic district. That was easy. I think the whole town is a historic district. After finishing our dinner, we walked out on Main Street into the middle of a faux gunfight. The sheriff had just arrested Jack McCall for shooting Wild Bill Hickok. The sheriff then tagged me as a witness to the killing. He marched McCall up the street to a courtroom where a judge was waiting. It was called a "miners' court." In the process of the court, as instructed, I testified that I did indeed see Jack McCall shoot Bill Hickok in the back of the head while Hickok was playing draw poker in Nuttal and Mann's Saloon. Of course, it was all play and a lot of fun.

It was a reenactment based on the actual historical event. McCall did indeed shoot Hickok in the back of the head in the saloon. When Hickok fell, he was holding the five-card poker hand that contained two pairs, aces and eights. To this day, in poker, two pairs of aces and eights is known as the "Dead Man's Hand."

Incorrect Correction

**Predictive: relating to or having the effect
of predicting an event or result.**

Here's a double-edged problem that will cause you to pull your hair out. You have all done it at some time. It is on your phone and is "auto-correction" and "predictive text." You type something, and auto-correct changes the spelling to something you didn't intend. The <u>predictive</u> text assumes the word you intend and completes it for you, and it often does it incorrectly. You finish your quick message and hit the enter key, and it is gone. Then you look and find that it didn't say what you intended.

My wife, a realtor, was corresponding with another realtor by text and asked, "Is your buyer ready to move forward?" She pressed enter, then, to her astonishment, her question appeared, "Is your uterus ready to move forward?" Instant Panic? Time to turn off the auto-correct!

LAST FRONTIER

**Stampeder: Someone following a
stampede for a gold rush.**

I knew Alaska so well back in the '60s that I spoke of it as though
the state belonged to me. I had worked on construction projects from
Ketchikan in Southeast Alaska to Kodiak Island, Anchorage, and
Fairbanks, and the end of the Aleutian Islands Chain.

A drive from the "Lower 48" to Alaska is always memorable. It
was 3,403 miles from Ventura, California, to Anchorage, and some
1,500 miles of it in northern British Columbia and Yukon were not
paved. I drove those miles in the spring of 1965. I wonder if those
roads are paved yet.

Following those early years, my work took me in different
directions, and I had not visited any part of Alaska in nearly 40
years. That is what made it exciting when I cruised there in 2004.

Skagway was an exciting stop. We booked an excursion on the
White Pass Railroad up to the top of the pass on the Chilkoot Trail.
The trip culminated at Lake Bennet near the top of the pass.

During the 1897 and 1898 Klondike Gold Rush, more than
100,000 gold prospectors, known as stampeders, climbed the pass,
working their way to Dawson City, where they boated and barged
on the Yukon River to the goldfields in the far North.

In 1898, a tent city of 15,000 people sprang up on the southern shore of Lake Bennett. The stampeders would wait for the ice to melt before crossing the Yukon River to Dawson City in wooden boats and rafts.

In 2017, I drove north of Whitehorse to Dawson City, hoping to cross the border from the Yukon into Alaska and continue to Tok and Fairbanks—no such luck. On May 3rd, the mile-wide Yukon River was still frozen from bank to bank.

I have made a couple more trips north, and I remain fascinated with the immensity and the challenges that can be found in Alaska, that "last frontier" of the United States.

A BUMPY RIDE TO TOWN

**Somnolence: A state of drowsiness or
the strong desire to fall asleep.**

In the 1940s, in Arkansas's northern Randolph County, relatively
few people had cars. Pickup trucks, vehicles that could significantly
help country farmers, were likewise rare. Many families' means of
transportation were the team and wagon. That's the way it was at
my home. Every Saturday, my stepfather, Aden, would harness up
our mules, Red and Sal, and we would load into the wagon for our
weekly shopping trip into town, some three miles away. The steel-
rimmed wheels of the wagon made it a rough ride on the gravel road.
My mother saved her egg and cream money to buy a spring seat for
the wagon. That helped her and my stepfather, but my sister and I
bounced on the floor of the wooden wagon bed. Aden often threw
a forkful of hay into the wagon, making the ride easier for Jo Ann
and me.

The town was full of life on those Saturdays as it was everybody's
shopping and visiting days. The two pool halls and three cafes were
brimming with people on Saturday evenings. Those were fun times.
It was fun just to sit on the steps of the **grocery** store and speak to
the people who were always milling around.

Those days are gone now. People have cars, televisions, and air conditioning. They stay at home in the evenings and drive to the county seat to do their shopping. My little hometown is the epitome of <u>somnolence</u> from the time the sun goes down until the following morning when people awaken and head to their place of work.

Old Man Weaver

Spasmodic: Occurring or done in brief, irregular bursts

I called them cuss-fits. I don't think they are as common as they once were. Folks in the city live too close together to put up with neighbors ranting and raving in decibels akin to that of a rock concert. But it was different a generation ago out in the country. (It's that old story – a different time and a different place.)

When I was ten years old, we lived about three miles from town out on a gravel road. Our nearest neighbors were Baird and Sally Weaver. Baird was an inveterate cusser. He could cuss whether things were good or bad. "Well, I see that blankety-blank sun is up again." "I've got to get to the blankety cornfield and chop them blankety-blank weeds." Then he would laugh. Baird was actually a nice fellow.

Baird would get frustrated about some aspect of home life, whether it would be chickens out of the pen or his dog ran off and he couldn't find it. Anyway, he would go stomping around the yard, cussing with every breath at the top of his lungs. Of course, way out in the country where there was no noise pollution, a loud person's voice could carry a quarter mile. My mother would ask, "What's going on out there?"

I would tell her, "Old man Weaver's having another cuss-fit."

One time, I recall that he got so mad he threw his false teeth on the ground and a chicken ran off with it. That made for an entertaining tirade.

Baird would have us believe that they were involuntary <u>spasmodic</u> spells, but I believe he just wanted Sally to hear his frustrations.

MADRID

Strumpet: A woman who has many casual sexual encounters or relationships, a female prostitute

We had driven into Madrid from Toledo – and so you know, Toledo in Spain is pronounced "toe-LAY-though." We had an afternoon to kill. We were advised that there were lots of shops and cafes on Calle de la Montera. We found it to be true, but there was something else.

There were cottonwood trees spaced out up the center of the pedestrian street, at least two or three in sight from any given point. We noticed that near each tree was an attractive lady seemingly passing the day. Eventually, a man would come by, converse briefly with the lady, and they would leave together. Almost immediately, another lady would emerge from a nearby portico to fill the vacancy at the tree. We could soon see that there was an unending supply of ladies at the portico waiting for their turn at one of the cottonwoods.

We are told the strumpets are as common here as in Amsterdam. From what we observed, we can attest to the validity of that claim. We were also advised that the ladies' closest friends and protectors are the Madrid beat-cops.

We wondered whether the ladies shared their wares or shared their fares.

America has an
Abundance of Power

**Superfluity: An unnecessarily or excessively
large amount or number of something**

We continue hearing concerns about our nation's ability to handle high demands for electrical power. Concerns rise in the dead of winter when the country experiences a prolonged cold spell. And then again in the summer when a bubble of infernal heat settles over a significant part of the country. And then there are the pundits who claim our country's power capability cannot support the change from combustion-powered cars to electric vehicles. The naysayers have no basis for their fears. There should be no need for concerns during extreme weather events.

I worked much of my career building power plants. From diesel generators in Alaska's Aleutian Islands to natural gas-powered turbine generators in South Florida, with nuclear, coal, hydro, and lignite plants in between. I have maintained that the industry will create and supply surfeit power if regulators permit them to do it profitably.

A lot of detractors tend to poo-poo wind and solar power. They are ill-advised. California is the leading state in the United States for solar power production, generating more than double the amount of electricity from the sun than any other state. In 2023, California had 46,874 megawatts of solar capacity installed, which is enough to power 13.9 million homes and accounts for 28% of the state's electricity. California's solar power industry also employs more than 86,000 people.

Texas is the leader in wind power production in the United States, generating more than twice as much as the next state. In 2023, wind accounted for 28.6% of Texas's energy generation, and the state has over 15,300 wind turbines, the most of any state. Texas's wind power generation surpassed nuclear in 2014 and coal-fired in 2020. Power is power, no matter where it comes from.

We are surprised to learn that California now has so many solar power farms and people with rooftop solar panels that they are producing a superfluity of electrical power and are having to throw it away. According to Independent System Operator data, in recent years, the amount of renewable energy curtailed or wasted has skyrocketed from both oversupply and so-called congestion. So far this year, the state has lost out on nearly 2.6 million megawatt-hours of renewable energy — most of it solar — more than enough to power all the homes in San Francisco for a year.

So, America, lighten up! America has an abundance of power. We'll keep your heaters and air conditioners working.

THE DITCH

Tasman: The Tasman Sea is a marginal sea of the South Pacific Ocean

It was not "smooth sailing." I looked out just after daybreak, and the view that greeted me reminded me of my working days out on Alaska's Bering Sea. But we are on the <u>Tasman</u> Sea, 36 degrees of latitude south of the equator. The temperature was 68 degrees, it was raining, and the wind was blowing at Force 7 – "Near Gale.". I went to the 7th deck and opened a door to the promenade. The wind nearly sucked me through the doorway. I decided to stay inside. It was Day 65 of our Grand World Voyage.

The Tasman Sea is referred to in Australasian English as The Ditch; for example, 'crossing The Ditch means traveling to Australia from New Zealand, or vice versa. The diminutive term "the ditch" used for the Tasman Sea is comparable to referring to the North Atlantic Ocean as "the Pond."

I suspect old Abel Janszoon Tasman, the Dutch explorer who discovered and crossed the passage in 1642, might be a mite miffed to know that folks called his sea a ditch.

We first crossed it in 2008, cruising east from Dunedin, New Zealand, to Sydney, Australia.

Noble or Ignoble

Imposter: A person who pretends to be someone else in order to deceive others, especially for fraudulent gain.

Where do you live? What's the name of your town? Your county? Is it named after a nobleman? A guy who built the first mercantile? Or the ferry or a grist mill? Many towns are named after local or national heroes. Crockett, Texas, is named, of course, for Davy Crockett. Hays County, Texas, my home county for two decades, is named for the great Texas Ranger, John Coffee Hays.

We find that occasionally, we, trusting Americans, can be guilty of ascribing some degree of honor to someone and finding out later that the person was not quite as honorable as we had thought. That is not the case with Davy Crockett, Jack Hays, or Captain John Maynard, the namesake of my hometown in Arkansas. These men were honorable.

Now, let's look at the case of a couple of other locations. Bastrop, Texas; Bastrop County, Texas; and Bastrop, Louisiana, are all named in honor of Baron de Bastrop, a nobleman from Holland. But just how noble was he?

Philip Hendrik Nering Bögel was born in Dutch Guiana, November 23rd, in 1759. He grew up in Holland after his parents moved there. By the time he was 23 years old, he was married, the father of five children, and working in Friesland as a tax collector. However, the next year, he was accused of embezzlement of tax funds, and he fled the country, leaving his wife, kids, and the Dutch lawmen behind.

He fled to Spanish Louisiana and posed as a Dutch nobleman. He assumed the name Baron de Bastrop and started a new life. When things didn't suit him in Louisiana, he moved on to San Antonio in New Spain. He sucked up to the Mexican authorities and got himself appointed alcalde (mayor or chief judicial official) of the Spanish town. He helped Moses Austin and Stephen F. Austin obtain grants to bring Anglo-American settlers to Texas. He made such a name for himself that towns in Louisiana and Texas were named after him, as was Bastrop County, just east of where I lived.

Even in his last will and testament, Bastrop continued to claim noble background, giving his parents' names as Conrado Lorenzo Neri, Baron de Bastrop, and Susana Maria Bray Banguin. Some of his contemporaries believed him to be an American adventurer; historians have thought him to be a French nobleman or a Prussian soldier of fortune. Only within the last century have records from the Netherlands been found to shed light on Bastrop's mysterious origins.

So, the great Baron de Bastrop was a farce, a total <u>imposter</u>. He was a thief, a fugitive from justice, and he abandoned his wife, who was left to raise five kids alone. Not very noble, would you say? Yet two towns and a county proudly bear his name.

GOOD GUYS WEAR WHITE HATS

Persona: A character played by an actor

Spring was a beautiful season to visit in Missouri, and there's an abundance of enjoyable scenery in the Show-Me State. I remembered having first driven across Missouri back in 1961. My trip on that occasion was straight across the girth of the state from Kansas City through St. Louis. Since that time, some 65 years have faded into the twilight of the past.

Back then, I was traveling with my young wife from Washington State to North Carolina to visit my sister in Winston-Salem. We saw a lot of beautiful country on that cross-country trip, and when we were through and back in our Tacoma, Washington, home, I told Elaina that Missouri was the prettiest state. I repeated the claim many times over the next half-century.

But this time, it was to be a leisurely trip. We were not due in Banff, Alberta, for more than two weeks. After a lovely visit with dear friends Joe and Judy Pryor at their home on Lake of the Ozarks, we were ready to continue our trek northward. Joe and Judy had been my dear friends for decades. Time has passed and Joe has now passed on from this world. Judy was the younger sister of my earlier wife, Sue Steen Cates, who was several years deceased by the time of this trip. Judy remains my dear friend today and will be so forever.

We looped around Kansas City, Missouri, then stopped in Clay County at the little town of Kearny. Kearney holds its place in American history and folklore as the birthplace of one of the American West's most notorious characters, Jesse James, and the home of his parents for many years.

There's something magically alluring about the name and character of Jesse James. An example of the popularity of Jesse James is that Hollywood has made no less than twenty-five major motion pictures about him, starting as far back as 1921. A film about Jesse James has been released in every decade since the 1920s.

In my younger years – my "Cowboys and Indians" days, my friends and I sometimes assumed the <u>personas</u> of Jesse and Frank James, as well as their friend, Cole Younger, and their cousins, Bob, Frank, Emmet, and William Dalton of the notorious Dalton Brothers Gang. The good guys wore white hats, but we kids were fascinated with the bad guys, too. They were that exciting.

We drove out to the James Farm in the rural countryside northeast of the village. The original but restored James's farmhouse, where Jesse was born in 1847, is preserved in good repair. When we visited on May 30th, 2006, there was not a soul around but us. We walked around the house and visited Jesse's fenced-in grave. It was a beautiful day with serene stillness known only to locations such as this, far from the bustle and traffic in the towns and cities. As I stood for a photo next to the gravesite, I remembered scenes from at least a dozen movies that I had seen about the famous outlaw.

With a world of outlaws' history swirling around in my head, we left the James farm and drove north through the countryside, headed for St. Joseph in the far northwest corner of the Missouri Pony Express country.

THE ROAD TO
SIOUX CITY

**Fraught: Filled with or likely to
result in something undesirable**

St. Joseph, Missouri, is chock-full of early frontier and old-west
history. French fur trappers traveled up and down the Missouri River
from St. Louis to the Rocky Mountains. The river was a busy artery
in the latter 18th century.

By the turn of the 19th century, a Frenchman of the St. Micael
family had established a campground on the west side of the river.
Meriwether Lewis and William Clark and their Corps of Discovery
camped there on their way upstream in 1804 and again on their
return trip in 1806. Joseph Robidoux, a French fur trader, established
his Blacksnake Hills Trading Post in 1826, where he bought furs
from Indian trappers and sold them downstream to fur wholesalers.
On July 26, 1843, Robidoux filed the plan with the clerk of Common
Pleas in St. Louis and named the town after his patron saint, Saint
Joseph. Robidoux began selling lots shortly after that.

St. Joseph, Missouri, also known as "St. Joe," was a key starting
point for westward expansion in the 19th century. The city's location
at a bend in the Missouri River made it ideal for travelers to outfit
their wagons and cross the river by ferry into modern-day Kansas.

From there, they would continue on the St. Joe Road to connect with the Oregon or California Trails.

St. Joseph was busy serving the needs of pioneers during the westward expansion. There was great excitement when the Hannibal and St. Joseph Railroad arrived on February 14, 1859. This city was on the western edge of civilization. Settlers heading west faced a 2,000-mile trip by wagon train that often took three months, three months fraught with hardships. Equally exciting, on April 3, 1860, the people of St. Joseph gathered to witness an event as exciting in those days as our space travels are to this generation. It was the start of the Pony Express.

William H. Russell, William Bradford Waddell, and Alexander Majors were already in the freighting business with 4,000 men, 3,500 wagons, and 40,000 oxen in 1858. They held government contracts for delivering army supplies in the West, and Russell envisioned a similar contract for fast mail delivery. Their proposal was a fast mail service between St. Joseph and Sacramento, California, by a Pony Express with letters delivered in the unheard time of 10 days.

They advertised for "young skinny riders, preferably not over 18 years old. Each rider carried the mail about 75 miles a day, changing horses at stations every ten to fifteen miles. The Pony Express operated for only 18 months, from April 1860 until the fall of 1861. It ceased operation on October 26th, 1861, two days after the Transcontinental Telegraph connected the East and West Coasts.

We toured the Pony Express National Museum on 914 Penn Street for a couple of hours. There is so much to see, read, and try to absorb. We then drove to the Jesse James Home Museum at 1201 South 12th Street. This is the last home where the famous Outlaw lived. He had planned to live out the rest of his life there in peace. However, his violent past caught up with him. Robert Ford later said he believed James had realized that the Ford brothers intended to betray him. They were all living together in the James home.

Instead of confronting them, James walked across the living room and laid his revolvers on a sofa. He turned around, noticed a dusty picture above the mantle, and stood on a chair to clean it.

Robert Ford drew his weapon and shot the unarmed Jesse James in the back of the head. The .44 Caliber Smith and Wesson bullet passed through Jesse's head and left a ragged hole in the wall. For over 50 years, tourists were even allowed to touch the hole. That was a bad idea, as the hole is now a fist-sized blob, enlarged by generations of groping fingers. It has been said that it looks as if Jesse James was shot with a potato. Jesse James was 34 years old.

We drove to a Stetson Outlet, where I bought a nice Stetson Panama straw, and then we said goodbye to the historic city of St. Joseph and continued north. Sioux City, Iowa, would be our next destination. Isn't travel wonderful?

FOURCHE RIVER CRUISE

Impediment: A hindrance or obstruction in doing something.

Fun came from all directions and new adventures. It was along about the dog days of the 1952 summer that I and a couple of friends embarked upon a curious adventure.

The Fourche River was a significant stream that flowed out of Missouri west of Middlebrook, Arkansas, and curved around between Maynard and Pocahontas, then joined the Current River a few miles farther east. I say the Fourche was significant in that I've seen it more than a half mile wide at Brockett Lane after heavy rains.

Always looking for a new adventure, I had become interested in exploring the lower reaches of the Fourche. My idea was to take one of the wooden johnboats that were always tied up near the Brockett Highway Bridge, and float downstream to the little town of Engleberg, and then catch a ride back to Maynard on the highway. The boat's owner would find it at the Engleberg Bridge and take it back to where he had left it.

I submitted this idea to a couple of comrades, Junior Talbott and Lester Pease. Both Junior and Lester were about my age, all of about 14 years. They liked the idea immediately and we set out for our new adventure. My plan was flawed, however. In my appraisal of the Fourche being a large, free-flowing river, I expected it to be easy sailing all the way to the Engleberg road. We would paddle through the pools and drift across the shoals. That's the way I had done it on the upper Current River.

We selected a good, sturdy boat, rounded up three paddles, and shoved off. We hadn't gone a half-mile when we rounded the first bend, and lo and behold, the whole surface of the river was blocked by a bank-to-bank drift reinforced by a sycamore tree that had fallen across the river. It took a good half hour to portage the heavy johnboat across the obstruction.

Back in the channel and making downstream progress again, we reveled in our fun and freedom. This had been an excellent idea. In no more than another half mile, we encountered another similar <u>impediment</u>. We traversed a couple more of those water-moccasin-infested piles, and we were beaten. Junior said, "That damned boat can stay there until it rots." We abandoned the boat against a large sweet gum drift, climbed out of the riverbed, and started thrashing through brush and bamboo thickets, looking for a way to get downstream to Engleberg.

We finally found some cornfields where we could walk along the edges and turn rows. We'd eaten nothing since morning and it was now late in the day. We'd been drinking the murky river water to satisfy our thirst, but now our stomachs were telling us they needed some real food. We picked corn in the fields but didn't have any dry matches to build a fire and cook it. I learned that afternoon how sickening the taste of raw field corn is. I can remember the taste to this day, and to eat even a bite of it now would cause me to retch. We got back to Maynard late in the evening, sunburned, tired and hungry.

Junior and Lester are both gone now. Junior is the same Junior with whom I made a memorable trip back to Arkansas from Chattanooga, Tennessee, earlier that year – 450 miles of hitchhiking. Junior and I both went into the army in 1954. Junior died somewhere in California a few years later. I never saw him again. Lester became a long-haul truck driver. He died just a few years ago in Southeast Missouri. I have often wondered if they enjoyed recalling our Fourche River excursion as I have.

Is it Broom or Gorse

Subcutaneous: Beneath the surface, or medically - under the skin

Adelaide, to me, is the most beautiful name there has ever been for a city and the most beautiful there will ever be. Compare it with a name like Portland, a city name that we have an overabundance of in our country. There is no comparison. As a charming name, Adelaide far surpasses names like Sacramento or Jefferson City, both capitals of American states.

Throughout most of my life, I have had an underlying desire to visit Adelaide, Australia. I unadvisedly assumed that there was only one Adelaide, and it was entirely the province of South Australia. With only a smattering of research, I learned that there are nine towns in the world named Adelaide, and five of them are in the United States.

As eager as I was to visit the real Adelaide, as I considered it, once I got there – taking nothing away from the city of Adelaide, it presents as a beautiful city – I wanted to get out of town. Every city has a unique character and personality; however, it is most frequently subcutaneous. Upon entering the center of commerce, they all look alike. You wouldn't be able to tell Cleveland from Buffalo. On a short visit, you might never see the uniqueness of a city, the true character that distinguishes it from all others. It is hidden beneath all the superficial scenes you see in every city.

I traveled northward from the city into the Mt. Lofty Range of mountains to the German town of Hahndorf. As we motored into the foothills, I commented to our driver about the brilliantly blooming brush at the edges of the fields and groves. I said, "The Scotch broom is beautiful when fully abloom." He responded, "That is not Scotch broom; it is gorse." He had me there. It looked just like the scotch broom that grows in Western Washington. I made the mistake of asking, "Are you sure?" He then, in his characteristic Crocodile Dundee accent, assured me that he indeed knew what he was talking about. He explained that South Australia had both broom and gorse, and the broom was not from Scotland. It was French broom, imported from England.

The Mt. Lofty mountains were so appealing that we used much of our free time touring with little left over for Hahndorf. We motored to the top of Mt. Lofty, 3,000 feet above the nearby Gulf St. Vincent on the Indian Ocean. That's pretty high when sea level looks to be hardly more than a stone's throw away. It was a perfect photo-op.

Following a great German dinner in the town of Hahndorf, our driver deposited us back at the cruise terminal so we could board our big Queen Mary 2 and sail for Perth. COVID-19 was breaking out all over the world, and we didn't know when, or even if, we would ever get back to Texas.

ZADAR

Peerless: Having no equal; matchless; unrivaled

In the past few decades, I have taken over thirty ocean cruises, a couple of them to the far side of the globe, and I have enjoyed every one of them.

Some folks talk about days at sea and assume they are boring as the scenery never changes. Perish that thought. I have seen a thousand sunsets that I wanted to photograph and post on Facebook. I will try to restrain myself. A number of our friends have become seasoned travelers in recent decades. They can attest to the plethora of peerless sunsets that one can see, whether in the nearby Caribbean, the distant Bay of Bengal, or on the high plains of the Texas Panhandle.

My favorite sunsets will always be in the town of Zadar on Croatia's Adriatic Sea coast. Zadar's sunsets are so famous that the great English film director Alfred Hitchcock made special trips to Zadar. The "Master of Suspense" once said," Zadar has the most beautiful sunset in the world, more beautiful than the one in Key West in Florida."

We were unaware of Zadar's famous sunsets when we drove into town from a week of touring the Julian Alps in Slovenia. I was primarily interested in Zadar's long history on the upper Dalmatian Coast. Luckily, we got swept up in the crowd as they moved toward and assembled on the Riva, a beautiful stone promenade facing the sea.

We soon found ourselves surrounded by people from all over the world. Couples holding hands, parents taking photos of their children, and elderly couples gazing at the horizon. They were all waiting for the sun to go down, and when it finally met the line that separates the earth from the sky, they started clapping. Indeed, it is a performance that deserves a standing ovation, and luckily, it takes place on that beautiful coast every evening.

VERONA TO VENEZIA

Parasol: A light umbrella used to give shade from the sun

One will readily observe that the myriad of churches in Italian cities is overwhelming. There seems to be a church every two hundred yards. That only seems strange to us unsophisticated Westerners. In Europe, when a church will no longer accommodate the multitudes, they simply build another church rather than blasting the old one down to build a bigger one. That explains why one can see several centuries-old churches within walking distance of one another.

We enjoyed our stay at the Agriturismo le Case di Compagna in Verona. Our hosts, Frederico and Simonetta Pasquetto, had hosted us royally and walked us to our little Peugeot station wagon and bid us farewell with characteristic Italian hugs and cheek pecks. (il saluto)

We drove eastward through pleasant farmland to the town of Vicenza, then turned on the route to the town of Padua. (The town is shown as "Padova" on the Italian maps.) I was overjoyed to have the opportunity to visit the Basilica of Saint Anthony of Padua. Our city, San Antonio, Texas, is named in honor of the saint. San Antonio was a little Indian settlement alongside the stream in 1691 when Father Damián Massanet first visited. He named the settlement San Antonio de Padua for his favorite saint.

The exterior of the Basilica at Padua, like so many of the great cathedrals of Europe, was shrouded with scaffolding for renovations that were in progress. It is hard to get good photographs in those cases. But the interior? Oh my goodness! We were amazed at the immensity and beauty of the 800-year-old complex. My wife and I agreed that the Basilica of St. Anthony rivals that of St. Peter's in Vatican City. It was hard to tear myself loose to continue our journey toward Eastern Europe.

We drove northward to the walled city of Cittadella. (Think Citadel) We had never seen a completely walled city. The original town is surrounded by massive stone walls 46 to 52 ft. tall. The walls, double in gate locations, are complete with functional gates and drawbridges. The fortress also featured the requisite "murder hole" or meurtrière in the ceiling of a gateway through which the defenders could pour boiling oil on attackers. A water-filled moat surrounds the whole complex. The fortressed city was founded in 1220 and has been a functioning city for more than 800 years. It is clean as a pin, with colorful flower boxes beneath every window.

Our pleasant vine-covered Hotel Due Mori was within walking distance of the Old City. We walked the couple of blocks to the drawbridge, stopping at virtually every house to snap photos of the flowers and flowering vines and shrubs. Local folks probably thought that I was an idiot or somebody to keep an eye on. We found an outdoor café in the walled city and enjoyed a couple of glasses of local wine and a light European-style dinner.

The following day, we drove to Mestre and caught the train to take us to Venice. There is no parking place in Venice, as the streets are all waterways. Upon arrival at Santa Lucia Station, we went to the Vaporetta Dock and caught one of the boats to St. Mark's Square, the center of everything Venezia. The vaporettas are like a city bus system, but these boats haul up to 100 folks at a time.

The waterways, canals, and channels are constantly alive with activity. They, for Venice, are what the downtown streets are for New York City: full of traffic. The variety of sizes and shapes of the boats is inestimable. I could perch myself at a shaded table overlooking the Grand Canal and spend the afternoon. It is a boat-lovers paradise.

The outstanding attractions to see are overwhelming. On previous voyages, we had visited the Doges Palace, St. Mark's Cathedral, the Rialto Bridge, the Bridge of Sighs, and the Campanile. It was good to visit St. Mark's Square again and remember these attractions from years earlier.

We shopped and lunched at St. Mark's Square. My wife bought two new parasols at the same market where she had shopped previously. It is good to visit this unique city again. It is a city full of romance and known as "The Queen of the Adriatic." Venice is always crowded.

Back at Cittadella for a final evening, we strolled back down to the walled city for another look and an excellent Italian dinner. What a fascinating place! We will probably never see this ancient city again, but the memories are indelible.

We breakfasted with our hosts the next morning, May 20th, 2011, and said goodbye to this evocative, historic city. We headed north toward the Julian Alps and Austria. Our tour of Central and Eastern Europe was just getting started.

THE GREAT DEPRESSION

**Parsimonious: penurious, stingy,
ungenerous, unwilling to spend**

During the early days of the stock market crash of 1929 and
the following Great Depression of the 1930s, Donna was living
in Birmingham, caring for her two small children and working as
a housekeeper. Her husband, my father, was serving time at Fort
Leavenworth, Kansas, federal prison. That is another story.

When the family that Donna was working for could no longer
pay her, she took her two small children and went to Arkansas to
live with her father. He lived about four miles south of Pocahontas
on the Imboden Road in Randolph County.

She remembered years later how <u>parsimonious</u> her father was.
He didn't spend even the smallest change unless it was absolutely
necessary. The government's "Relief" program doled out some
"commodities," but old granddad wouldn't take charity. So, Donna
walked all the way to Pocahontas and carried a 50-pound bag of
flour home on her back. She never forgot how frugal my grandfather
was, and she shared it with us children.

We hope there will never be another Great Depression.

NOT A THANKSGIVING
TO BE RECOMMENDED

**Venerable: Accorded a great deal of respect,
especially because of age, wisdom, or character.**

My trip back to civilization would not go as planned. I had been working on a contract on the island of Shemya, 1,500 miles from Anchorage, out on the Aleutian Chain. It was remote by any standard. This island was so far out that it was actually south of the Russian Peninsula, halfway between Anchorage and Tokyo. The International Date Line that extends down through the center of the Bering Sea has a kink in it to keep Shemya in the same day as the rest of the United States.

Our only way to travel between Shemya and civilization, which was Anchorage, was Reeves Aleutian Airlines. Reeves used propeller-driven planes to service the island chain. Major airlines had switched to jet planes by that time, but Reeves had not made the switch. They used DC-6s to service the outer islands and DC-3s for some of the inter-island flights. These airplanes had been built just after World War II by Douglas Aircraft Company in Santa Monica, California, between 1946 and 1958. By 1965, they were showing their age.

Reeves had a government contract to deliver mail to the islands where military personnel and government employees were stationed. Reeves earned extra bread and butter by hauling passengers and freight. During the summer, when I flew out to Shemya to start the job, Reeves was flying two trips each week. They would stop at Adak on the way out, then fly all the way to Attu, at the end of the chain, drop off mail and supplies for the 32 people stationed there, and then fly the 52 miles back to Shemya where they had quarters in a World War II hangar. They would spend the night there and then fly back to Anchorage the following day.

The flight crew comprised the pilot, co-pilot, flight engineer, and two stewardesses. Often, the Head Stewardess from Anchorage would accompany the flight. That conveniently created a complement of three men and three women. This balanced crew would dependably spend the evening partying at Shemya's NCO Club. Hang the regulation that said airline pilots were prohibited from drinking in the 24 hours prior to hauling passengers.

The NCO Club was a lively place on evenings when Reeves was on the islands. The population on the island was some 300 men – Air Force personnel, government contract workers, and construction workers. There were no women on the island except, of course, when Reeves was making their turnaround. These couple hundred flyboys would spend a year on that tiny island without seeing one woman, other than the Reeves stewardesses. They would flock to the NCO Club just to see the stewardesses. It was exciting. One doesn't realize the need for a man to see a real woman until he goes an extended time without seeing one.

My job at Shemya that summer was three-fold. Besides finishing and painting the interior of several rooms in a hangar for Air Force flight personnel, I had to service the lighting on three giant radar antennas and construct offices and metal stairs in the power plant building. The power plant building work was the last of my activities, and I worked long hours the week before Thanksgiving to finish it.

Almost too late, I learned that Reeves had shifted its service from the summer schedule, which was two flights per week, to the winter schedule, which was only one flight per week. That flight would be on Tuesday, November 23rd. My plan was in place. I would, at all costs, work through the weekend, if need be, and finish my work on Monday. I would fly back to Anchorage on the Tuesday flight, get my car out of storage the next morning, and ship it to Seattle with Alaska Steamship Company. Then, I would catch an Alaska Airlines flight to Seattle. Then, on Thursday, I would be celebrating Thanksgiving with friends in Tacoma. I was almost giddy with excitement.

I worked all night prior to my flight just to get the job done. I packed my clothes and had my friend Jack Hefner take me to the airplane terminal. The Reeves DC-6 had already left the terminal and was taxiing to the runway. The ground controller called the pilot, who stopped the plane to wait for us. Although it was about 9 AM, it was still pitch dark. At the controller's instruction, Jack drove down the taxiway and pulled alongside the airplane. The stewardess opened the door. I climbed atop the cab, threw my bag in the plane, and climbed in. Goodbye Shemya, forever.

It was at about this time that I started to realize that my plan had some serious flaws. Since the days had grown so short in November, the flight couldn't make it to Attu when they flew from Anchorage. It was dark by the time the flight arrived, and Attu didn't have runway lights. Thus, the crew would spend Monday night at Shemya, and then we would have to go to Attu the following morning before we could head for Anchorage. That would put us at least three hours behind my hoped-for schedule.

I settled and strapped in for the ride. There were no more than a dozen passengers, all workers, who were heading back to the mainland to observe Thanksgiving with their families.

As we approached Attu, the Captain glided toward the runway but didn't flare out for the landing. Instead, he flew low over the runway at full speed. Then, as there were steep mountains just ahead of us, he put the plane into a hard-turning climb. Arlene, one of the stewardesses with whom I had become acquainted, was close to me, so I asked, "What the hell was that about?"

She explained, "When there is snow on the runway, Captain

Kelly flies over it to look, for himself, to see if it is safe to land."
She went on to relate that once previously, the snow was deeper on
the runway than had been reported, and the landing damaged the
landing gear. She continued that we must land if at all possible.

She said, "There are only 32 personnel on the island, and they
want their mail and their beer." After the go-around and another
approach, we landed so I suppose the men stationed on the island
got their mail and their beer.

Captain Kelley, a <u>venerable</u> pilot, was well-known in the
Aleutians. He is reputed to have once landed on Shemya in an 80-
knot wind. Why would he take the chance to do that? He had no
choice. He had burned his fuel just getting there. With scheduled
stops at Adak and Amchitka, it is a 12-hour flight from Anchorage
just to get to Shemya. He couldn't turn around and go back. I
remembered both Captain Kelly and Arlene from my first flight
into the Aleutians.

Finally, we were in the air again and headed for the mainland.
My schedule had been compromised but I was still hopeful that
I could work it all out in Anchorage and still get to Tacoma for
Thanksgiving.

Then Captain Kelly's familiar voice came over the speaker. He
said, "You may have noticed that the right-side inboard engine isn't
running. A hydraulic pump has failed, so I cannot feather the prop.
We will have to go back into Shemya and make repairs." Now, my
plan was really in the toilet.

By the time we reached Shemya, another storm had blown in off
the Bering Sea. The wind was so strong that the plane couldn't turn
crosswise to the wind in order to taxi into the hangar. So, Captain
Kelly taxied up to the leeward side of the hangar, actually in the
back of it, as close as he could get, to let the hangar block some of
the wind while they replaced the hydraulic pump. Sleet was blowing
into drifts around the plane as we waited for the needed part to be
flown in from Amchitka and for the repairs to be made.

It was early afternoon when we got into the air again, and dark
by the time we reached the mainland near Dutch Harbor. It was

nearly midnight when we landed and deplaned at Anchorage. My plan was probably impossible from the start due to the shortness of the days in the far north. Coupled with that and the just plain lousy luck about the hydraulic pump, I had to resign myself to spending Thanksgiving alone in Anchorage.

I rented a room at the Captain Cook Hotel, got a few hours of sleep, and celebrated the 1965 Thanksgiving on grungy Fifth Avenue in downtown Anchorage with a lunch-counter dinner and a few scotches in the bars that I remembered from early in the summer when I was working in town. I hired a cab to take me to my boss's house to get my car. It had 19 inches of snow on it. I took it to a car wash, where they steamed the snow and ice off it.

Bright and early the following day, I went to Alaska Steamship Company and arranged to have my beautiful 1964 Galaxie delivered to Seattle. That afternoon, I caught an Alaska Airlines flight to Sea-Tac Airport. It was an exhilarating feeling to get on the jet headed for civilization. I was ready for some fun. I had not even seen a woman in the two months at Shemya, except the Reeves stewardesses who came through there once or twice a week.

It was an unforgettable Thanksgiving. Was there a blessing in all of this? There were actually two. One was that I got to watch the Northern Lights from my airplane window for more than an hour while flying between Cold Bay and Anchorage. The second blessing was that I would never have to go to Shemya Island again.

NOT A HOLIDAY DESTINATION

Penurious: extremely poor, poverty-stricken, supplicating

What's in a name? Chennai is an enormous city we'd hardly heard of before the trip. The British founded the city back around 1640 and named it Madras. (Leave it to the British to give an Indian city a Portuguese name.) Madras was a British colony for three hundred years. After India gained independence in 1947, it started grumbling about some of the names. Eventually, they changed Madras to Chennai and Bombay (another Portuguese name) to Mumbai.

Chennai is the capital of the Indian state of Tamil Nadu. As of July 2024, Chennai, India's fifth largest city, has an estimated population of 12 million and growing daily, as is the whole country. India is now, as of 2024, the most populous nation in the world, with a population just shy of 1.5 billion.

We spent the day in Chennai. I vow to give thanks and advised my Facebook and email friends and kin to give earnest thanks. I mean, down on our knees and give thanks – that we were born in the USA rather than India. If there is a city that is uglier than Chennai, I don't want to go there. Don't show us pictures. Don't even tell us

303

about it. If Manila was "third world" (and it was), then Chennai is fifth or sixth world. We cannot describe it, but if you've seen Tijuana, Juarez, or Matamoras, you'll have an idea of what I am talking about; however, this is worse than any of those.

It started as we approached the harbor with a scheduled docking at 8 AM. But there were cranes that had to be moved, and it took over an hour to get them out of the way. As we reached our berth, a military band on the dock started playing. The San Marcos Salvation Army band would have been an improvement.

The half-mile-long dock was covered with wet, greasy grime from one end to the other. Half a dozen little old Indian ladies were bent over sweeping the dock with whisk brooms. They must have been prisoners. No imaginable effort could have looked more futile. We left the ship at about 10:30, and after walking about 60 yards through the wet muck, I ruined a pair of Dockers khaki slacks before I could even get onto the bus. Before we left the dock area, a waif-like little Indian woman climbed inside the bus. She looked like an emaciated street beggar. It turned out that she was our guide. Thinking back now, she could be counted among the better-looking people we saw that day. She tried to use the microphone, but all that came through the speaker system was loud engine noise and an echo. Abandon that idea.

We left the harbor and drove along the waterfront past miles of slums. These were shacks with walls of woven thatch and standard palapa-type thatched roofs. The farther we went, the worse it got until they were just ragged tents, side by side along the main road. We won't try to think of sanitary facilities for this population. There was none in evidence. Trash and garbage were strewn in every unoccupied area, and scavengers were plundering through it.

As Barbara, our "Port Talk" authority, says, "There are over twelve million people here, and all of them have two vehicles." (mostly motor scooters) It seemed that seven million of them were driving around today, and the other five million were just milling around. Our (supposedly) two-hour excursion stretched into more than four hours, the vast majority of which we were stuck in traffic with horns blowing all around us. Some of it was laughable, but one dared not laugh.

The part that wasn't laughable was the people. India has apparently recovered from the days when it was reportedly possible to see bodies dead from starvation littering the sidewalks. That didn't just happen in Calcutta, where Mother Teresa labored to help the helpless; it happened in all of the major cities of India. However, it doesn't look much better now. One cannot imagine the conditions that these people face every morning that they awaken.

We snapped pictures until the battery in our camera failed. We'll not email them, though. It is too sad.

We had intended to ride the shuttle back into the city to shop after our excursion was finished. However, after four hours of looking at Chennai's ugliness and sadness through the windows of the bus, we had seen enough. We went to the Lido deck for a salad and some pizza.

Later, we went to the Lido afterdeck and sipped Cabernet during the 6:00 PM sailaway. We chatted with our friends, Jerry and Siri Bernstein, and discussed what we had seen during the day. They had taken the shuttle to the Taj Hotel and had briefly ventured out on the streets to some shops. There, they were confronted with the armless and legless beggars, some with distended stomachs and many with deformities. Many of the beggars are women carrying their babies, babies that they never should have had to start with. Then there were the street vendors hawking beads, bracelets, postcards, and figurines.

Sounds bad, doesn't it. It is! By the time we left the city of Chennai, I was convinced that it was the most horrid city that I had ever visited. The plight of the people of Chennai saddened me then, and it saddens me to this day any time that I recall it.

The Canterbury Plain

Gurgler: A drain, as in a sink or toilet bowl

"Nice day for ducks!" That's what I told my wife as we cruised slowly into the Lyttelton Harbor. The heavy clouds were hanging just above the twin stacks of the Amsterdam, and a cold wind was blowing sheets of rain across the deck. We dressed for breakfast and hoped the weather would improve by the time we docked and were ready to go ashore. It could hardly get worse.

As we disembarked the ship, we saw that the weather had improved ever so slightly. The wind had decreased from gale force to a brisk breeze, and the rain had become a cold drizzle. Just beyond the port of entry, the government offices, immigration, customs, etcetera, we could see an impregnable-looking range of high hills. Where is the city, we wondered?

Port Lyttelton is precisely that: no more, no less. It is the port for Christchurch, New Zealand, and the interior, as Christchurch actually sits inside a giant volcano crater. Port Hills is a volcanic ridge that protects Christchurch from the bitter weather that blows northward from the Southern Ocean. I imagine, only with difficulty, the challenge of traveling over these hills – some more than a quarter mile high – between the city and the port before a tunnel was built through the base of the hills in 1964.

Shortly after 7 AM, we boarded excursion buses at dockside

and headed for the city of Christchurch. By way of the mile-long Lyttelton Tunnel, we passed under a line of mountains into a pretty sheltered valley and the town of Christchurch. Charming seems to be the appropriate word for the town. All neighborhoods looked clean and well-kept. Homes were modest in size but modern in appearance, and yards were not just lawns but rather landscaped gardens. Flowers and flowering shrubs were in abundance. One could imagine that each home employed a professional gardener.

Christchurch is as English as the Pope is Catholic. The city was named after Christchurch, Oxford, England.

Founded in 1848, immigration soon followed. The First Four Ships were chartered by the Canterbury Association and brought the first 792 of the "Canterbury Pilgrims" in 1850. The city now boasts some 400,000 residents. It is situated in what became the Canterbury Region.

Our coach took us through the city and deposited us at the train station. Our prearranged Trans-Alpine Train and Tea excursion was a rail trip across the Canterbury Plain and up into the Southern Alps. We boarded quickly and chose comfortable seats with broad windows for viewing the scenery.

Christchurch sits at Canterbury Plain's eastern edge, spreading from the narrow coastal mountains 65 miles inland to the foot of the Southern Alps. This Canterbury Plain is as flat as a conference table and is an attractive farmland. It is all sheep or cattle pasture or grain fields for the production of livestock feed. Although flat, one can never see a horizon. That's because there are lines of trees for windbreaks. These are single or double rows of either evergreens or poplars. They are aligned precisely from east to west. They are pruned so that they form a sort of hedge fence 20 feet high or higher and so thick that one cannot see through the row. We are told they are called snow breaks as well as windbreaks, and they are the only protection from the weather that animals have. There are no barns. The fields are small, so these hedges are everywhere. New Zealand has only four million people but has forty million sheep.

Another note about New Zealand is that there is not much

wildlife. There's no such thing as elk, bears, wolves, coyotes, or, for that matter, any kind of predatory animal. Europeans, either by bad choice or accident, introduced possums and rabbits. Both are considered nuisances, mainly the rabbits on the South Island and possums on the North Island, where there is a widespread extermination plan to thin the population. There are no snakes in New Zealand.

The weather improved but never really cleared up as we traveled westward. After about an hour, without warning, the mountains rose abruptly from the plain. The mountains are aptly named the Southern Alps. They are a range that runs from north to south down the spine of the island, separating the western slopes from the eastern plains. They are somewhat similar to the Sierra Nevada Mountains of northern California. Many peaks are over 10,000 feet high. Vistas from our rail carriages were breathtaking as we crisscrossed the Rakaia River several times. The river, although crystal clear, was snowmelt from higher in the mountains. Stretches of it are reminiscent of Arizona's Colorado River before the dams tamed it. Other stretches reminded us of the Tanana River in Alaska, where the gray gravel river bed was up to a mile wide.

We enjoyed our tea and crumpets while traveling through the Waimakariri Gorge on our way to the crest of Arthur's Pass National Park. We never reached the summit as we went through a five-and-one-half-mile tunnel under the pass. At the little village of Otira, we left the train and boarded our waiting buses. This time, we went back over the pass and got to fully experience the Alpine views through the park. We could sometimes see half a dozen waterfalls at a time, some of which were several hundred feet high.

About halfway back to the East Coast, our three buses left the road and pulled through a gate into a sheep pasture. There, a large tent was set up, and we were served a sumptuous meal complete with wine and hot coffee. It had been catered from somewhere, and they took good care of our hundred or more hungry fellow travelers.

Back in Christchurch, our driver and guide gave us a city tour.

What a beautiful, clean city it was. Did I say that Christchurch was English? The Avon River meanders through the heart of the city.

These New Zealanders are fun to listen to with their unique speech and accent, as well as their choice of words. Our guide talked about money being wasted as "money down the gurgler." An announcement on the train was that we would "make a short stop at the next village to set down a group," meaning let a few people get off the train. Our guide on the bus talked of "berating" herself for failing to give us some piece of information. Our drive across the sheep pasture was on wet ground. The guide and driver agreed that it was "a bit greasy."

My heart was broken three years after my visit to hear that Christchurch experienced a catastrophic earthquake. It was February 22nd, 2011. Some 185 people lost their lives, and much of the beautiful city was devastated. Recovery continues to this day under the auspices of The Christchurch Central Recovery Plan, which was published in July 2012 and defined 17 anchor projects.

The Cement Plant was Interesting

Athrob: Athrob means pulsing or throbbing

It was July of 2024, and much of the world was <u>athrob</u> with excitement swirling around the Olympic Games of the XXXIII Olympiad in Paris. Opening ceremonies involved a flotilla on the River Seine. I was reminded of my own cruise on the Seine.

It was back in 2005. We flew into Barcelona, Spain, and rented a car to tour France. Of course, our first challenge was to get out of Barcelona and Spain and into France. I had assured my wife that I could read the road signs. I knew a smidgeon of Spanish from my 18 months of driving jeeps hauling army officers on the roadways in Panama. Also, I had employed a good number of Hispanic or Mexican carpenters and laborers, many of whom spoke little or no English, on construction jobs in Texas.

My rude awakening was immediate when I found that the highway signs were in Catalan, not Spanish. I had not been aware that Barcelona and the extreme eastern region of Spain are part of the autonomous community of Catalonia, and they have their own language.

Touring France was interesting with its expansive vineyards in the central and south, wheat and canola fields in the north, and its planted poplar forests. All the trees are in straight rows. I suppose natural forests had become extinct some centuries earlier.

The next day, we continued northward through the Bordeaux and Nantes regions and found a little B&B in Saint-Lô. The lady at La Crémaillère couldn't speak English but held up her fingers to show that the room rate was 3 and 6. So the rate was 36 euros, and that's about all the tiny upstairs room was worth.

Although the town of Saint-Lô didn't show it, it was completely destroyed by Allied bombing during World War II. The process, which included the landing on the Normandy Coast, was the Allied forces liberating France from Hitler's German Army. Saint-Lô had been a regional headquarters of the German army. It is recorded that one of the bomber pilots said to his comrades after virtually leveling Saint-Lô, "Well, we sure liberated the hell out of that town." It was also in the Saint-Lô area where my wife's uncle was killed in action in fighting related to the D-Day invasion.

After spending the night in Saint-Lô, we drove on to the Normandy Coast, where we toured the battlefields, saw the thousands of bomb craters, and actually walked inside the concrete German artillery bunkers. After viewing the cliffs of Utah and Omaha Beaches, where over 4,000 of our soldiers died, we drove to the Normandy American Cemetery and Memorial at Colleville-sur-Mer.

We parked and went into the Visitor's Center and were met by Katia, a young lady from Russia. My wife gave Katia the name of her uncle, who had lost his life in the Normandy Campaign. Katia looked in her books for a few minutes and said, "I've got it. Come with me."

We piled into a little golf cart-type vehicle, and Katia drove us down a pathway between thousands of gleaming white cross monuments. She carried a little pail of wet sand and took us right to Eleanor's uncle's monument. Katia took the dark, wet sand and rubbed it into the lettering on the monument, highlighting the inscriptions for us to read and photograph.

It was an emotional moment as we read on the stone, Iris L. Bradshaw, PFC 23 Inf 2 Div, Texas, July 14, 1944.

———

Having finished with Normandy, a primary reason for our trip, we toured northward through France and Belgium to The Netherlands and Amsterdam. There, after touring Holland and much of the Low Country, we boarded a cruise ship and headed back south.

Our big ship put us ashore at La Havre and we bussed up the Seine Valley to Paris. After the mandatory visits to the Arc de Triomphe de l'Étoile, Notre Dame Cathedral, and several statues of Napoleon, Joan of Arc, etc., we visited the guillotine where Marie Antoinette and some 700 of her followers forfeited their thinking caps. That's a sobering thought.

We made our way to the excursion dock on the Seine River, boarded the large restaurant boat, and enjoyed an anniversary dinner while cruising past the Louvre, Eiffel Tower, Notre Dame, and a cement plant. The cement plant was interesting.

THE SERPENT MUST
BE VANQUISHED

**Layed by: "Layed by" is an old farming term
that means tending a crop for the final time and
allowing it to mature without further cultivation.**

Summertime in North Arkansas had at least three beginnings. It started in late spring, and as soon as the days got hot and sticky, thunderstorms were occurring with regularity, and many of us spent the days chopping cotton or hoeing corn and swatting mosquitos. That was Start Number 1.

Start Number 2, usually about May 30th, was the final day of the school year.

Start Number 3 was the summer solstice, the official start of summer. That start could be ignored as insignificant. It was meaningless. The actual start of summer, the one that we were waiting for, was Start Number 2.

The start of summer was an exciting event. School was out, nearly all of the crops were layed by, the water in the creek was warm enough for swimming, and we had the time and freedom to take full advantage.

My friends, the Cox family, lived in their home in the delta of two creeks. Lemmons Creek flowed south from the Supply,

Arkansas, road, and Spring Creek, as the name implies, flowed from some springs in the hills a mile upstream. The two streams converged just beyond Mr. Cox's hay barn. The children of the Cox family, three boys, and two girls, were my best friends.

Spring Creek was too small for serious swimming, but it was an ideal stream to take small children to picnic and let them play in the chilly water, catching crawfish and minnows.

Lemmons Creek (later known as Smith Creek as Clarence Smith had a large farm on it.) was our Shangri La, the place where we spent at least some fun time nearly every day of the summer. A half-mile up the creek and across the fence into Pearl Redwine's farm was the swimming hole. It was about six feet deep in the deepest part, right below the high bank. We could dive, jump, or belly-flop off the high clay bank or wade into the water from the gravelly shoal on the downstream side.

No girls ever joined us. It was strictly our hole. Skinny-dipping was the standard. We didn't carry swimsuits. There was no danger. Our rollicking fun made so much noise, with splashing and commotion, that snakes, of which there were many on the creek, probably wouldn't come within a hundred yards of the swimming hole.

On one of those hot afternoons, Leon and Levon Cox, the well-known "Cox Twins," and I were headed up the creek to the swimming hole. As we crossed a spring branch near Pearl's fence, we encountered a rather large water moccasin in the shallow water. When an encounter like this occurs, God-fearing boys like us bear a heavy burden to slay the serpent. You see, we'd all heard the scriptures and knew that the blame for the fall of mankind rightly fell on such a creature.

As I recall, Eve had hardly drawn a second breath after ratting on the snake when God took up the matter. After upbraiding the evil perpetrator, he tore the snake's legs off and told it to crawl and eat dust. He then pronounced great enmity between Eve and the snake and told Eve and her grandkids to hereafter and forevermore crush the snake's head. The snake was not clueless and was determined to bruise her heel any time he got a chance. According to the scriptures, Adam kept his mouth shut. That's the only thing we know of that Adam did well.

Anyway, on this summer afternoon, neither Eve nor any of her immediate progeny was available to carry out God's vengeance on this hapless moccasin, so we dutifully vanquished the evil monster with rocks. When it was down to just enough strength to twitch its tail (We know that dying snakes always do that until the sun goes down.) I had an inspiration that was sure to magnify the adventure.

I had heard that Melvin Shores could pop a snake's head off by grasping it by the tail and snapping the snake like a bullwhip. The snake's head would go flying, so we had heard. I tried several times to make it happen, but the snake's head stayed firmly attached. Finally, out of anger and frustration, I decided to teach the old snake one more lesson. I would warp it around a fence post as hard as I could. That would surely separate his brain from his body.

I swung the big snake as hard as I could. Trouble was, I was standing a little too close to the post. As I caught the post with the snake's midsection, the front third of him whipped around the post, and the snake's head slapped the underside of my forearm with a sound like a rifle shot.

Now I had a real problem. I thought I had made the snake bite me. The stinging red welt on my arm added credence to my fears. Luckily, though, it was apparently the back of his head that stung my arm, and he had his fangs turned the other way. Anyway, I lived on to endure the hoots and hollers of my friends, who seemed to see a whole lot more humor in it than I did.

BATTLE OF THE CRATER

Impasse: A situation in which no progress is possible

It is not likely that many folks these days are familiar with the Civil War "Battle of the Crater." But it was very real to the soldiers who fought there a century and a half ago.

Every July 30th, we have the opportunity to celebrate the anniversary of the Battle of the Crater, although I don't know of anyone who actually does it. And if one chose to observe the anniversary, would he celebrate it or abhor it? One would need to identify, within the realm of the battle, which side was the antagonist and which one was his adversary. Was it a debacle or a triumph? Again, that depends upon which point of view you happen to choose.

It was a tumultuous day, some 160 years ago, in the American Civil War. During the Siege of Petersburg, opposing armies were almost at a stalemate. Confederate troops under the command of Robert E. Lee were entrenched, and Yankee troops under the command of Major General Burnside could not manage to break what appeared to be an <u>impasse</u>. Some of Burnside's troops were miners from Pennsylvania. They devised the harebrained idea of tunneling under the Rebels' perimeter, loading the hole with dynamite, and blowing a hole in the defenses. The idea, of course, was that they then could rush in and shoot a lot of the southern boys.

The problem was that they loaded the charge with too much dynamite. When they set it off, the massive explosion created a giant crater. The Yankee boys rushed in, all primed up to shoot a lot of rebels, but instead, they found themselves in a big hole surrounded by Confederate Soldiers. It turned out to be a massacre as the southern boys picked them off from the rim of the crater. The Army of the Potomac lost nearly 4,000 soldiers that day. Commanding General Ulysses S. Grant described the event as "the saddest affair that I have witnessed in this war." He immediately fired General Burnside, who would never again command Union troops.

The Battle of the Crater, as it became known, is the same battle as depicted in the movie, "Cold Mountain," which starred Nicole Kidman, Jude Law, and Renee Zellweger. It is a great movie.

This battle is of particular interest to me as my great grandfather, John Outlaw, fighting under General Robert E. Lee in the Army of Northern Virginia, was severely wounded in that battle. He spent the rest of the war in a hospital and was crippled for the rest of his life. He was awarded the Confederate Cross of Honor for his bravery during that battle. He was supposed to receive a pension for his service and his disability. However, Confederate dollars had little value after the war.

UNDER THE MISSISSIPPI

**Vivacious: attractively lively and
animated (typically used of a woman)**

It was back in the early 1980s, and I was assigned as a project
engineer on a construction project in southeast Arkansas. It was
an interesting project that was designed to provide water for the
operation of a giant paper mill that was being constructed a mile or
so away by another contractor.

What made the project interesting was the challenges presented:
to construct large intake pipes and anchor them 30 feet below the
surface of the water in the middle of the Mississippi River, then build
a pump station to pump all of that water under a large flood control
levee and a mile of soybean fields to the paper mill.

As the project engineer, I was strapped with a thousand
responsibilities. I was responsible for budgeting, purchasing, hiring
and supervising surveyors, recording the weather, payroll, and – worst
of all – the accounting of a couple of hundred bid item activities.

I needed help. I got a young lady from the local jobs program.
She should have been a student in special education herself, so she
didn't last. Then, I hired the superintendent's son, a second-year
college student. With another couple of years at the university, he
may be qualified in physical education. I wouldn't advise him to aim
too high. He was no help to me.

Then Karen came along. What a blessing. Her hand was like lightning on the ten-key. She could do more data entry on the cost sheets in 30 minutes than I could do in three hours. Bonus! Karen was nice looking. My wife swore that I hired Karen because she was "<u>vivacious</u>." Not so! But she was. I will not soon forget Karen.

National Day
of Prayer

___

Vestige: A trace of something that is disappearing or no longer exists

May 2nd has been designated National Day of Prayer. Since prayer has been removed from schools, and the Ten Commandments have been denigrated and removed from many public places, the National Day of Prayer is one of the last <u>vestiges</u> we have with Christian connotations. Let's take full advantage of it.

There are plenty of things to pray for these days. We might start by praying for the people who have been killed or wounded and are starving to death in Israel and the Gaza Strip. Let's pray for the folks in Ukraine who are suffering at the hands of Russia. Let's pray for the poor and hungry who have accumulated at our southern border, seeking an American way of life.

And let's not forget to pray for our country, our beautiful country that has been mismanaged by our elected government officials for decades. I am praying for a significant change.

I frequently reminisce about my early days when I lived in what was then dirt-road Arkansas. We were surrounded by good people—people who were fiercely American. I recall that we periodically met at the rural schoolhouse where I started school for a "singing."

We sang songs like "America the Beautiful," "God Bless America," "My Old Kentucky Home," "Carry Me Back to Old Virginny," "Old Black Joe," and "Way Down Upon the Swanee River."

When we pray on "National Day of Prayer," or better yet, when you pray every day, let us beseech the Lord to guide us back to what we were when we were surrounded by God-fearing people who love the Lord and love our country.

They Sailed from Plymouth

Bangers and Mash: Sausages and Mashed Potato – A British comfort food

It started in England, left England, went back to England, and eventually wound up in New England.

The Separatists didn't believe that a church, the only church that they were allowed to attend, should be one that was started by one man. In this case, that one man was King Henry VIII, and his church was the Church of England.

Seeking freedom to worship in their own way, they fled England and settled in Amsterdam, Holland. After a dozen years in Amsterdam, they still had not found the freedom of which they dreamed. Many of them moved on to the city of Leiden. Little had changed. Life was hard in the Netherlands, and there was an intensifying threat of war between the Dutch and the Spanish.

They had been hearing for several years that disenchanted Europeans were fleeing the Continent for the New World. The leaders of the Separatist movement traveled to London, where they contracted with the owners of the Mayflower to transport them to the colonies of America. They would depart from Southampton, the major port city 80 miles south of London on the English Channel.

The Pilgrims, as they had become known, hired another ship, the Speedwell, to haul them from Delfshaven, a port town on the Nieuwe Mass River just south of Leiden, to Southampton. There, they would load and outfit both ships for the journey across the ocean to the New World. They departed on July 22nd, 1620.

The Speedwell, an older ship, leaked badly on the trip to Southampton. With new planking and loads of tar, the Pilgrims patched up the old ship. They declared it satisfactory for the trip, so they loaded up and embarked from Southampton on both ships on August 5th. As soon as the ships got into the rough seas of the Channel, the Speedwell's repairs started failing. The ship was leaking again. Both ships headed for safe harbor and put in at Dartmouth to make more repairs. They had hardly made it a hundred miles, and it was now August 12th.

After what they thought would be adequate repairs, the two ships set sail again. The Pilgrims were exuberant. They were finally on their way. However, before they were three hundred miles out at sea, the Speedwell was leaking badly and in danger of sinking. The two ships put in to the port at Plymouth.

The frustrated Pilgrims determined that the Speedwell could not be depended upon to maintain seaworthiness across the North Atlantic. The leaders ordered that some of the supplies and some of the passengers, only as many as the ship could haul safely, be transferred to the Mayflower. Some of the devoutly religious Pilgrims had begun to have doubts as to the Lord's blessing on the voyage. They gave up and decided to stay in Europe. Finally, on September 6th, the badly overloaded Mayflower set out for the western horizon. It was alone.

Some 395 years later, I was among a group of modern-day pilgrims touring Jolly Old England. We set aside a day to tour the town of Plymouth. After checking in at the Holiday Inn, it was still early afternoon. A number of our fellow passengers/tourists – there were a couple of dozen of us, total – had signed on for a "pub crawl," which would include dinner. I didn't want to hang with our busload of tourists, and if there were anything that this old country boy would not relish, it would be a pub crawl with a bunch of Yankee tourists. Beyond that, I knew there was a lot of history in Plymouth, and I would likely never be there again.

Our hotel was sitting behind the "Hoe." The Plymouth Hoe, or "The Hoe," as it is locally called, is a green space and park above the limestone cliffs at the seafront. We decided to spend our afternoon exploring the area around the Hoe and the waterfront.

A major attraction at the Hoe is the beautiful red and white Smeaton's Tower lighthouse. At 72 feet tall and sitting high on the Hoe, the lighthouse, originally built in 1759, is perhaps England's most famous landmark on its South West coast. Historic lighthouses always deserve a visit. We were not disappointed.

While strolling the bucolic acres atop the Hoe, we happened upon a tournament of sorts. Gentlemen, and I suspect I should call them gentlemen – they looked like gentlemen – were playing "Bowls." Lawn bowling, I think some folks call it. These players were all wearing white shirts and trousers and white hats. We learned that lawn bowlers wear white, reflecting the sport's privileged heritage, much like cricket, tennis, and croquet. It is obviously played by people who have somebody else do their laundry.

The Plymouth Hoe is perhaps best known for the probably apocryphal story that Sir Francis Drake played his famous game of bowls here in 1588 while waiting for the tide to change before sailing out with the English fleet to engage with the Spanish Armada.

We strolled to the Pub on the Hoe for some pub food, as they call it, and a glass of red Bordeaux. I was immediately stumped. There was a whiteboard mentioning the day's special. It was "bangers and mash." I had never seen that on a menu before, so I was forced to question the publican about what bangers and mash is. It turns out that it is simply sausages and mashed potatoes. And it was served with "mushy peas." Go figure! And it was very good.

With our thirsts and appetites slated, we were ready to set out for another of Plymouth's famous attractions. Thankfully, it was not a great distance. We were there to see the famous Mayflower Steps. The Mayflower Steps is a stairway of sorts leading from the base of the Hoe down to the water. It is supposedly the last steps that the Pilgrims made on the European continent as they were heading for the Mayflower to sail away to the New World.

The attraction, as you will find it today, consists of a commemorative portico with Doric columns of Portland stone that was built in 1934 and a small platform over the water with a brushed steel rail and a shelf with nautical bronze artwork and historical information. It is on a small pier that is believed to have been built in the 18th or 19th century.

As we envision the Mayflower at anchor in the harbor, we can also see the wharf boats loaded with Puritans, who have just descended those steps, as they are ferrying back and forth from the steps to the ship.

When the ship finally sailed out of the harbor on September 6th, the Pilgrims had already been living on the ship for more than a month. During the 66-day trip, the venerable ship encountered storms, sometimes so violent that they had to furl all the sails and let the vessel drift in the wind. They reached the Provincetown Harbor, at the extreme outer end of Cape Cod, on November 9th. It was bitter cold.

There was virtually no timber on the outer end of Cape Cod. Explorers roamed south on both sides of the bay and finally determined the best place to build a settlement was on the west side of the bay at a location now known as Plymouth Rock, Massachusetts.

They didn't call it Plymouth Rock, but they did name it Plymouth, and they banded together and called their group the Plymouth Colony. But there is a Plymouth Rock. You can see it in Plymouth, Massachusetts. It is a tourist attraction and might induce a burst of laughter when you see it. It is a lone rock sitting in the bottom of an enclosure, and it has absolutely nothing to do with the pilgrims who came ashore near there some four hundred years ago.

Bums have come
a long way

Pitiable: Deserving or arousing pity

It would rank right up there with the worst job I have ever had. However, I thanked God that I had it. JC and I had gotten hungry a few times while trying to find steady employment in the San Joaquin Valley. We had finally found this job in Fresno. JC was working as a journeyman drywall finisher and getting paid $3 per hour. I was applying "flop" texture and being paid $1.50.

After a week and a paycheck, we were eating again. We bought a generator and voltage regulator at a junkyard, put it on my '54 Ford, and were driving again.

After I had received the second paycheck, I was starting to feel a little less destitute. On Monday morning of the third week, I had to meet the superintendent at the Melody Diner to get my assignment for the day. I parked my car in the railroad station parking lot since the diner lot was full. As I started to leave the car, I heard a deep voice. It startled me. I looked around. The voice said something like, "Hey, Buddy." I didn't see any other buddy around, so someone must have been talking to me. I expected someone would tell me to get my car out of his parking lot. The man came out of the shadow of a locked entrance and said, "I just got off a freight train, and I haven't eaten in two days. Can you help me?"

The man was as filthy and decrepit as the station. His hands shook, his eyes were hollow, and he smelled. Urine and body odor were not my ideal start for the day. The man seemed more <u>pitiable</u> than menacing.

I pulled out my wallet and gave him two dollars. That left me five. The man seemed genuinely appreciative.

"Where did you come from?" I asked him. Night trains have always been especially fascinating to me. Back in Arkansas, I used to listen to the faint sound of the whistle late at night. It came from somewhere over around Reyno or Biggers, probably a dozen miles away, across the Current River. It was a peaceful, lonely sound.

The man said he'd hopped the freight in Red Bluff, up in Northern California. He seemed anxious to get on his way, which made sense. After all, he hadn't eaten in two days.

He started to walk away, then turned and asked, "Do you know what time the liquor stores open around here?"

I went on into the Diner a bit wiser, having learned that in desperation, hunger always comes in second to thirst.

Some forty years later, I was in Whistler, British Columbia, a ski resort much like Aspen or Vail. It was early morning, and I was getting a cup of coffee for the road before driving north to Cache Creek. A homeless man sat on a bench across from the exclusive Blackcomb Lodge. His bag of belongings was beside him on the bench, and he was reading the financial section of the local newspaper. He even had a pencil and a pad and was making some notes. Bums have come a long way in the last forty years. Well, haven't we all?

His ear is missing

Elude: Avoid or escape by being quick, skillful, or tricky

We motored into Amsterdam the previous day after driving across the low country from Brugge, Belgium. Our stay in the "Venice of the North" would be short. We booked two nights at the Mercure Hotel near the airport.

On our first morning, we went to the Anne Frank House at Prinsengracht Canal, 263 to 267. This is the home where Anne Frank, her parents, and her sister, Margot, <u>eluded</u> capture for more than two years. One can imagine the terror felt when German soldiers raided the home, arrested the Frank family, and deported them to their deaths in concentration and death camps. One cannot leave a visit such as that with a cheerful demeanor.

Our next stop was at the Van Gogh Museum. I have never been a fan of Vincent Van Gogh's art, but since he and his art have been so popular, I figured a little exposure to the genre might be beneficial. In the end, I didn't get that feeling. Being aware that old Vincent was known to have gone crazy and cut off his own ear, I could surmise that he looked at a couple of his paintings to see what he had done, and that was when he fell off his wagon. After a bit, I felt like they might have the same effect on me if I kept looking at them.

Joe the Aleut

Prankster: Practical Joker, someone
who likes to play tricks, especially to
make other people **look silly:**

The Aleutian Islands is a chain of islands that reaches halfway
from North America to Japan, separating the North Pacific Ocean
from the Bering Sea. The "Chain," as it is commonly known, is
named for the native tribes who populated the islands prior to the
Second World War.

The climate is unforgiving. Trees will not grow there. There
are no people living on the outer chain. At the start of World War
II, the Allied Forces moved the Aleut Indians off the islands to the
mainland. This was necessary. The Japanese occupied Attu and
used it as a submarine base for a few months. They bombed Dutch
Harbor, which was near the mainland. There was a significant battle
between the Allied Forces and the Japanese Imperial Army on the
island of Attu. It lasted nineteen days, from May 11th to May 30th,
1942. When the war was over, the Aleuts were allowed to return to
the islands. They refused to go. Now, you can find them any evening
on Fourth Street in Anchorage.

We had one Aleut worker on our project in Shemya. He's the
only one I ever saw work anywhere. Joe never smiled, at least during
the daytime. After we were paid every Friday night, the poker games

would start in the day room. Joe was probably making about $800.00 per week. By Saturday morning, he was broke and hung over. This routine never varied.

I never saw Shemya after 1965. I returned to Alaska and worked on projects on Adak Island during the following two years. The people I worked with in Alaska in the '60s were an adventuresome and interesting lot. Many of them were foreigners, and several were immigrants. The Irish had settled near Ketchikan. Their names were fun to learn. I worked with Sean O'Laughlin, Shamus O'Flarrity, and Bill O'Shaughnessy. Most of the Americans were from the Northwest or Texas.

On one Adak job, I became friends with a couple of pipe insulators. They were longtime friends and inveterate pranksters, constantly pranking each other. They both lived in the Seattle area. Hugo was a German, and Aaron was a Swede. (Everybody is something in the Northwest, rather than just people like they are back in Arkansas.) These guys were funny, and they were fun. They were always playing some kind of practical joke on someone or on each other.

They and I finished one job on Adak at the same time and caught the same flight to Anchorage. These guys couldn't wait to get on the Alaska Airlines jet in Anchorage and start drinking. They had made a poke full of money and were going to celebrate for about a week. They planned to get a head start on it on the evening flight to Seattle.

On the jet, Aaron and I sat together in a seat toward the rear of the plane. (The door was near the rear of the Convair 880.) When the stewardess came by, Aaron stopped her and asked, "Do you see the big guy on the aisle near the front?" He identified Hugo to her and continued, "His name is Hugo. He has epilepsy. He will want to drink, but if he does, it may trigger an epileptic seizure and could endanger his life."

The stewardess accepted Aaron's story, and when taking drink orders, she passed Hugo by without comment. Hugo weighed about 270 pounds and had a voice to match his size. He was not going to allow any good drinking time to be wasted. He called the stewardess, "Hey, I need a drink too." Upon her explanation that she couldn't serve him, Hugo went ballistic. He caused such a commotion that, in the end, she told him she wouldn't serve him under any circumstances. Hugo sulked and cursed Aaron all the way to Seattle while Aaron and I enjoyed our drinks at the back of the plane.

I questioned Aaron just to get a rise out of him, "Hugo wouldn't do that to you, would he?"

"Hell," he said, "Hugo would have put sugar in Lindberg's gas tank."

These two guys were constantly amusing. I never saw or heard of either of them after 1966.

The Dalmatian Coast

Stipend: A sum of money paid at regular times for services or expenses.

We were driving southward from Slovenia toward Croatia's Dalmatian Coast. It was approaching noon as we entered the town of Karlobag. We hoped to find a place to get lunch. We didn't even know if the Croats ate lunch at noon. Not every country does.

Road signs are all written in Croatian, which uses the Latin alphabet, and have a lot of Latin symbols that render them gibberish to an American.

Presently, we came across an unusual structure. We checked it out. It was evident that it was ruins of a church with little of the structure remaining standing.

We found a nearby café and decided to give it a try. It might have been the only one in town. We parked our Peugeot with Spanish license plates directly in front. It was like a patio café in that the dining room had no front wall. A gentleman, a few years past middle-aged, apparently sized us up as tourists. He called out in his language into an adjacent room, and presently, a young man, about college-age, emerged. His heavily accented English worked, and he explained that his uncle didn't speak English and that he would help us.

We said we would like to get something to eat. He described

some kind of sandwich that they could fix. We didn't recognize any of the ingredients that he mentioned. We still had a good distance to drive that afternoon and didn't know what lay ahead, if anything, so we ordered two of what he had described. Glasses of some white wine were offered. Somewhat sweeter than chardonnay, it was quite tasty.

We talked with the young man while "uncle" prepared our sandwiches. The young man – I'll call him Luka – became excited when he learned we were from Texas. He had seen some John Wayne movies. He explained that his family had a cow. The Croatian government gave them a stipend of $800 as a subsidy just for them to own a cow. It was a government program intended to make rural families more self-sufficient. I could see the wheels turning in Eleanor's head. We had about 130 head of cattle at that time, including cows, bulls, and heifers. (Let's see, at $800 each, that would be OMG!) No need to think about it. Our government doesn't give us diddly for owning cattle.

We inquired about the monolith that stood just across the street. It turned out that it was what was left of the St. Karlo Boromejski church that was bombed to ruins by Allied bombers in the Second World War. Local history tells that it was bombed out of existence on August 31st, 1944, because it was believed that it was being used for ammunition storage by Nazi forces. The remaining fragment of the structure only contains part of one wall, as well as the tower and belfry.

Although the Church intended to rebuild, the communist government that came into power after the war removed much of what was left and built a road through it. The St. Karlo Boromejski was an active church from 1710, built on the foundations of the church of St. John (1615).

Karlobag is the northernmost point of Dalmatia, a town where three regions are connected (Dalmatia, Primorje, and Lika). It is extremely well connected with the rest of Croatia because it is located along the Adriatic highway.

The town's history goes back to 1387 when it was first mentioned as "Bag," founded by the Holy Roman Emperor Charles IV. By his name, Charles, known in Croatian as Karlo, the town got the prefix Karlo.

The Turkish invasion of Lika changed Karlobag's development course. In 1525, the Ottoman Turks destroyed the town. The only building left was a fortress for a small military presence. Austrian Archduke Karl rebuilt the town in 1579. Following that rudimentary restoration, the Venetians took over the fortress and destroyed it again. Right up until 1683, Karlobag was inhabited only by military units.

Next to the church stands the monument of Šime Starčević, father of the first Croatian grammar.

Šime Starčević was a Croatian priest and linguist. He came to Karlobag in 1814. He knew Latin, French, Italian, and German and could read Slavic languages. In 1812, he published his French grammar in Trieste. He revised and translated from German, using domestic terminology for linguistic terms. His grammar of "Illyrian" was the first Croatian grammar describing the four-accentual system of the Neoštokavian dialect.

Karlobag is now a tiny coastal town located on the Adriatic coast, with a population of just 917 folks. Its attractive beaches, clear waters, and rich history remain a secret to many. I am glad that we stopped to inquire about the church ruins. We could so easily have missed it.

We enjoyed our couple of hours in Karlobag, visiting with Luka and "uncle" and learning a little about Croatian life. The wars and strife that have bruised and battered that part of the world can only be imagined. Aren't we glad that we live in a country that has never been destroyed? So far, at least.

IT WILL WARM
YOUR INNARDS

**Porter: Porter is a dark brown beer brewed
from malt that is partly charred at high
temperatures. It was first brewed in London,
England, in the early 18th century.**

It was a cool, misty Sunday morning in Belfast. May is a little early for visiting that far north unless one enjoys being cold. I don't. We checked out of the Stormont Hotel, loaded our bags into the "Luxury Coach," as our Welsh guide referred to it, and headed for our next adventure.

Belfast has long been the center for the linen industry, tobacco production, rope-making, and shipbuilding. The city's leading shipbuilders, Harland and Wolff, built the ill-fated RMS Titanic. We strolled the concrete pad where it was built and fitted out. In its heyday, the Harland and Wolff shipyard was the largest and most productive shipyard in the world.

We spent a good two hours touring the Titanic Center in Belfast. Titanic Belfast is a visitor attraction and a monument to Belfast's maritime heritage on the site of the former Harland & Wolff shipyard in the city's Titanic Quarter. It tells the stories of the ill-fated RMS Titanic, which sank on her maiden voyage in 1912, and her sister ships RMS Olympic and HMHS Britannic. The building contains more than 130,000 sq. ft. of floor space, most of which is occupied by a series of galleries, plus private function rooms and community facilities. A visit to this museum is a must for folks touring Belfast.

After Belfast, we motored to Downpatrick in County Down for a visit to St. Patrick's grave. It is easy to visit and pleasant to sit in the cemetery beside St. Patrick's Cathedral.

I was glad to visit St. Patrick's gravesite. Anyone who can spread Christianity to a whole country/island, an area populated with violent heathen Celtic tribes, had to have been quite an inspired and inspiring preacher.

We enjoyed our visit to St. Patrick's Cathedral. It is now an Anglican church. It was built in the 11th century, so it was Catholic when it was built. Poor old St. Patrick. He didn't know that the British would turn him into a Protestant some thousand years after he was buried there.

We motored south from Downpatrick, along the shore of the Irish Sea, crossing the border from Northern Ireland back into Ireland near Dundalk. In another couple of hours, we entered the city of Dublin. It is time to put away the British money and get the Euros out again. This gets to be confusing.

Every beer-guzzling Yankee who visits Dublin, Ireland, feels that he has to visit the Guinness headquarters and drink Guinness beer as if it is different from the Guinness that he could get back in Wichita. Maybe it is. I am not a beer drinker.

Of course, you won't run into the canaille of Irish beer drinkers at the Guinness Brewery. They are down the street at a local pub drinking <u>porter</u>. Porter is especially favored in the winter as it is said to warm your innards. And, of course, the climate in Dublin is winter-like nearly all year long. Cheers!

THEY MIGHT BE FROM DES MOINES

**Indelicate: Having or showing a lack
of sensitive understanding or tact.**

It is interesting and sometimes amusing to see the couple from
Wichita recoil when confronted with Michelangelo's anatomically
correct sculptural rendering of David. Non-Wichitans, but of the
same ilk, who likewise see as <u>indelicate</u> any display of a male body
with genitalia intact, will forgive me for categorizing them along
with the citizenry of Wichita. They might, in fact, be from Des
Moines.

LET'S CALL IT WHAT IT IS

Providence: the protective care of God
or of nature as a spiritual power

It was a pleasant fall day in Georgia, November 19th, 1994. I had a weekend off from work and was eager to go sightseeing. Georgia has such a fascinating history. The project, like all construction jobs, is temporary. I might not be in Georgia for more than a year or two so I would try to see as much as possible.

I was working on a big concrete paving project at the Hartsfield-Atlanta International Airport. Our job was to construct nearly a hundred acres of reinforced concrete aprons and taxiways for the new International Concourse.

We set our sights on Andersonville in southern Georgia. Andersonville is famous, or infamous, because of the notorious Civil War prison there. The largest and most famous of 150 military prisons of the Civil War, Camp Sumter, commonly known as Andersonville, was the deadliest landscape of the Civil War. Of the 45,000 Union soldiers imprisoned here, nearly 13,000 died. At its most crowded, it held more than 32,000 men, where forced overcrowding compounded problems of supply and distribution of essential resources.

Some folks scoff at why people would visit a place with such a sad history. Probably the same reason that folks visit the site of the Battle of the Little Bighorn.

The prison camp at Andersonville was a hell-hole of the worst kind. I suspect that all Civil War prisons were hell-holes. Two of my kinsmen died in northern prison camps. But Andersonville was the most notorious. Thousands of prisoners died, mostly of diseases exacerbated by lack of food and good drinking water. It wasn't because of evil guards. They didn't have enough food and water either. There were simply too many prisoners and too little food.

In the summer of 1864, the prison's wells dried up, and prisoners were dying of thirst. Then, there came a miracle. Accounts are mixed on how the spring first appeared on that August night. The more dramatic tales have it bursting out of the ground after a lightning strike from a towering storm cloud. Other accounts say it sprung up after a heavy rain storm saturated and shifted the grounds underneath the prison. Still, others say it just appeared during the night while the prisoners slept. Either way, to the Andersonville prisoners, the sudden emergence of a bubbling spring of fresh water on the north side of the stockade felt like the work of divine Providence. They named it <u>Providence</u> Spring.

Following the initial preservation of the prison site in the 1890s by the Grand Army of the Republic, the Woman's Relief Corps arranged to have a spring house constructed to cover the site of the spring. The Providence Spring House was dedicated on Memorial Day, 1901.

The photos we snapped that day show Providence Spring still running a nice stream of crystal-clear water. Regardless of what caused the spring to start flowing, it is flowing. Let's call it what it is—Providence!

HAVE WE FORGOTTEN HOW TO BUILD?

Genesis: The origin or mode of formation of something

Ocean cruising was among my primary recreational activities in this century's first couple of decades. I have been forever fascinated by the architecture, engineering, and construction of these giant cruise ships. And almost every year, newer and bigger ships are added to the world's fleet. And they enthrall me to an even greater extent.

This started with my first major cruise in 2003. It was on the Crystal Harmony. The first day I was on the Harmony, even before the lifeboat drill, I encountered a plaque on a bulkhead adjacent to the promenade deck that said that the ship was built in 1992 in Japan by Mitsubishi Heavy Industries. I wondered why an American company uses a ship built in Japan. Is it because it is cheaper? Do the Japanese craftsmen work for less wages? Or do they have better skills?

I have found that all cruise ships have plaques showing the genesis of the vessels, where and when they were built, and by whom. The second cruise that I took was early the following year. It was on Royal Caribbean's Rhapsody of the Sea. I sought out the plaque and found it was built in 1997 in St. Nazaire, France, by Chantiers de L'Atlantique. It was the same for Vision of the Seas, which was my third cruise. That was interesting. The beautiful cruise ships aren't built in India, like my Rockport shoes, or Cambodia, where my Jockey briefs come from, or Bangladesh, where my Izod khaki slacks were stitched. No, and France is not a third-world country.

The fourth cruise was on Princess Cruises.' The Grand Princess is a Grand-class cruise ship built in 1998 by Fincantieri Cantieri Navali Italiani in Monfalcone, Italy.

We took the Amsterdam around the southern tip of South America in 2005. It was built in 2,000 at Fincantieri Cantieri, Navali Italiani SPA, Maghera, Italy

Fast forward a few years to our 13th and 14th cruises, both of which were out of Galveston on Royal Caribbean's Voyager of the Seas. The Voyager, like a baker's dozen of other cruise ships, was built in Finland. And that includes the grandest of them all, the colossal Icon of the Seas that is now in her first full year of service. She carries 7,000 passengers. That's as many people as live in the county seat of my home county in Arkansas.

It boils down to the fact that the cruise industry is a giant industry, employing hundreds of thousands of workers, and America is not a part of it, except as paying passengers. Politicians talk about bringing jobs back to America, but nothing changes. It has been that way for years. We Americans have forgotten how to build nuclear power plants. I worked on one of the last ones that was built in the United States, and that was 40 years ago. And America apparently never learned how to build cruise ships. Not one of the hundreds of cruise ships plying the oceans worldwide was built in America.

I am determined to avow my support for national leaders who will actually do something to bring back manufacturing jobs to America, and I loathe any of them who won't.

HUNTER-GATHERER, OR WARRIOR

Euphemism: A mild or indirect word or expression substituted for one considered too harsh or blunt when referring to something unpleasant or embarrassing.

It was an excellent day for a drive to the Northwest from West Yellowstone. The "Big Sky" of Montana was clear, and the scenery was beyond beautiful.

The route was familiar to me from previous trips, although not all of them had been pleasant. The route was generally the same, but the highway was not. I will clarify.

We were driving Interstate Highway 90, a wonderful superhighway. I didn't have that when I drove the route in 1957 in my old 1954 Ford. It was US Highway 10, a two-lane road, and it was in a snowstorm. A year later, I drove it again, but this time, I was on a Harley Davidson trying to get back to Tacoma from Upstate New York, and I was colder than I have ever been at any other time in my life. I remembered these experiences as we cruised across the border into the Panhandle of Idaho.

I had my sights set on the town of Coeur d'Alene. I knew the town, which by now had grown to some 50,000 folks, was amid some beautiful scenery. It, like the Coeur d'Alene Mountains, is named after the Coeur d'Alene People, as they are known, a tribe of supposedly hunter-gatherers who occupy a territory of four million acres from eastern Washington to Montana.

I chuckle at the "hunter-gatherer" term. It is an overworked euphemism for most American Indians whose young boys grew up to be warriors and periodically made war on other tribes.

We located a modern hotel adjacent to a small park right on the shore of Lake Coeur d'Alene. The view was exceptional. At a nearby visitor's center, we learned that there was an excursion boat service for scenic cruises on the lake. We eagerly rushed to the dock and caught the last cruise of the day, during which we were treated to a stunning sunset just before returning to the dock.

The following morning, we checked out of our hotel and said goodbye to the beautiful Lake Coeur d'Alene. By nightfall, we would be in Mukilteo, Washington. My wife and I agreed that we had a new favorite American city in Coeur d'Alene, Idaho.

MINISKIRTS WERE POPULAR

Indecorous: Not in keeping with good taste and propriety, improper

My English teacher at Ventura College, Professor MacNaughton, was a linguist, etymologist, and stickler for vocabulary. He seemed to have a command of more words than Roget. When he admonished my fellow students to refrain from sitting at our desks in an <u>indecorous</u> manner, he left it up to us to know precisely what he meant. It was, as I recall, the days when miniskirts were popular.

THEY BIVOUACKED IN THE CEMETERY

Forage: Of a person or animal, search widely for food or provisions.

General Sherman's infamous March to the Sea should not be relegated to the distant dark pages of history. It was a ruthless sixty-mile-wide path of destruction that started November 15th, 1864, near Jonesboro, just south of Atlanta, Georgia. It culminated on the outskirts of Savannah on December 21st. In 1864, Dr. Richard Arnold, the mayor of Savannah, signaled to Sherman that the city would surrender. He felt more prudent to surrender the city than to have Sherman's troops burn it to the ground as they had done in Atlanta.

Sherman agreed. He surveyed the scenery of Savannah and reputedly declared it "too beautiful to burn." He subsequently messaged President Abraham Lincoln news about his campaign. His telegram of that date stated, in part: His Excellency President LINCOLN: I beg to present you, as a Christmas gift, the city of Savannah, with 150 heavy guns and plenty of ammunition, and also about 25,000 bales of cotton. (signed) W.T. Sherman, Major General.

That was quite noble of the General. His swath across Georgia was not against the Confederate soldiers but rather against the region's impoverished citizenry. The troops burned their homes and confiscated their food. Relics from the campaign existed for decades as lonely fireplace chimneys standing where homes and mansions had previously stood. They became known as Sherman's Sentinels.

The actions of Sherman's troops were incredibly cruel, and they were sanctioned by their commanding officers. Soldiers, known as foragers, rode in advance of the columns. Their jobs were to <u>forage</u> for foodstuffs. They did this by riding to farmsteads, which women and children typically occupied because the men were off at war, and robbing them of all of their food, such as canned goods, potatoes, and apples, that they had stored up for winter.

I visited Savannah in 1994 after driving down from my home in Atlanta. I recall, in particular, the Colonial Cemetery, a nearly three-hundred-year-old cemetery in downtown Savannah.

When Union troops occupied Savannah in December 1864, the graveyard served as a bivouac area for hundreds of Union soldiers. According to local lore, these soldiers did more than camp. Soldiers displaced and defaced nearly all of the stone markers and monuments. They had fun altering the information carved on the monuments and headstones in their spare time. Soldiers changed headstone dates, sometimes adding digits to make people appear much older than they were. For example, one soldier might make someone appear 421 years old instead of 42.

When I visited, I spent more than an hour reading the inscriptions on the hundreds of headstones leaning against the inside walls surrounding the cemetery. Once the Union soldiers were gone, nobody knew where the headstones belonged, so they rest, to this day, against those outer walls.

Washington DC

Spiffily: In a stylish, attractive, or pleasing way.

I had just finished my training: Eight weeks of basic infantry training at Camp Gordon, Georgia, and another nine weeks of antiaircraft artillery radar operation training at Fort Bliss, Texas. I had five months of the military under my belt, and it had all been training.

But now I was at Camp Kilmer, New Jersey, awaiting my ship to take me to the Panama Canal Zone. It was the yuletide season of 1954, and it was cold and lonely. I had never before been away from home at Christmas. In a rare stroke of luck, I had no duty assigned on the Christmas weekend, so I was granted a three-day pass. It was like, "Get out of here. We don't need you and don't want to feed you." I immediately called my sister, Donna Dean, in North Carolina, and she wired bus fare to me. I caught a bus and headed south for Winston-Salem.

The bus ride from Newark was uneventful. It felt good to get away from the army camp and be among civilians. Bus passengers are not an over-friendly lot. That was okay.

In Washington DC, the bus pulled into a big terminal. I would have a couple of hours before the next bus would pull out for Winston-Salem. I bought a cup of coffee and found a seat away from the traffic. There were a number of uniformed soldiers and sailors obviously

---

347

heading home for visits with families. I was nervous because my pass was just a standard little pass card with stock information that said such things as "Not valid after 2330 Hours" and "Valid only within 50 miles of base". The orderly at Kilmer had scribbled on the back, "Three Day Pass." I wondered if that would satisfy an MP. I was hoping that I would not see one. Surely enough, here came a Marine Military Police and a Navy Shore Patrol.

These young men approached me in a serious military manner, and the <u>spiffily dressed</u> Marine said, "Let me see your orders and ID card." I handed him my pass and ID card and told him that was all I had. I was afraid I was in big trouble. He studied the card for a long minute, then asked, "Are you from Arkansas?" I told him that I was.

He then asked, "Did you attend school at Richardson?" Again, I told him that I had. He said as a statement, "You have a sister named Jo Ann." I nodded. He then asked, "Do you remember Miss Romack?"

I said, "Yes, I started my first grade there, and she was my first teacher. He said with a smile, "Miss Romack is my mother, and I was also attending school there. I was in Jo Ann's class." How coincidental! Richardson was a little rural one-room schoolhouse, and Miss Romack taught all eight grades at that time.

The military police wished me well and went on their way. I had a warm feeling inside. It had seemed that I was a million miles from home. Now, it didn't seem quite so far.

BILLY THE KID

Ristra: Also known as a sarta, the ristra is an arrangement of drying chile pepper pods

Old Mesilla, south of Las Cruces, ranks right up there with my favorite locations that I have ever visited. I love the unusual history of the small town. It used to be in Mexico and thought it still was until the Treaty of Guadalupe Hidalgo moved the U.S. border south of town, thus placing Mesilla in the United States. It upset some folks so much that they moved farther south to stay in Mexico. But don't kid yourself; Old Mesilla (pronounced meh-see-yah) is still Mexican and beautifully so!

Even more extraordinary, my favorite Mexican restaurant sits in the middle of Old Mesilla. La Posta de Mesilla calls me back every time I travel through southern New Mexico. For over a century and a half, those adobe walls have withstood the attack of elements and man, sheltering personalities such as Billy the Kid, Kit Carson, General Douglas MacArthur, and Pancho Villa.

The heart of the picturesque village of Mesilla is much the same as it was one hundred years ago. Thick-walled adobe buildings, which once protected residents against Apache attacks, now house art galleries, restaurants, museums, and gift shops. Today, tourists stroll on the peaceful plaza and imagine life as it might have been a century or more ago.

After the Treaty of Guadalupe Hidalgo concluded the Mexican War in 1848, the Mexican government commissioned Cura Ramon Ortiz to settle Mesilla. He brought families from New Mexico and from Paso del Norte (modern Ciudad Juarez) to populate the Mesilla Civil Colony Grant, which by 1850 had more than 800 inhabitants.

On November 16, 1854, a detachment from nearby Fort Fillmore raised the U.S. flag here, confirming the Gadsden Purchase; thus, the Gadsden territory was officially recognized as part of the United States. In 1858, the Butterfield stage began its run through Mesilla. During the Civil War, Mesilla was the capital of the Confederate Arizona Territory.

Mesilla's most notorious resident, Billy the Kid, was sentenced to death at the county courthouse just down the street from La Posta, but he escaped before the sentence was carried out. Legendary hero Pat Garrett eventually tracked down and killed the Kid; later, Garrett was mysteriously murdered in an arroyo just outside of Las Cruces. He is buried in a local cemetery.

San Albino Church, on the plaza, is one of the oldest churches in the Mesilla Valley. The nearby Gadsden Museum houses Indian and Civil War relics and Southwest New Mexico artifacts.

Throughout Mesilla, colorful <u>ristras</u> of red chile peppers strung together decorate homes and businesses, symbolizing the hospitality of the Southwest. A visit in Las Mesilla transports a visitor into another era!

My son, Tim Cates, and I motored into the historic village of Old Mesilla on June 15th, 2024. We were there to meet my friend, Laura Stadjuhar, for lunch at my favorite restaurant in the world. I will visit Old Mesilla and La Posta any time that I have the opportunity.

My Uncle

Profligate: Recklessly extravagant or wasteful in the use of resources.

Thankfully, I am not aware of any of my family members being particularly <u>profligate</u>, except one. My Uncle Sam is a hopeless spendthrift. How could one otherwise explain a national debt of $35.17 trillion?

Baden Baden

Insolent: Showing a rude and arrogant lack of respect

Eleanor had visited Baden Baden once before and loved it, so she looked forward to seeing it again. We had toured almost to the extreme north of Western Europe, so it was time to start working our way back to the South of France.

We drove southward from Remich, in Luxembourg, down to Strasbourg, France, then back up the valley to Baden Baden.

I had heard about Baden Baden before. My favorite author (the Twain fellow) had toured Baden Baden in 1880 and found the shopkeepers, hoteliers, and bathhouse attendants to be insolent and lugubrious. To exacerbate an already bad situation, he found that the German population of Baden detests the English and despises the Americans. We didn't find that hostility. Maybe a century and a half had ameliorated their malevolence, or was it Hitler?

It is hard to explain a funny double name like Baden Baden. Baden translates to bath. That doesn't help. Bath Bath makes no more sense than Baden Baden. There are other Badens scattered around Europe: one near Vienna in Austria and one near Zurich in Switzerland. So, Germany just doubled down and called theirs Baden Baden.

Baden Baden reminded me of other bath centers that I have

known. Hot Springs, Arkansas, has cured people of their ills for nearly two hundred years. It still has the same eight bathhouses that it had back when it entertained mobsters and politicians alike. It still has horse races, but the speakeasies are gone.

Radium Hot Springs, in the mountains of eastern British Columbia, also has bathhouses but caters primarily to the well-fixed population of Vancouver.

I don't know that the Germans of Baden Baden still despise Americans. They do make it plain that they are liberal and love all liberal Americans and loathe folks such as the Bushes and Donald Trump. I didn't argue with them. They are bigger than I am.

We enjoyed dinner and a couple of local beers, then spent the night at the Heliopark Quillenhof Hotel. After a breakfast of boiled pork and eggs, we charged into the mountains of Switzerland.

No, we didn't do the baths at Baden. We are too American to parade around in the nude. They call it au naturel, and it doesn't seem to mean a lot to them. We call it bare-assed naked, and it means a lot to us.

THE AMAZON

Suffice: Be enough or adequate; be sufficient.

Rivers are special to many of us, whether as short as the Roe River in Montana, at 201 feet long, or as magnificent as the Father of Waters, our great Mississippi River. We love our rivers. We dam them up. We channel them with revetments. We dredge them to keep them deep enough for tugs and barges. We suck water out of them to irrigate the rutabaga farms, water our lawns and gardens, flush our toilets, brush our teeth, and wash our bodies. Rivers are our blessings. They were also used for dueling.

In earlier centuries, among other uses, men who saw themselves as having their honor damaged sought satisfaction by dueling on islands in the middle of the Mississippi River. It seemed that there were state laws against dueling, but islands in the Mississippi that were more than a mile from either shore were outside any state jurisdiction. It takes a big river to satisfy that need. But the mighty Mississippi is 11 miles wide at its widest point, so <u>suffice</u> it to say, it is more than adequate.

We have already seen the shortest river and how broad our biggest river is, but how might they rate on a global scale? Old Man River, at 11 miles wide, registers embarrassingly small compared with the Rio de la Plata on the Uruguay and Argentina border, at 140 miles wide.

How about navigability? Can you imagine a Cruise ship going up the Mississippi River to St. Louis? No, he would tear the funnel off on the Hughey P. Long Bridge before he even got out of New Orleans. By contrast, cruise ships regularly navigate 1,000 miles up Brazil's Amazon River from the Atlantic Ocean, then turn into the Rio Negro, a tributary, and cruise on to the city of Manaus.

Should you choose to make that journey upriver to Manaus, be mentally and psychologically prepared. The entrance to the Amazon is at the city of Macapá, smack-dab on the Equator. In addition to the characteristic equatorial heat, the Brazilian rainforest surrounding the entire voyage length renders it insufferably humid all year around.

We made that voyage in 2012. My wife and I agreed that probably no one in history has ever volunteered to do it twice.

VIA DOMITIA IS OLD, REALLY OLD

**Primeval: Of or resembling the earliest
ages in the history of the world.**

After driving southward over the Swiss Alps into France, we
intercepted the Via Domitia at Gap and determined to follow it as
closely as possible down into Provence.

I wondered why a highway had a name like that. I found that
Via Domitia is old, really old. We thought Historic Route 66 was
old. Via Domitia was built by the Romans a couple thousand years
before Route 66. In fact, it was built over a hundred years before
Jesus was born.

Via Domitia was the first road built from Gaul to Hispania.
That means that it stretched nearly 500 miles from the French Alps
down through present-day Switzerland and Provence and into the
Iberian Peninsula. One can only wonder what kind of tools and
equipment the Romans used to build a roadway through the highest
mountain ranges in Europe. It was completed in 118 BC.

Gap is a commune of the Hautes-Alpes department, in Provence-
Alpes-Côte d'Azur, Southeastern France. We intended to spend
some time in the town, but we found ourselves in the middle of a
portion of the Tour de France. Bicycles, carloads of bicycles, and

busloads of bicycle-race aficionados were everywhere. There was not even a place to park in the town. We decided to move on.

We deviated to Aix-les Bains on the shore of Bourget-du-Lac to spend the night. We were directed to a delightful restaurant overlooking the lake just as the sun was falling beyond the mountains that shade the western shore of the lake.

Our Campanile Hotel in Aix-les-Bains was a pleasant three-star boutique hotel with just 59 rooms. The bed was a nice surprise. It was almost like an American queen-size bed. We had already observed that most Europeans don't sleep together. Several of our hotels had rooms with two single beds. In a couple of the hotels, the twin beds were pushed together to make it look like one bed. However, the bedding is separate – separate bottom sheets and separate duvets. Our hotel in Rüdesheim am Rhine, Germany, had a near queen-size bed, but it had a two-by-six plank down through the middle of it to separate the two sides. How Victorian is that?

The following day, we drove to the summer home of our Texas friends, Bob and Iris. They hosted us for a couple of days, and we toured the surrounding villages together. I told Bob that I wanted to visit the Roman Bridge, Pont Julian, that had been built for the Via Domitia Road in the third century BC. Anything that has existed since before Jesus was born and is still in use fascinates this old country boy.

The Pont Julian is a stone arch bridge - right pretty, I think - that spans the Calavon River. The Calavon flows generally west-southwest. It is a right tributary of the Durance into which it flows at Caumont-sur-Durance, near Cavaillon.

The Roman Bridge, as local Provençals know it, was only three miles from my friends' house in Roussillon, near Bonnieux. We parked near the north end of the bridge and then set out walking. Pont Julian was used for vehicular traffic until 2005, when a new bridge was built nearby to relieve the old bridge from wear and tear of cars and trucks. Pont Julian is now a favorite crossing for hikers and bikers.

I didn't need to drive across or even walk across it. I was happy to stand on the bridge, which has been in constant service for over 2,000 years, and visualize the columns of Roman soldiers crossing the bridge and marching south to conquer Hispania.

WORLD CRUISE 2020 – EPISODE 1

Ungainly: Graceless, awkward, clumsy.

New York City is always an experience. People who live and work there take it in stride, but for an out-of-towner, the city might as well be in a foreign country. The people of the Big Apple don't just talk differently; they are different. Of course, I am just one, and there are umpty-squat million of them, so who is different?

We knew that we wouldn't spend time touring New York City. We had done enough of that before. We were here for one purpose: to start our second around-the-world cruise.

I had brought a bottle of wine from Texas. We ordered pizza to be delivered to our room. It was a good New York-style pizza, and it went well with our bottle of Merlot. I took the half of the pizza that we didn't eat and gave it to the diminutive Guyanese desk clerk. It was still hot, and she looked like she needed the nutrition.

It was Thursday, January 2nd, 2020. We would vacate the city on the morrow, hopefully avoiding the infliction of too much New York-style foreignness. Our wheelchair pusher at the airport was from Ethiopia, and our cab driver was from Eritrea. I am left wondering how this <u>ungainly</u> ape managed to get from that tiny country on the

Horn of Africa to New York City and learn to drive a taxi. I suspect them all as hereditary brigands.

The following morning was our occasion to board the big Queen Mary 2 and embark upon our cruise, a cruise which would end up being the most unforgettable yet and the furthest thing from what was planned.

Friday, January 3rd: The Cunard folks processed us aboard our new home away from home in a timely and courteous manner, quite different from the chaotic procedures when boarding a Carnival Line cruise ship. Embarkation operations can be equated, as best, to something like herding cats. We were compactly ensconced in our Stateroom 5185 by 1:30 pm. There's room enough to sleep but not enough to swing a cat, even if we had one, and if we wanted to swing it.

WORLD CRUISE 2020 – EPISODE 2

Solicitous: To show concern for someone and ensure they are comfortable, well, or happy.

We ducked our heads as we sailed under the Verrazano-Narrows Bridge, and soon, we began to feel the gentle lift and fall of the big ship as she rode the waves of the Atlantic Ocean.

The first time that I sailed out of New York Harbor was 55 years earlier. That was in a little U.S. Navy troop ship, and we were headed to Puerto Rico and Panama. The beautiful Verrazano-Narrows bridge had yet to be built at that time.

This time, we were excited to be traveling in luxury and style. We were aboard the Queen Mary 2, the flagship of the historic Cunard Line. The QM2 is not a cruise ship. Instead, it is an ocean liner and the only ocean liner still in existence.

Our crossing was without incident of any huge kind, speaking for myself. But there are always the other stories. We didn't get far out to sea the first evening before having to turn around and swing into Halifax, Nova Scotia, to drop off a sick person. We feel <u>solicitous</u> for that person, or that family, whom we have never met, nor ever shall. World cruises, such as this one, require long-term

---

361

planning and a considerable outlay of cash. Most world cruisers are more than a trifle superannuated, and many have health concerns.

It is all too typical. A cruise like this is, for many, a once-in-a-lifetime experience. Following the long wait, the embarkation date approaches. The person will proceed with the voyage, come hell or high water. But then it happened, and the ship had to drop them off at a hospital in a foreign country before they even got a full day into the trip. How sad!

On Saturday, we attended a 2 p.m. lecture in the Royal Court Theater. The British lady told us what we should do in Southampton—at least, I think that is what she was talking about. With her strong British accent and some kind of cockney cadence, she may as well have been speaking Ojibwe. I gained nothing from it.

On Saturday evening, not 24 hours after docking at Halifax, Nova Scotia, to evacuate a sick woman, we were beset with another predicament. We were thrashing along in a winter storm in Newfoundland's Grand Banks, and another lady fell deathly sick. We turned back toward Sydney, on Cape Breton Island, Nova Scotia. We made it to the Laurentine Channel and rendezvoused with the Nova Scotia Coast Guard. A large helicopter picked the lady and her husband off the heaving deck in 80 miles-per-hour winds. We hoped and prayed for that couple.

The storm never let up. By bedtime that evening, we were in a blizzard. We watched the snow build up in drifts on our veranda until we fell asleep.

We were just two of the eleven hundred guests on the ship. We would pick up another 700 at Southampton on Friday.

The surroundings on the big Queen Mary 2 were gay and enlivening. Our hosts obsequiously, but respectfully, and with great dignity, went to great lengths when necessary to ensure that even the most careless guest would avoid any discommoding mishap. The waiters hovered over us like bumble bees.

Our hosts preferred to call us guests rather than passengers. After all, one of the most important positions on the ship was Hotel Manager. That tells you something.

Monday was the first formal evening of the "crossing," which is what they call it between NYC and London. Due to the discomfort of the rough seas, we forewent the gala cocktail party. However, we enjoyed the sumptuous formal dinner. On formal evenings, the dinner menu in the Britannia Dining Room always included lobster and escargot, my favorites.

Some 400 miles east of the Grand Banks and the shallow water of the Flemish Cap, we cruised above the wreckage of the Titanic. I suppose that it should be no surprise that favorite shipping lanes haven't changed in the last 112 years. Our route takes us above or near the Titanic route on nearly every crossing. Icebergs floating south from Labrador haven't changed either. I made this crossing eight years earlier on the Caribbean Princess, and we had to deflect our course 120 miles to the south to avoid icebergs. And that was in the warm month of May.

The sea smoothed a bit. We crossed above the Mid-Atlantic Ridge on Tuesday. After a day and two nights cruising above the Porcupine Abyssal Plain, on Thursday, we entered the Celtic Sea.

Our dinnertime table-mates included Renee, Faud, and Bobbie. What a fun menagerie!

Renee was a true British lady. She hailed from somewhere north of Liverpool. She was a British version of Aunt Bea, of the Andy Griffith show. Renee was the epitome of pleasant. Her smile is constant and genuine. We had no doubts as to its authenticity. Renee was a bank employee until she started having babies. Babies didn't mix well with work schedules, so she quit banking and raised her kids. Eventually, her nest became empty, and for something to do, she started teaching cooking to the local shire ladies. When her ladies had learned all that Renee had to teach, the sessions changed to friendly visits. They kept coming. They still come. They are now old friends.

Fuad was an entirely different story. He is a citizen of Oman and was born in Kenya. We don't know how that happens, but somehow, things work differently in the Middle East. He got an education in Oman and wound up as an Ambassador to the United Nations.

Nepotism abounds in the diplomatic corps in his part of the world, and after Fuad's retirement, Ms. Fuad, or whatever her name was, became Madam Ambassador. Fuad was Oman's gift to our dinner table, our very own Sheik of the Burning Sand—an Omar Shariff kind of fellow. Single ladies are drawn to Fuad's diplomatic manners, speech, and his immaculate attire. We didn't ask for details about why he was having fun on a cruise while Ms. Fuad was doing her diplomatic stuff in New York City.

This brings us to Bobbie. She was hitched, for some 30 years, to some wayward son of a powerful Italian Mafioso. She somehow escaped with some money because of the son's wayward ways. It seems Godfather held Bobbie in higher esteem than he did his firstborn son. So, Bobbie was traveling the world exquisitely coifed, wearing the finest clothes, and having fun on some of the old mob money.

Bobbie seemed fascinated by Faud. Bobbie was slightly older and a staunch Midwestern conservative, and Faud was a Trump-hater. That made for some interesting exchanges.

It was nearly noon on Friday when we made port in Southampton. I caught a free shuttle to the West Quay Shopping Center, then struck out walking through the Old Town. The most interesting part of the Old Town was the preponderance of brick and stone walls. The still-existent city walls extend to the Bargate, through which visitors and attackers have passed since Medieval times.

World Cruise 2020 – Episode 3

Superfluity: an unnecessarily or excessively large amount or number of something

Some of our Continental guests, or maybe it was just the Brits, managed to delay our departure from Southampton. The Brits are superior about formalities, but they are sorely lacking when it comes to punctuality. We didn't take in lines until nearly midnight on Saturday, the 11th.

The Sunday morning church service was very British, very Church of England. Our new captain, Aseem Hashmi, whom we had picked up in Southampton, was the minister who conducted the service. It was my first experience in a pure Anglican meeting. Captain Hashmi did a good job, and I didn't question him about his church having been founded by the ultra-ungodly King Henry VIII. I still wonder how the Church of England adherents resolve that question.

We made port early at Lisbon, and I went ashore shortly after 8 a.m. I had visited Lisbon several times previously and had seen the well-known tourist attractions, some more than once.

I loved those earlier visits to the Belem Tower, the Monument to the Discoveries, the 25 de Abril Bridge, the neighboring towns of Cascais and Sintra, and, best of all, the Christ the King Monument.

Lisbon is a gritty city that most folks don't find attractive. I actually enjoy that earthy grittiness of the city and its people. Some of the dirt might have been left there by Ferdinand Magellan when he sailed away in 1519. From the looks of some of the areas. It seemed entirely possible.

If I were a younger man, which I once was, and had a <u>superfluity</u> of spare time, which I never had, I would rent an apartment for a month right in the center of the city. I find Lisbon that interesting.

I went ashore and caught the free shuttle to the Placa de Restauradores. After walking around for about 15 minutes and seeing nothing of interest, I hired Alexandra Silva and her tuk-tuk for a 40-minute tour. I remember, primarily, the teeth-rattling tuk-tuk ride on the cobbled streets.

Back at the Placa de Restauradores, I fulfilled a long-nurtured goal by finding the famous Fábrica da Nata to enjoy one of their famous pastéis de nata. The Pastel de nata, or pastéi de nata, is a Portuguese egg custard tart pastry dusted with cinnamon. Famous worldwide, I dared not miss the opportunity. It remains a highlight memory.

My last responsibility in my Lisbon visit was to fetch a bottle of real Portuguese port wine. Garrafeira Estado d'Alma's motto is "Life is too short to drink bad wine." I knew they would not disappoint me. The resident sommelier recommended a Royal Oporto 10-year Tawny. My wife and I would enjoy a post-dinner sip of that for several days.

World Cruise 2020 – Episode 4

**Desiccated: Having had all
moisture removed, dried out.**

We cast off from Lisbon on Monday afternoon. It was cool. Lisbon has the same north latitude as my hometown in Arkansas. Lisbon's temperatures are moderated by its proximity to the sea. However, it was still mid-January, and the wind across the deck was piercing.

By evening, we had sailed out of the Tagus River Estuary. We said goodbye to Cabo da Roca, the westernmost extreme point of mainland Portugal and, in fact, Continental Europe. The beautiful red and white Faro del Cabo de la Roca lighthouse was casting its warning beam from high above the Atlantic Ocean. We had visited it from the mainland four years earlier when we drove there from Sintra.

We spent Tuesday morning cruising south along Portugal's Atlantic Coast. At noon, we cruised by the Farol do Cabo de São Vicente, near Sagres, another lighthouse that we remembered from our auto tour in 2016. The Farol do Cabo de São Vicente was Portugal's first lighthouse, built in 1515. In those years, the light was fueled by olive oil and the beacon could be seen six miles out at sea when the wicks were clean. Improvements have been considerable in the last 500 years. The Cabo de São Vicente Lighthouse is now equipped with a 52 inches hyper-radiant Fresnel lens, producing a single white flash with a period of 5 seconds and a range of 32 nautical miles, being the biggest optic of all Portuguese lighthouses and one of the ten biggest in the world.

After rounding the Cabo (Cape) near Sagres, we turned to the east and headed toward the Strait of Gibraltar and the Mediterranean Sea.

The Strait separates Europe from Africa by the busy channel that is only eight miles wide at its narrowest. The Strait is full of vessels almost constantly as all shipping between Mediterranean ports and the countries of the Western Hemisphere pass through that narrow body of water. History? Yes, Spanish and Portuguese explorers, such as Christopher Columbus, Cabeza de Vaca, Ponce de Leon, and Hernando de Soto, sailed through the Strait.

The famous Rock of Gibraltar loomed to our left as we entered the Strait. To the right, we could see the traffic on the hills of Morocco. Soon, we were abreast of Tangier, my favorite Moroccan city.

We cruised along the Barbary Coast of North Africa for another day and two nights. From our veranda, we could see the dry mountains of Algeria and Tunisia and wondered what timeless mysteries were hidden in the deep canyons and <u>desiccated</u> land beyond.

Late Wednesday, we turned away from the Tunisian coast and watched the mountains recede into the horizon. We entered the Tyrrhenian Sea and sailed past the Sicilian city of Palermo. By morning, we had steered into the Strait of Messina and docked in the city of Messina.

Messina is home to Italy's most famous astronomical clock. The Messina Bell Tower, with its 157 feet for the clock and 40 for the pinnacle, is just short of 200 feet tall, has a square base of 103 square feet, and is considered the world's biggest and most complex astronomical and mechanical clock. The clock is built into the campanile of the Messina Cathedral.

The clock displays a 12-minute-long performance composed of various carousels and moving statues that make the watcher feel completely hypnotized while Shubert's Ave Maria propagates through the air. The performance narrates biblical and allegorical scenes linked to the city's history.

The Messina Cathedral is much older than the clock. Built by the Normans, it was consecrated in 1197 by Archbishop Berardo. Henry VI, Holy Roman Emperor, and Constance I of Sicily witnessed the ceremony.

We made our way to the Cathedral in time to join three or four hundred others in the plaza waiting for the 12 o'clock performance. We had seen performances of other astronomical clocks in Strasbourg and Prague but Messina garners our vote as the best that we have seen. There are many astronomical clocks in Europe but none in the United States.

Our afternoon excursion took us to the Tempio Votivo di Cristo Re, Italy Shrine of Christ the King, Messina. As we approached the magnificent shrine, I suddenly realized that it was familiar. I had been there before. I didn't have my diaries with me, so I couldn't tell when. I later checked my diaries and found that I had visited it on my way to Athens in 2015.

Before returning to the ship, we stopped by an al fresco café for a brioche and caffè latte.

I engaged in a discussion with a couple from Peekskill, New York. In conversation, I shared that I was disappointed we didn't go to Naples. I wanted to have a pizza in the hometown of pizzas, where they originated.

The lady told me: "You'll have to be careful. Their pizzas are not like ours."

I didn't say it aloud, but "Hey, lady! Do you think pizzas started in New York and eventually spread to Italy? And maybe the recipe got corrupted before it got to Naples?"

Messina represented a change in our itinerary. We had been scheduled to visit Naples instead of Messina, but a change was made after we left New York. We never did know why.

WORLD CRUISE 2020 – EPISODE 5

Adjudged: Determined to be true or otherwise.

We sailed for two days and three nights in the Ionian Sea between Messina, Italy, and Haifa, Israel.

On Friday, we sailed between the island of Crete and the Mediterranean shore of Libya. As I gazed southward from our starboard veranda, I could visualize the Libyan city of Tripoli just beyond the horizon.

Twelve years earlier, on our first world cruise, we had been scheduled to make a port visit in Tripoli, on the north coast of Africa. However, about this time, the United States accused Libya of being a terrorist state. Its leader, Moammar Gaddafi, was disaffected by our State Department and <u>adjudged</u> guilty of harboring terrorists. Diplomatic relations went into the toilet. The State Department issued travel warnings against Libya, and our planned visit fell casualty.

Colonel Gaddafi never regained status on our Christmas card list, and our military saw to it that he would never be a threat again. They executed him in 2011.

Looking the other way, beyond the Greek Isles, the Dardanelles, and the Sea of Marmara, I recall sailing into the Golden Horn, tying up to the dock, and visiting the most despicable country imaginable. It was several years earlier, and our agenda was to make a two-day visit to Istanbul before continuing north into the Black Sea.

In the early days of Christianity, the land that became Turkey was populated by Christians. After Jesus's crucifixion, his disciples, or apostles, fled persecution and settled in that land. The gospel spread north to Antioch, where believers were first called Christians. The region was part of the Roman Empire in those days, and the capital was Byzantium. Constantine the Great set up headquarters there and, with his power and influence, renamed the city Constantinople. That was in 330 AD. Constantinople remained the center of Eastern Christianity for more than a millennium and remains that to this day, but only in a titular manner. Islam has spread throughout the country until Christians are now a tiny minority, with less than one percent of the population. Constantinople was renamed as Istanbul in 1930.

It was in Ukraine that I first learned of the slave trade in Turkey. During the Ottoman Empire and earlier, Turkish slavers traveled across the Black Sea to the Caucasus region of Circassia, Ukraine, and Georgia. They raided towns and captured young girls, and took them back to Istanbul to be sold as slaves. That practice has not entirely ended. Walk Free, an international human rights group focused on the eradication of modern slavery estimates that there are 1.3 million people, primarily women, who are held in slavery in Turkey right now. I am glad not to be visiting Turkey on this trip.

On Sunday morning, the sky was dark. It would be an hour before old Sol would show his countenance over the Mount Carmel mountains just beyond the city of Haifa if he were to do it at all. Captain Hashmi eased the big ship to the dock and gave orders to secure it with the ropes. We felt not the slightest reaction as the big QM2 touched the bumpers. That says a lot since it was still dark except for the flashes of lightning. Hard winds and driving rain were no challenge for our experienced Skipper.

There was only a brief respite from the rain as we made our way to our special excursion bus. We were confident that the sun would soon show her sweet face and start warming the streets of Haifa and we would have a pleasant shirt-sleeve visit in the Holy Land. But no! The sun angel did not come calling. The rain continued. Oh well, we had come halfway around the world to visit the land where Jesus was born, grew up, and ministered some two thousand years ago. We would deal with it.

We were on a "wheelchair-adaptable" excursion. The excursion was limited to four couples, meaning four occupied wheelchairs and four spouses. We chose it because some of these excursions require a great deal of walking. My wife was by no means wheelchair-bound, but her less-than-successful back surgery a couple of years earlier had left her with some severe pain if she were on her feet for an extended length of time. For that reason, we rented a little battery-powered scooter to allow her to get around more comfortably.

It took some doing to get two lovely wheelchair-bound ladies and one typically snarly New Yorker and their wheelchairs snugged down in a center aisle and the rest of us seated. My wife's little jitney was the easiest part of the load.

Our guide, Aichiya, was a good enough workaday guide with a somewhat typical guide's accent. I can't tell you what that accent was, but if he didn't have one, he would sound like a Texan, which he did not.

Sedan was our driver who had the duties and responsibilities of loading and securing the wheelchair folks, in addition to navigating Israeli traffic, something that I wouldn't want to tackle. Now, Sedan's name is not pronounced like the body style of your grandma's four-door Chevrolet. I won't try to explain it. Sedan only knew four words in the English language. They were, "I only speak Hebrew."

Our primary destination for the day was the Sea of Galilee. People and denominations can argue about where precisely the manger was where our Savior was born. and where was the location of the burial site. And they do. But no one argues about the Sea of Galilee being the place where Jesus walked on the water, calmed the sea, and told experienced fishermen where and how to catch fish.

The Sea of Galilee is as real as the story of Jesus himself. That is why we were determined to see it.

Without getting too longwinded about our day, which I am sometimes inclined to do, I'll just share that seeing that body of water that we had heard preachers preach about all of our lives was just reward for our braving the rain. I will have more to say about it later. It was a big event for my wife and me to go down below sea level from Tiberius and visit the Jordan River, where John the Baptist baptized our Savior.

Mark Twain famously said: "Travel is fatal to prejudice, bigotry, and narrow-mindedness."

It is true. We learned that the center of the universe is not in our hometown or even in our state or country. We learn that 95% of the people of the world don't give a hoot about George Washington, Abe Lincoln, or Oprah Winfrey. They have never heard of them. We learn that soccer is more popular than NFL football, and cricket is dearer to people's hearts than major league baseball. We find that some of our friends are gay, and yet they are nice people. We find that refugees are not bad people. They are desperate people, and they have been through danger and suffering that you and I can only imagine.

We see the poverty in so many places around the world, and our hearts cry that we cannot help them. We see where people in European countries celebrate their history of Christianity and wonder why ours at home is under attack. We find that the Vietnamese people treat us kindly even though our army killed hundreds of thousands of them in "The American War," as they call it. We find that there are good, caring people everywhere, except maybe in Turkey.

Travel is also fatal to our perspectives, and we all have them. In this case, based on what I had read and seen on TV, my perspective of the Holy Land was that it was so desolate and desert-like that God indeed could have picked a better place to originate the history of Christianity, like maybe somewhere around foothills of the Ozark Mountains. My perspective was shattered on our visit.

As our excursion motored out of Haifa and up the Yizre'el Valley,

I watched field after field of commercial vegetable farming slide past my excursion bus window. It reminded me of the Salinas Valley in California. As we left the valley and started climbing to higher elevations, we saw vast expanses of lush green wheat fields like one would see in eastern Montana or eastern Washington. These Israelis are pretty smart. They built their villages on the rocky hilltops, planted olive trees on the rocky slopes, and saved the best land for agriculture. California could take note.

We bypassed Nazareth and started downhill toward Tiberius, and at 200 feet below sea level, we turned south toward Poriya. From there, the descent intensified. The narrow switchback road reminded me of the old road from Boulder City, Nevada, down to the crossing on Hoover Dam. Deeper and deeper we went with our ears alternately stopping and opening again, popping, and doing it all over again. By the time we reached the Jordan River, we were 700 feet below sea level. Just think, if the water level dropped 700 feet at Galveston, you could walk from there to New Orleans. Well, that's silly. You'd be in mud past your knees, and the mosquitos would eat you alive.

Anyway, it is a different world down there. The air is thick. The oxygen is rich. The avocado and mango trees eat it up and produce fruits as plentiful as manna was for the refugees from Egypt.

As we circled the Sea of Galilee, we found the valley of the Jordan River and the sea to be a rich land with vast citrus farms. When we drove along the base of the Golan Heights, we traveled through mile after mile of banana plantations. I suspect that area would match Costa Rica in terms of the production of bananas. That is not the picture we had in our minds of what the war-torn, disputed territory of the Golan Heights would look like.

Somehow, when I read how Jesus found John baptizing people in the River Jordan and Jesus requested John to baptize him, I pictured a rocky desert and a sandy or rocky beach, something similar to Boulder Beach in Nevada, for Jesus to wade out into the water. What we found was a significant river not that different from the rivers back where I grew up in Randolph County, Arkansas. However, the

Jordan is surrounded by citrus and banana plantations rather than the rice, cotton, and soybean farms that prevail along the rivers of my youth.

So, a new perspective awakens. The rocky desert-like hills I envisioned our Savior walking through are not that at all. These Arabs, Bedouins, Israelites, or whoever lived here for thousands of years before Jesus walked out of Nazareth as a young man might have already cleared the rocks out of those fields. They had had thousands of years to do it while their kinsmen, along with other slaves, were making mud bricks down in Egypt.

We all know the story of how Jesus fed the multitudes with five loaves of bread and a couple of fish. (They seem to have called them "fishes" instead of just "fish," as we call them today.) Of course, the people were Israelites, too, rather than Israelis, as they are called today. (I may lie awake trying to figure that one out, too.) But on our trip around the Sea of Galilee, before we reached the village of Capernaum, we came upon the location where some five thousand folks came to hear Jesus preach and didn't bring a sack lunch. So, Jesus broke the loaves of bread into little pieces that swelled up like exploding Nissan airbags, so he broke them again and was able to feed the whole "multitude," as they were called.

Some folks, way back, figured out where this all happened, so the Catholics did what they always do: they built a church on the spot. It is known as the Church of the Multiplication. That was 1,670 years ago. Then, the Persians destroyed it in 614. That was the Muslims of Baghdad. They made sport of destroying anything Christian. They still do that.

After the Persians destroyed the church, the Jews were not interested in it, and the exact site was lost for some 1300 years. Then, the German Catholic Society bought the property in 1888. Archaeological surveys were done, and full excavation began in 1932.

These excavations resulted in the discovery of mosaic floors from the 5th-century church, which was also found to be built on the foundations of a much smaller 4th-century chapel. Since 1939, the property has been administered by the Benedictine order as a daughter-house of the Dormition Abbey in Jerusalem. The current church, inaugurated in 1984, was built on the same floor plan as the 5th-century Byzantine church, and some of the ancient black basalt walls have survived and remain visible.

Our visit to Israel was fulfilling and satisfying.

It is good that we went when we did. It is a dangerous part of the world now.

WORLD CRUISE 2020 – EPISODE 6

Aweigh: Nautical, the anchor is raised free of the seabed or riverbed.

The day started early on January 22nd. We had cruised overnight from Haifa, Israel, and gotten into our queue at Port Said for our passage through the Suez Canal.

At 3:30, the captain gave the order to "Weigh Anchor." "Weigh Anchor" is the term that gives rise to the term "Anchors <u>Aweigh</u>." That shouted announcement signals that the anchors are clear of the sea bottom and, therefore, the ship is officially underway. And, of course, there's the old Sailors' Song, "Anchors Aweigh." Definitely not "anchors away," an egregious misspelling.

By 4:30 am, Captain Hashmi had steered our ship into her assigned spot in the convoy of ships to transit the Suez Canal today. We are number 3 in the convoy of 19 vessels and the only passenger ship. We traveled at a regulated speed of 9 knots and maintained an interval of 1.5 miles between vessels. A ship like this, at umpty-squat million pounds, doesn't stop just by the captain stepping on the brake pedal.

It was still dark when we entered the 120-mile-long canal. The Suez Canal has no locks. It is the longest sea-level canal in the world. It is a thrill to cruise through it, just as is transiting the Panama Canal. This time, we are transiting north to south, from the Mediterranean Sea to the Red Sea. I have cruised it once before, but that time, we were crossing south to north, with mainland Egypt on our left and the Sinai Peninsula on our right. This time, it is just the opposite.

Along the upper reaches of the canal is the vast agricultural region that likely stretches westward to the Nile Valley. We see field after field of vegetable farms interspersed with large groves of date palms.

At 8:05 A.M., we passed under the giant Egyptian/Japanese Friendship Bridge. It is the only bridge that crosses from the African continent to Asia. The bridge was closed except for military use because of concerns about possible terrorist attacks. This is a violent part of the world. In fact, Security people have been on both sides of the ship all day, with binoculars, scanning other vessels.

At 10 am, we reached the city of Ismailia, the headquarters of the operational authority of the canal. An hour later, we entered the Great Bitter Lake. This is a natural lake that the canal passes through. It is wide enough that the northbound convoy and the southbound convoy pass each other at that point. The original lanes of the canal are only wide enough for one-way traffic.

The system is simple. Convoys: that means every vessel that has paid to make the crossing starts every morning at each end of the canal. They meet and pass each other at Bitter Lakes, then continue the rest of the way through the canal. When the last vessels have cleared the canal, it is closed to traffic until the following morning, when it will all happen again.

We enjoyed seeing the contrasts – the Sinai desert on the left and the developed cities and farmland on the right. There were military installations and guard posts throughout the length of the canal. There are reinforced stone and concrete walls that would probably turn President Trump green with envy. But these Egyptians are as serious as a heart attack about security. Just notice the size of the guns they carry.

By nightfall, we had completed the canal transit, passed Port Suez, and were cruising in the Gulf of Suez. It was an interesting day. Besides that, it is warmer. It is nice to put away the fleecy sweats and slip into shorts and tee shirts.

Through the night, after completing the Suez Canal transit, we cruised south through the Gulf of Suez into the Red Sea, steered around the tip of the Sinai Peninsula then north through the Gulf of Aqaba to the city of Aqaba at the southern tip of Jordan.

We arrived at the dock in Aqaba at 8 A.M., and by 9:30 A.M., the ship had regurgitated onto the dock more than 2,000 citizens of the lost tribes of the world.

We were given three strong recommendations prior to visiting Aqaba, Jordan.

1: Go to Petra. Everybody on the ship is here to go to Petra.

2. If you don't go to Petra, go to Wadi Rum. Everybody on the ship who doesn't go to Petra is going to Wadi Rum. However, our good friends back in Texas told us not to bother with Wadi Rum. There really isn't anything interesting to see once you get there.

3. At any rate, don't get mugged, robbed, or waylaid in the city of Aqaba.

Well, Petra is beautiful but crowded beyond imagination. There's a lot of walking involved. There are camel jockeys, donkey jockeys, and carriage captains – villainous hucksters, one and all. We are advised to avoid them like a plague.

We chose to forego visits to 1 – Petra and 2 – Wadi Rum. We watched from our balcony while the lost tribesmen boarded 44 giant buses and were soon on their way to the desert locations. We were okay with our choice. We will go to town.

Aqaba is considered a sort of crossroad of the world. When we arrived at our berth, we had four countries visible from the ship. Egypt is on our port side (left), Israel to the front, Jordan on the starboard (right), and behind is Saudi Arabia.

Aqaba has a long past history. This was the land of Edom that you have read about in the Bible. The Edomites were bitter enemies of the Israelites in the early days. In fact, God told Moses to avoid crossing through the land of Edom as Moses was leading the Israelites out of Egypt to their promised land. I will leave it to you readers to get those details from the biblical book of Numbers.

Aqaba sits at the extreme tip of the Gulf of Aqaba, an extension of the Red Sea, boxed in by treeless mountains and an immeasurable desert. It was a year after our visit when I really got interested in the city.

Have you read the book or seen the movie, "Lawrence of Arabia?" Colonel Thomas Edward Lawrence was a British archaeologist, army officer, diplomat, and writer who became renowned for his role in the Arab Revolt (1916–1918) and the Sinai and Palestine Campaign against the Ottoman Empire during the First World War. The breadth and variety of his activities and associations, and his ability to describe them vividly in writing, earned him international fame as Lawrence of Arabia, a title used for the 1962 film based on his wartime activities.

It so happened that a significant battle in that campaign against the evil Ottoman Empire happened right where we docked our ship. That historic battle, the Battle of Aqaba, happened on July 6th, 1917.

Try to imagine the ferocity and tumult of the battle when Lawrence and Sherif Nazir led 600 soldiers on camels into battle against twice that many Turks. Lawrence and the Arabs prevailed. Lawrence was not perfect, though. During the battle, he accidentally shot his own camel in the head.

Historical dates and places are abstract when one sees them in a movie. It puts a real perspective on them when you visit the location.

Since I had never been to Jordan, I was determined to go ashore at least. I wanted to buy a new cinturon and some shoelaces. My wife and I caught the shuttle to the city center and started doing what every other tourist was doing, essentially, standing around looking stupid. But eventually, we found and engaged a cabbie. (the very thing we had been cautioned against.) Sometimes, these "cry wolf" cautions are as baseless as some recent impeachment hearings. Our cabbie, Loay, was everything we needed. He drove us across town to the Mall of China. He helped us into the mall, took us to shops, explained what we were looking for to the bilingual Chinese and monolingual Jordanians, and helped us make our purchases. He did all of this, knowing how to speak neither English nor Chinese.

We were a spectacle in the mall – me with my pale honky skin and a Panama straw hat and my wife with her big Texas blonde hair. She was riding her little blue electric scooter. We were a scene beyond anything any Jordanian citizen had seen since Sarah kicked Hagar and Abraham's bastard child, Ishmael, out of Abraham's mortgage-free tent.

We got smiles from the souk ladies and big-eyed stares of astonishment from the children of the burqa-covered ladies shopping there. Needless to say, we were off the grid. There were no other guests from the QM2 within a mile of the China Mall.

Aqaba had nothing more to offer, so we returned to our big ship, took our place on our tiny veranda, sipped our double-malt, and watched the sun set over the fluted mountains of Egypt's Sinai Peninsula.

WORLD CRUISE 2020 – EPISODE 7

Backscatter: The scattering of radiation or particles in a direction opposite to that of the incident.

We cruised out of the Gulf of Aqaba during the night, then through the Strait of Tiran toward morning, and then into the Red Sea.

Saudi Arabia and Mecca were to our left as we continued cruising southeastward. I don't think many Americans visit Mecca. It is the holiest city for Muslims. One cannot get more into Salafism than that. Every adult Muslim who is physically and financially able to make the pilgrimage is obligated to do so at least once in their lifetime. However, only if their absence will not place hardships on their family. Muslims face Mecca when they pray because they turn towards the Kaaba, a sacred shrine in Mecca, Saudi Arabia, during their daily prayers.

We were treated to a novel experience that one might make jokes about but shouldn't. We were entering waters where piracy has been the order of the day for the last few years. For three days crossing the Bab el Mandeb and the Gulf of Aden, we would be under the protection of an International Task Force assigned by the United

Nations mandate to protect merchant ships from a piracy threat. The Task Force has provided armed personnel trained to repel piracy attacks. Additional defensive procedures were in place, but we were not privy to the details.

What we did know was what we should prepare for. That novel experience was a piracy drill. In the case of a piracy alert, we were to close shades, extinguish all lights, and go to an interior location of the ship.

During our time in hostile waters, possibly three days, at night, we would be running dark – that is, no exterior lights on. Outer decks were closed. The reason is to allow lookouts to maintain full night vision to the sides and aft end of the ship without any backscatter from deck lighting.

We were not to expect anything, but it has happened, mostly to tankers, but some passenger ships had been hijacked, certainly none as big as this one.

The previous week, we had cruised the last little bit of the east end of the Mediterranean. I was saddened that we did not stop at Alexandria. The last time we had cruised here, we put in at Alexandria and then took a coach excursion to the Giza Pyramids and Cairo. At the end of the day, after our dinner at a floating restaurant on the Nile River, we roared right through Alexandria and back to our ship.

Alexandria has held a palpable allure for me ever since the days back in the '70s when I was studying the source/sources of our Holy Bible that we hold dear. The Bible, as we know it, was coming into being just before, during, and immediately following the beginning of the Christian era. Scholars who compiled the first full bible into one collection used the Alexandrian Canon of Scriptures that was maintained in Alexandria, a center of higher education at that time. That bible, completed by Saint Jerome in 405, became the official bible of the Catholic Church and remains so to this day and for all time.

The great city was founded by none other than Alexander the Great, so it bears his name. Now, if that ain't a historical link, I don't know what could best it.

On Saturday, the 25th, we continued steaming southeast in the Red Sea. About all most of us know about the Red Sea is how God parted the waters for Moses to lead his followers across it. From watching Exodus, one might get the idea that the Jews scurried across a mile or two and then wiped the mud off their sandals on the clean sand of the Sinai Desert. The Red Sea is way bigger than that. It is 1,400 miles long and 221 miles wide at its widest spot. It took us three days of sailing before we sailed through the perilous Bab el-Mandeb Strait into the Gulf of Aden.

One could have panic attacks just looking at who our neighbors were. We took a good look at the African country of Sudan as we passed. (Thank you, Captain, for not stopping here.) We continued past Eritrea, Ethiopia, and Djibouti. I didn't want to stop there either. Saudi Arabia was still lurking in the distance off our port side.

The Red Sea is a busy waterway. At any time, we could see two or three vessels. No two of them are alike, and neither of them came from the same place, nor are any of them going to the same place. One wonders about these things. Who are the people on those ships? What language do they speak? Trains and planes elicit scant interest. But ships and the people on them are a murky mystery; the whole world is their oyster.

We had been, and continued to be, treated with some of the greatest entertainment in the world. But on quiet afternoons, when we were being lazy and flirting with borderline torpidity, we started to miss the music from home. At one point, my wife asked, "Don't you have music on your phone?" Oh my goodness! Why hadn't I thought of that?

WORLD CRUISE 2020 –
EPISODE 8

August: Marked by majestic dignity or grandeur

As the Red Sea is large, the Arabian Sea is several times as large. It would take seven days to reach our next port in the United Arab Republic. Our interesting group of dinnertime tablemates would change at that point. Renee would complete her contracted portion and fly home to jolly old England. Fuad would fly to his ancestral home in Oman. We enjoyed learning at least some snippets of our friends' lives and backgrounds. Fuad was, for twelve years, Oman's Ambassador to the United Nations. One might think that a retired former ambassador would be a senior citizen. Not necessarily so. Fuad was just maybe the youngest one at our table, certainly a lot younger than I was. What an interesting life he has surely had, far different from that of the rest of us.

We spent Monday and Tuesday steaming northeast off the coast of Yemen. I didn't want to get too close there. We don't like those people, and they don't like us. For two more days, we continued off the coast of Oman. Pakistan was dead ahead by a couple hundred miles, and India was off to our starboard beyond the horizon.

Do you remember in the story of the birth of Jesus, the Magi came from the East with gifts of frankincense? Well, this is where they came from. This is where frankincense grows. I must have been over-enthused about it the last time we visited Oman. We bought a suitcase full of frankincense and burners and took them home as gifts to our family members. Nobody was interested. The stuff is still at home in some cabinet.

Our professional mariners, the ship's officers, dress beautifully with a wide array of uniforms and insignias. We never learned to interpret the stripes and doodads. A couple of weeks earlier, about the time we crossed the 25th parallel of north latitude, the officers laid away their blue uniforms and came out in dazzling white. That would remain their dress as long as we sailed in warm climes and seasons.

There can be no better dresser, though, than our tablemate Fuad, the former Omani Ambassador. He is polite and courteous even to courtliness. The ladies love him. Of course, we, in this <u>august</u> company, are all dressed in our best and on our best behavior. There are no coarse jokes or indelicate or intemperate language. That didn't keep us from having fun.

This is a hairy part of the world. Yesterday, we cruised the Gulf of Oman. Today, we have the halfway-friendly country of Oman off our port (left) side and the decidedly unfriendly Iran off the Starboard side. You can bet I won't do anything to make them mad. The sons of Ishmael here are convinced that we, not they, are the infidels.

There were a couple of incidents on this cruise that brought to mind an old idiom that I consider now and then. It is this. "Not all women are ladies, and not all men are gentlemen." That is my thought for the day, and I am serious about it.

Blatant misuse of words is an intense peeve of mine. In this instance, I am thinking of the titles "Lady" and "Gentleman." And remember, they are titles. I had a respected English professor several years ago who said it quite succinctly. "A man should be referred to as a man unless there is reason to appraise him as a gentleman. Likewise, a woman remains a woman unless, and until, she has done something to indicate that she deserves to be called a lady."

Here's an example of the error that grabs my attention. A TV newscast is reporting about a robbery and shooting. The reporter gets the words from a witness who gives his version of the event. "I heard the shooting and saw these two gentlemen run out of the store with guns in their hands and jump in their car and leave." Here's the point. These two guys were not "gentlemen." They were quite likely hoodlums, and hoodlums don't deserve to be called gentlemen.

Here's another example. A witness said, "These two ladies started cussing each other, then they started swinging fists and pulling hair." No, Mr. Witness. These were not ladies. Call them women.

I am thinking of an occasion a couple of weeks ago. We attended the Burns Night ceremony in the ship's Queen's Room. It was a gala evening, and patrons were dressed in their finest. It was crowded. All the seats were filled, and a lot of people who didn't find chairs stood along the walls behind the tables where others were seated.

At the start of the program, four women formed a group at the edge of the dance floor, blocking the view of about a dozen people seated at tables. At least four people, including myself, told them that they were blocking our view and asked them to move. They heard but ignored each person's complaint, and it was all for naught. They remained defiantly in place. Handicapped ladies at our table completely missed seeing the event, as well as the Master of Ceremonies and the speakers. Their only view was of the backsides of these obstinate women. Here's my point. These women, regardless of how well-dressed they were, were not ladies. Ladies would not have acted like that.

I realize that political correctness precludes me from pointing out the ethnicity of the women, but dammit, I wouldn't want you to think that they might be Texas women. They were not. Perish the thought that some Texas women might be that inconsiderate. Indeed, Texas ladies would show more class.

It was Sunday, January 30th, when we arrived at the unreal city of Dubai in the United Arab Republic. I describe Dubai as unreal because it is. There is nothing else like it in the world—the place reeks of money. A Mercedes Benz taxi is standard. If one wants something better, a Rolls Royce is always available.

All of the Cunard excursions to the Miracle Garden were full, so we went on our own. We chose a taxi out of the line-up that was an SUV with space to haul Eleanor's little electric jitney. Noman, our driver, was from Pakistan. He spoke very little English, and of course, we didn't even know what his native language was, much less how to speak it.

It was a long drive through the city to the Miracle Garden out in the desert. The drive was pleasant, though, because it was so interesting. It was along a wide divided-lanes avenue, thankfully not an expressway where one sees virtually nothing. Our impressions were that everything was new, clean, and bright. The businesses, apartments, and homes were joined side by side with no space in between. That is good. I suspect that throughout history, not one blade of grass has sprouted here without being planted and watered. If it has ever rained here, there remains no evidence that it ever happened.

We arrived at the Miracle Garden at 10 am and spent the rest of the morning just being awed by the man-made beauty of a trillion flower blossoms and giant topiaries. You will not imagine the beauty. I'll share more about it later. I'll just say for now that the attractions in the 17-acre park included a giant Boeing 737 airplane, complete end to end and wingtip to wingtip, completely covered with flowers.

We then had Noman take us to the Mall of the Emirates, a shopping mall like none other. Get this! We didn't need to shop. We went there to see the ski slope that is built inside the mall. Ski Dubai is a real skiing facility with a slope, snow, chairlift, and all the gear that is needed for one to spend the day skiing. Do you want to ride a toboggan down the steep, crooked track? You can do that too.

WORLD CRUISE 2020 – EPISODE 9

Panegyric: A public speech or published text in praise of someone or something

We cruised overnight out of the Persian Gulf, around the bend through the Strait of Hormuz, and into the Gulf of Oman. Shortly after daybreak, we were moored to the dock at Muscat, Oman. The serried ranks of tour busses – there must have been 40 of them – were waiting for the hordes of pilgrims to start gushing from the gangways.

We were still overwhelmed by the city of Dubai, and I suspect we will remain so for the rest of our conscious years. A century ago, Dubai was a Bedouin community, probably with people living in tents. Now, it is a city almost the size of Los Angeles and still growing at an astounding rate. My panegyric of Dubai is entirely based on its man-made beauty. In natural beauty like that of the Ozarks, Cumberland, or Adirondacks, that is a different story.

There is nothing old in Dubai. There are no old buildings or old cars. Everything is sparkling clean. Even the cars are clean. We are told that if your car is dirty, they will arrest you. I suppose if there were a second offense, they would beat you. We have already learned that in Islamic countries, they don't like to lock criminals up and feed them. They would prefer to execute them or beat them half to death so that they will be good from now on. The practice of garroting has ridden these countries of career criminals. We should try it in the US.

Our driver, Noman, who took us to the Miracle Garden on Thursday, is from Pakistan, so naturally, he is a Muslim. As he drove us through the city, we noticed that there was a mosque with towering minarets at the end of almost every long block. We saw dozens of them, and they are, admittedly, all beautiful in architecture and form – not like Christian cathedrals but very appealing in a modest way. We know so little about the Islamic practices. We knew that the Muslims are called to prayer from the minarets five times a day. I asked Norman if he was driving his taxi and heard the call to prayer what would he do? He said if he didn't have a fare, he would go to the nearest mosque and pray. If he had a fare, he would pray later. Of course, here in Dubai, his fare would likely be another Muslim, in which case he and his fare(s) would go to the mosque and pray together. However, and this is important: only if his fare is male. Men and women do not pray together in a mosque.

Another characteristic of the Muslim faith is they donate heavily (it is required) to help the poor. In this area of oil-rich madness, I am wondering who and where are these poor people that they are donating for. Maybe a poor family has just one oil well.

It is interesting to see how people dress here. We see women wearing all black and men wearing all white. For men, it is a kind of dress that is an ankle-length collarless gown with long sleeves, called a dishdasha. I wouldn't dare let them know that I called it a dress. And then I saw one chauffeur driving a large Mercedes SUV, who could pass for all the world for a resurrected Yassar Arafat.

As we were walking through the parking garage at the Mall of the Emirates, we saw a rather large lady. I think she was large. Her burqa had to have been 10 square yards of black material that covered every inch of her body except an area around her eyes. She whirled by us and stepped into the driver's seat of a Porsche Cayenne. Somehow, that all just didn't fit in this old country boy's brain.

Our most vivid memory of Dubai will forever remain our visit to the Miracle Garden. Exploding with color, the world's most extensive garden boasts over 250 million plant varieties.

It was a beautiful morning when we reached Oman., as it seems they all are in this part of the world. We watched from our balcony as the QM2 snuggled up to the dock in Muscat, Oman, and deployed the mooring lines. Our view revealed not the city but some of the roughest, ruggedest mountains that one can imagine. The rocky Western Al Hajar Mountains dominate the landscape and crowd the city of Muscat to the water's edge. Surely, nothing grows here but rocks. We see many landscape flowers, but I suspect they are planted in artificial dirt. Our cabbie said last year was a good year. It rained four times.

I'll back up. Before we left the ship, I went to the Purser's office and asked if they had any local currency. The young lady informed me that they had none because, in Muscat, all the shops, taxis, etc., accept American money. That's convenient. In Dubai we had to use United Arab Emirates currency. The Purser lady failed to tell me, however, that the Omanis would not accept American currency dated 2008 and earlier. It turned out that half the cash that we took ashore could not be used.

We disembarked the ship at a few minutes before 10. Our first haggle-fest was with the taxi boss. He was a sort of broker. All deals go through him. We came to an agreement for a two-hour tour of the city, but Eleanor's little electric jitney wouldn't fit in the trunk of the car. That meant we had to use an SUV or a minivan. A minivan was summoned. Then, we were told that the price of the minivan was just about double what we had agreed on for the car. Unacceptable! Time to renegotiate or walk. Ahab, the Arab didn't want to lose the fare, so he decided that he would negotiate. I thought I was a pretty good negotiator, but Eleanor put me to shame. We soon had a new agreement. We put Eleanor's electric pony in the Hamood's minivan and were on our way.

Our first impressions of the city of Muscat showed us a gleaming white city. It is so new and white that it glitters. It is a beautiful city.

Like Dubai, everything is new. And it is immaculately clean. There was not a speck of dirt or trash to be seen. There seems to be nothing old. And as we learned, that included money.

Hamood was a pleasant fellow. He seemed proud that his nearly new Toyota had been made in America. We had some good discussions, even with the language barrier. I am sure he spoke Arabic fluently. But sadly, his English was lacking. Hamood has seven children and several grandchildren. Like virtually all Omani men, Hamood wears a snow-white dishdasha, those floor-length dress-like robes with sleeves that completely cover the arms. He could choose to wear a certain kind of cap or wrap his head with some kind of scarf. He chose the wrap. The Omani men apparently never let their hair show. I asked Hamood if his wife wore all black. He assured me that she does.

Hamood is a proud Arab and a proud Omani. He said that Omanis were the only ones allowed to drive taxis in Oman. That's different from Dubai. I suppose the Dubai residents are far too rich to stoop to driving cabs. They let the Pakistani immigrants do that.

Oman is a fascinating country with a stunning contrast of beaches, mountains, and deserts. It is one of the hidden treasures of the Middle East. Add over a thousand ancient forts, castles and watchtowers, lively souqs, and the Bedouin culture, and it is an unforgettable traditional Arabian experience.

Muscat, the capital of Oman, is a city of just over a million. I was hoping to feel welcome as I strolled in the city. It is hard to feel it when I am the only person in sight who is wearing britches. People were nice, though. I was not made to feel unwelcome. I just know that I looked out of place.

There's much history in this part of the world, most of it I don't identify with or understand. On our first visit to Oman, we learned that Oman supposedly contains the biblical Job's tomb. Well, they claim that anyway. They also claim to have the burial site of Nabi Imran, Mary's father. We're talking here about Mary, the mother of Jesus. And then some say old Nabi was the father of Moses, not

Mary. Anyway, his tomb is located in downtown Salalah, in the Dhofar Region, which we visited in 2008.

I will have more to write about our visit to Muscat. It was a good experience. The only conflict was back at the dock when it was time to settle up with Hamood and the Mafia-type Taxi Broker. That is when we learned that half of my cash is not legal tender in Oman. We hammered out an agreement, and in the end, I had only two dollars left that I could spend in Oman. I handed them to Hamood.

WORLD CRUISE 2020 – EPISODE 10

Prate: Chatter, to talk at great length with little or no meaning

It was February 3rd, 2020. We were 32 days into our GWV, and we were sailing away from the Islamic Middle East.

Religion is a big thing everywhere. As we continued east, we would be facing Buddhism and/or Hinduism, or Shintoism, or Daoism, or Confucianism, or whateverism. Even after visits in both India and China, I can still say I don't really know any of those religions or the differences between them.

Down through history, criticisms of one religion by another have been standard fare. Wars have been fought over religious beliefs, and it continues to this day. Bob Mumford, a noted Christian speaker whose presentations are reliably laced with profundity, said it so well. "You cannot accurately evaluate another person's belief, looking at it from the outside. You must get inside that belief or religion and learn it throughout in order to relate it to someone else without distorting it." We can all benefit from Mumford's profound words.

I cannot say enough about the people that we encountered in Dubai and Muscat. They are both representative of the Muslim world. I know that many in our country have the preconceived feeling that these people are somehow a bit suspect. Please reconsider. By comparison, I think our country produces hordes of disrespectful larrikins that some of these countries would probably execute – either that or lay on a severe attitude adjustment. We were treated with the utmost level of respect. The young people that we encountered on the streets and in the shops were clean-cut, polite, and respectful. It seems to be the Arabic way.

Other observations: No pierced, punctured, and tattooed faces like an NBA star. No obnoxiously loud cars, trucks or motorcycles. No thousand-watt speaker systems to rattle your car or house windows. No pants or shorts so loose and low that the wearer has to hold them up with one hand as he walks.

The cleanliness of the Arabian cities that we have visited gives me pause to question why their cities are so clean and our American cities are not. There is not a speck of graffiti anywhere. That is impressive, and I love it. So, what is the explanation for their cities being clean and graffiti-free? There is not a McDonald's wrapper, plastic bag, or uneaten French fry to be seen anywhere. Is it because these Arabs are better people? Or is it because of the severity of punishment under Muslim law? I have to suspect it is the latter. Young Abdul will think twice before picking up a spray can if he got beaten severely the first time that he did it. There is something to be said for sensible law enforcement and respect.

Another interesting thought: In two days of touring these cities, away from the port area, we did not see one police officer. It was equally true on the streets and sidewalks and the highways. They don't patrol the highways and write tickets. They control the traffic with excellent design and construction and with traffic roundabouts and well-marked speed bumps. The USA could learn much from what is successful in other countries.

We have lost our fun dinnertime tablemates. Fuad and Renee left the ship in Dubai to fly home. Norma didn't like eating dinner so early (6 pm), so she switched to late dining. Bobbie switched to another table to be with new friends. Elmer disappeared. He may have left the ship in Dubai.

We gained a new couple in Dubai. Bryan and Sheila are from Birmingham, England. With Sheila's soft voice and hard British accent, along with my hearing impairment, for two evenings, I spent most of the dinner hour offering only perfunctory nods to Sheila, not wanting to admit that I understood less than ten percent of whatever it was that she was telling me. I finally asked Eleanor to sit next to Sheila. Her ears worked better than mine. Monday, we gained one more tablemate. Hazel is from the Toronto area. Surely, she won't talk as incessantly every evening as she did that first evening. I don't think I have ever heard one person talk that much during one meal. We listened to her <u>prate</u> about everything from her enrollment in a flower arranging seminar to how bright her eldest granddaughter is. Hazel is 77 years old and has been widowed seven years, as she related to us at least a half-dozen times. Blatherskite! She is probably a nice lady.

WORLD CRUISE 2020 – EPISODE 11

Congeries: a disorderly collection, a jumble, a hodgepodge.

On the world map, Sri Lanka looks like India's detached garage. It is a teardrop-shaped island hanging just off the southern tip of India. It has been called "India's Teardrop." It is also called the "Pearl of the Indian Ocean."

The cityscape looks like southern India; the people look like Indians, their dress is the same, and their religion is the same.

If I can find one word to describe Colombo, Sri Lanka, I would choose "mystique." And I suspect that word could be applied to the whole country of Sri Lanka. The foggy haze that hangs over the city just adds to the effect.

Ever since the Silk Road days, Colombo has acted as the entrepot for the whole island, which was known as Ceylon until recent years.

We docked in the Colombo Harbor at 8 am, and I went ashore at 9 am. We have gotten so many time zones east now that it is confusing. We are 170 degrees of longitude from Texas – 190 degrees if you go in the other direction - so when it is 9 A.M. in Sri Lanka, it is something like a week before last in Fort Worth.

The shuttle took me out of the port and deposited me into a

flock of what we have called mosquitos in the past. They aren't actual insects. They are worse. They are cab drivers and hawkers of tours. They surround the tourists like a thick swarm of mosquitos. It is hard to even walk through the swarm. Most of them were hawking tours by Tuk Tuks, the favored vehicle in Colombo. I chose Tharindu out of the group and engaged him for a two-hour tour of the city.

My initial impression of the city was that it is just another Indian city, and it certainly bears some of the trademarks of some Indian cities that we have visited. A difference, though, is that I didn't see the abject poverty that is evidenced in Chennai and Mumbai. This is a pleasant surprise because a travel show presented here on the ship described Colombo as "one big slum." It is that, but India is worse.

It is slummy-looking. It is tropical. It is hot, sweaty, and grimy the year around. It is not overstated to say that Colombo is not a pretty city. The picture that stands out for me is the industriousness of the city. The port where we docked is busy as a hive of bees. It has long been a shipping interchange on what became known as the Maritime Silk Road.

This island provides tea for the entire world, and it is all shipped right out of this port. Even in the city, there is an industriousness. Everybody is actively involved in some form of service or commerce. No one is sitting around. Are there homeless people like we see in Austin, Los Angeles, or a hundred other American cities? Maybe, but I didn't see any.

Who could possibly sort out the <u>congeries</u> of people in this city? It has been a crossroads of the world's trade routes for thousands of years. Although Buddhism is the predominant religion, the area has previously been ruled by the Anglican British, the Catholic Portuguese, and the Muslim Moors.

Tharindu wheeled the little Tuk Tuk through horrendous traffic to the attractions of the city, with particular emphasis on the Buddhist temples. I didn't even want to go, but everything about a Buddhist temple is so beautiful to a devoted adherent. Tharindu wanted to show me that beauty. So, I took my shoes and hat off and followed him past shrines and relics until my socks were filthy and my feet sore. Tharindu was happy to show me all this stuff that he thought was so beautiful. I smiled and told him that I thought it was beautiful, too.

We had feared that this visit was never going to happen. Five years ago, there was a big terrorist attack in Colombo. On Easter Sunday, April 21st, 2019, a coordinated series of terroristic suicide bombings targeted three churches and three luxury hotels. We were afraid Cunard would cancel our visit to Colombo. Anyway, 259 people were killed that day, mostly Christians. The suicide bombers, naturally, were identified as "Islamic State Fighters." It is a forever mystery why extremists will go into a foreign country just to kill Christians who have done nothing to them.

WORLD CRUISE 2020 – EPISODE 12

**Discommode: To cause inconvenience
to disturb, trouble, or bother.**

On February 7th, we cruised eastward, placidly crossing the Bay of Bengal. The "Fresh Breeze" slips through the haze without enough friction to raise a serious wave on the surface of the water. The ship was so steady that I think if we had a billiards table, we could have hosted a pool tournament, and the pool balls would roll as true as if we were in a parlor in Cincinnati.

Saturday, the 8th, like Pearl Harbor Day, stands in infamy in our consciences. It was a shocker! I awoke and turned on our stateroom television. The navigation channel shows our route, what port we came from, the port we are headed to, and a progress line showing where we are. The progress line showed that during the night, our ship doubled back for a couple of hours, drifted a bit, and then started forward again very slowly. What could this possibly mean?

It was nearly noon before the captain's voice came on our stateroom speakers, and he explained. A "coronavirus" had broken out in China and was spreading around the world, threatening to turn into a pandemic. Countries were closing their ports to foreign vessels.

We were due to dock in Phuket, Thailand, in two more days. What about that? Thailand's health minister lashed out at "Western Tourists" - That would be us - for not wearing face masks and suggested that such tourists be expelled from the country for "putting others at risk during the coronavirus outbreak." Then, they closed their port.

We would have significant adjustments to our itinerary due to the coronavirus. We would have to skip Thailand, Korea, Hong Kong, Vietnam, Namibia, South Africa, and a couple of islands in the Indian Ocean.

The cancellation of our intended visit to Hong Kong was not of significant consequence, that is, to Eleanor and me. Not so problem-free, however, for some other folks. We have visited Hong Kong previously and would much rather skip it than take a chance of the coronavirus coming among us on our ship. However, some of our friends are terribly <u>discommoded</u> by the change. They had planned to disembark the ship in Hong Kong and had arranged air travel from there to their homes, some in Germany, some in Australia, and who knows how many others to how many other countries. So, they have had to cancel all of those reservations and devise and schedule new plans from Singapore. We can only hope that they won't be adversely affected by any further changes. It could happen. And it did. Singapore closed its ports, too. Then, the people had to reschedule flights again.

The fallout from the coronavirus has impacted the QM2 and its itinerary, not the disease itself, but the fallout. February 9th was the date when we were scheduled to visit Phuket, Thailand. That is what was on the brochure for the cruise more than a year ago, so we looked forward to the visit. We had never visited Thailand before. However, this insidious disease, coronavirus, apparently came out of some pigpen way back in central China, so we were told, and it was now threatening the world. We were as clean as the driven snow on this ship, and Cunard intended to keep it that way. So, instead of going to Thailand, where someone might pick a germ, we spent the day treading water in the Andaman Sea, not knowing where we were going to wind up. If you want to check the location on the globe, we were south of Myanmar (Burma) and between the Malay Peninsula and the Andaman and Nicobar Islands.

We were told that we would also skip visits in two ports in Malaysia. We were not complaining about Cunard's decision. It is better to be safe than sorry. If the virus should spread through this ship, we could be quarantined until next summer.

You've heard it said many times and likely have used the expression yourself: "As a crow flies." But wait! The expression has a history. In the early sailing days, ship captains would take caged crows aboard before sailing out into unknown waters. After they had sailed for several days and possibly seen shorebirds in the air, they suspected they were near land. They would take a crow to the "Crow's Nest," the highest perch on the ship. There, they would release the crow, knowing that, by instinct, the crow would fly toward the nearest land. Then, they would alter their course and set out for land "as the crow flies."

WORLD CRUISE 2020 – EPISODE 13

Vexation: The state of being annoyed, frustrated, or worried.

On Monday, the 10th, we finally got some new directions. We were told that we would sail due south all the way to Australia. Australia was clean, and we were also. That would be the only place that we could land and go ashore. But here's the problem! We didn't have enough fuel to get there.

Captain Aseem Hashmi announced that we would sail south to Port Kelang, Malaysia, and hopefully take on fuel and stores there.

We made it to Port Kelang on Tuesday, February 11th, but that's less than half the story. We could not go ashore, and no one from Port Kelang could come aboard. The only people going ashore were those who completed their contracted tours at earlier cities but were not allowed to go ashore in those ports. At Port Kelang, they could get transportation to Kuala Lumpur – two cities that they likely had never heard of and certainly didn't expect to go there – and from there, they would fly back to their countries if – and here's the kicker – if they are allowed into their home countries. There were so many unknowns. Due to the coronavirus, some countries have closed their seaports and their airports.

Importantly for us, we were apparently running short of "stores," being, I suppose, things like chicken eggs, olives for martinis, and toilet tissue.

More importantly, we must have fuel. This bigger-than-a-battleship ocean liner burns a lot of fuel. And, believe me, they don't buy it by the gallon. The main fuel tanks hold 4,381 metric tons of heavy diesel. That is nearly 5,000 regular tons. It requires a tanker (ship or fuel barge) to come alongside and pump for several hours to top off our tanks. We would need to be full, too, since we would be running for a whole week to make Fremantle, Australia, on the 18th.

We paced the deck all morning, anxious to hear some positive report. After lunchtime, the fuel tanker still had not shown up. We can hear the <u>vexation</u> in Captain Hashmi's voice. The folks down in this part of the world remember that they were a British Protectorate until World War II came along. The British pulled out and left the locals unprotected. The Japanese came and literally slaughtered tens of thousands of men, women, and children. They depopulated towns and small cities. The Malaysians have hated the British and the Japanese ever since. Keep in mind that this is a very British ship. We may be lucky to get enough fuel to get to the next gas station.

Eleanor and I counted our blessings. We had just said goodbye to some folks who had become friends over the previous month. We wondered what happened to them. We learned later how Cunard went to extreme lengths to take care of their customers, those who were adversely affected by the changes made because of the virus.

You've heard it said many times, "over a barrel." Like, they had him over a barrel. But wait! The expression has a history. In the early sailing days, often a mariner tending a sail, repairing a halyard, or whatever would fall into the drink. It was a dangerous trade, and many sailors were lost at sea. However, when one falls into the sea and they drag him out, they try their best to resuscitate him. Remember, this was long before EMS, mouth-to-mouth, and chest pumps. Their method was to place the distressed victim on his belly on a barrel and roll it back and forth. The motion could cause him to expel water from his lungs and regain consciousness. Thus, the expression that they had him "over a barrel." I think our captain was feeling a bit over a barrel.

WORLD CRUISE 2020 – EPISODE 14

Phlegmatic: Having an unemotional and stolidly calm disposition

With all the news about coronavirus and the consequential changes they wreaked upon our well-thought-out itinerary, the conversations on the ship had become all of a general theme: Where are we going, and how will it end? Will we be marooned on the ship or on an island? How are we getting home?

"What do you think about all of the changes?" A lady asked me earlier.

I simply replied, "I am fine with it." I added, "I think it was a good decision. Cunard wants to keep us safe." I typically answer in that manner because, to be frank, I hate a bitcher. It is just as easy to provide a positive response.

To be sure, if my feelings are known, I am not as <u>phlegmatic</u> about cruising and travel as I might seem. And I was a little put out, myself, about what we would miss.

The beauty of any country is, more than anything else, its people. It is not the high Alps of Switzerland or the beaches of St. Moritz. It is the people. We don't see the noble, beautiful faces of a place like Sri Lanka, and the people, and the way they robe themselves in the dazzling Indian colors when we go to see a giant mosque or a Buddhist temple and have to shoo European and Japanese tourists out of the way to get a good picture.

No, the place to see the beauty is to get among the local people, the canaille, soak up the environment, witness the cultures, breathe the air, stroll the market where they shop, have a drink where they drink, and think about the histories of those peoples, which are so unlike the histories and background of yourself and your kin. That is what I intended to do in Malaysia and Indonesia, in particular, because their history, their lives, and culture are so different from our own.

So, what is left for me? Well, coming up is Australia. They speak the same language that I do (although they murder it in some beautiful way), they wear the same kind of clothes that I do, and go to the same kind of churches. No, I have missed my chance. I will make the best of it.

We have good friends in Australia – great people, a real fun-loving lot. We met them in the British Isles a few years ago. We are glad we are going to visit their island continent. We'll give a nod to Ken and Sandra Mahoney and Carol and King Alan Pailthorpe when we sail by.

Captain Hashmi, always thoughtful and perceptive, offered a general apology to us, who had paid for that service. He announced that since we could not make port in Hong Kong and buy flowers, we would not have the flowers needed to make the bouquets that should decorate the ship for Valentine's Day. It was a precursor of things to come.

We pulled into the harbor at Port Kelang, Malaysia, in the predawn darkness. Some of our fellow cruisers, the segment cruisers – those who only booked segments of the world cruise – were disembarked in Port Kelang. These passengers are those who were scheduled to be disembarked in Hong Kong and Singapore.

We waited, doing nothing, all morning and half the afternoon before the tanker finally showed up to fill our fuel tanks. He got started refueling us at 3 P.M. and continued until he ran out of fuel. We still needed another 1,700 tons of fuel to get us to Australia.

We motored out into the Strait of Malacca and dropped anchor to wait for another bunker. That's what small refueling tankers are called. That bunker would come from Singapore and would arrive after midnight. Actually, it was mid-morning before the tanker could get moored alongside to hook up the hoses and start fueling. It took until 3 A.M. the following morning to have us topped off. This is the first time that I recall ever being refueled while anchored in open waters. So, this delay gives us a late start on our already crippled revised schedule.

We ordered tacos for dinner and then learned that there were no more taco shells on the ship.

WORLD CRUISE 2020 – EPISODE 15

Acclaim: Praise enthusiastically and publicly

We spent Valentine's Day cruising through the Strait of Singapore and southward among the islands of Malaysia and Indonesia, south of the island of Borneo.

We were halfway around the world from our Texas home, 14 time zones to be exact. We crossed the Equator and suddenly passed from winter into summer.

As we travel around the world and visit so many countries, races, climates, cultures, etc., it causes us to look back at our home country from a somewhat more objective viewpoint. We are, and will remain, loyal Americans. However, our view of our homeland is different from what it has been in the past. It is hard to put it into perspective.

We have always been told that the United States is the greatest country in the world. And we are proud to continue to <u>acclaim</u> it. However, we have some struggles. We are told that the American worker is the best in the world. But we wonder. Assuming that is so, why can we not use American-made products to rebuild and improve our nation's infrastructure? We buy our appliances and electronics from China with money that we borrow from China.

We are supporting more people in prisons and on welfare than any other country. Our large cities are plagued with increasing homeless populations, with people sleeping on sidewalks and under overpasses and the resultant litter that accumulates in and near the homeless encampments. Fortunately, many of those problems are limited to the large population centers.

We are enjoying this beautiful ocean liner. It was built in France. Holland American's cruise ships, like Royal Caribbean's, are built in Italy and Finland. These are not third-world countries. There are thousands of cruise ships around the world, but we haven't built any of them. We don't operate them either.

As we cruised the Strait of Singapore, I walked around the Promenade Deck, and within view, I could see at least 40 ships. The captain later announced that we could see a hundred. In fact, some 2,000 merchant ships traverse this strait on a daily basis. I just pondered the likelihood that not one of them was built in America or owned by Americans. There is a great big, prosperous industry on this globe but the United States is not participating in that prosperity. Wouldn't it be wonderful if America could be made great again?

Had it not been for the coronavirus and the fact that we were running from it as fast as this big ship can go, we would be visiting Phu My, Vietnam, today; by the way, what we have been calling coronavirus now has a real name. The World Health Organization has assigned it the name CONVID-19. They have a new policy for naming outbreaks. They will avoid using a country or animal in the name of a virus. I wonder, did we hurt the feelings of folks living west of the big river by naming the "West Nile Virus?" Did pigs around the world get upset a few years ago when everyone was talking about the "Swine Flu?" Did chickens get mad and quit laying eggs over the "Bird Flu." Political correctness seems to have no limits. I'll wager that if I called an ant a pissant, a politically correct "Progressive" would take me to task about it. The pissant, however, would not likely show much concern.

Days at sea give me time to read and think, possibly too much. I like the way my favorite author, Mark Twain, finds the perfect words to describe what he sees. He told of an instance when he saw a dog of a type that he had never seen before. It is a particular breed of dog that he described as being a dog and a half long and only a half a dog high.

Twain writes of his concern about the dog that he saw. He worries that it is of a poor design, and structurally weak on account of the distance between the forward supports and those abaft. He is concerned that the "dog's back is likely to sag, and it seems that it would have been a stronger and more practicable design if it had had some more legs."

It reminded me of the time when I was building underwater structures in the Mississippi River and living in a mobile home park in Dumas, Arkansas. There was a neighborhood dog that everyone loved. We didn't know if any one person owned her or if she was simply everybody's dog. The loving, aging Bassett came and went as she pleased, and she reliably posted a new set of puppies every season, and everybody loved them. The lovely canine lady had done it so many times and over so many years that the baggy orifices from which she fed her babies had begun to drag the ground in their midrange. Her name was Marilyn.

WORLD CRUISE 2020 – EPISODE 16

Trumpery: Attractive articles of little value or use.

February 17th found us plowing south in the Indian Ocean in a violent storm. The wind was Force F7 on the Beaufort Scale, almost dead onto our bow. The hatches were battened, and the lounge chairs were lashed to the rails. I needed the exercise. I tried one lap around the outer promenade and was buffeted from bulkhead to rail. That was enough to convince me to stay inside for the rest of the day.

It was Day 46 of our cruise and I was starting to feel like a real mariner, an "Old Salt."

In the early days of merchant sailing, a captain was hesitant to grant shore leave to his crew, especially in the home port. He was afraid he would lose his crew. He was willing, however, to let his sailors' wives come aboard to visit their husbands. They were allowed to reconnoiter and socialize on the gun deck. It seems, though, that not all of the "ladies" visiting were wives. There were girlfriends, fun-seekers, and, it is suspected, even entrepreneurs. (Perish the thought)

Occasionally, one of those "ladies" wound up pregnant. She didn't know exactly which of the sailors was to be pegged as the father. The only thing for sure was that the child was conceived on the gun deck, so the child became known as a son of the gun deck, shortened to "son-of-a-gun." At least, that's the way they tell it in the maritime world.

We reached our destination, Fremantle, Australia, in the predawn hours of February 18th. Emotions ran the gamut from exhilaration for being in port to trepidation about what will happen next.

We lost some 800 of our fellow cruisers that day. These were the folks who were supposed to end their cruise segments in ports that we had bypassed. I had already said goodbye to my newfound friend, Knut. He was headed for his home in Berlin. We hugged Brian and Sheila the previous evening. They would fly to Singapore and then to their home in England. Maybe Hazel would leave, too. I could encourage it. If she's not from England, she should be. I had wearied of hearing her incessant bitching about not going to Thailand, among other subjects.

The fact that we were scheduled to visit Hong Kong on this day brings to mind earlier visits to China. I particularly remember a whirlwind trip that we made to the mainland several years earlier.

That was in the late fall of 2009. It was one of these Chamber of Commerce subsidized tours that Communist countries like to do. They are part of the so-called "Cultural Exchange Program." They welcome you with big smiles, take you to the places that they want you to see, and make freaking sure you don't see anything that you are not supposed to see. Their modus operandi is obviously to keep you so busy and tired that you won't have the energy to go snooping or misbehave otherwise. We didn't buy one piece of knock-off trumpery that China is known for. They ran us to death, seeing everything from the Ming, Ding, Ying Yang, and whatever other dynasties. Of course, they included the Great Wall, Forbidden City, Tiananmen Square, etc.

And then they boast of the good things they are doing for their loyal citizens. They dragged us through Beijing, Hangzhou, Suzhou, and Shanghai before turning us loose to go home. In Shanghai, we finally had some free time in a shopping center. By that time, we were too tired to shop, so we sought a place to sit down.

We were a spectacle, two pale-faced Americans in a place where such as we were seldom seen. There were three teenage girls who were bold enough, but hesitatingly so, to approach us and ask if they could have their pictures made with us. Of course, the communication was all by sign language and gestures since they only spoke in some unknown tongue and had no knowledge of Texas English. They were a pleasure.

Since we were in Fremantle a full two weeks ahead of schedule, we were blessed with two days before we would cast off again to who-knew-where.

We had to visit Fremantle to replenish fuel. We had cruised over a thousand miles, maybe two thousand, since Sri Lanka. During those several days, we burned a lot of diesel fuel and ate a lot of bacon, eggs, chateaubriand, and seafood – especially seafood.

Australia has some convoluted methods in dealing with tourists' passports, something like we had not seen since India a few years ago. Every person on the ship, nearly 4,000 of us, had to go ashore and meet, passport in hand, face to face with immigration authorities to somehow prove to them that we were not stowaway terrorists. No one could come back on board until everyone was off the ship. This stupefying "Chinese fire drill" used up the entire morning.

When we finally got ashore in Fremantle. We hired a taxi to get us out of the port and into a shopping area. We needed a grocery store to pick up a couple of toiletry items. Mustafa, our cabbie, was from Kazakhstan. (My goodness, am I back in New York?) Mustafa waited for us to shop and then drove us to the big Farmer's Market at the corner of Henderson and South Terrace. There are 150 markets, all housed inside a Heritage-Listed Victorian building where produce is protected from the harsh sun of Western Australia. Markets are an excellent place to mix with the local folks. We see how they talk, dress, and how they shop for produce.

We bought some tropical flowers for our stateroom, then summoned a cab to take us back to the port. The cabbie turned out to be a lanky Indian in a bright orange turban. He didn't speak English, but his license said his name was Jugraj Singh. I suspect folks named Singh in India would outnumber all the Smiths, Joneses, and Davises combined in the United States. Like Mustafa, he did a good job.

World Cruise 2020 – Episode 17

**Marooned: To leave (someone)
trapped and isolated in an inaccessible
place, especially an island.**

February 20th and Day 49 of our odyssey found us fully fueled up and surfeited with provisions for a two-day cruise to Darwin on the north shore of the island continent. Whatever was to happen after Darwin was yet to be determined.

The previous day, I enjoyed watching as truckloads of "stores" rolled onto the dock and the workmen loaded skidloads of all sorts of provisions into the belly of the big ship.

Hoses pumped wastewater from the ship into large tank trucks on the dock while on the other side of the ship, a tanker was pumping fuel into our tanks. I am fascinated at how much intelligent thought is required to make all of these things happen efficiently. Wouldn't you love to see the grocery list that is sent ahead to have these skidloads of broccoli, lamb, squid, cottage cheese, bacon and eggs, and hundreds of other foodstuffs and paper products sitting in containers when we pull into port.?

Maritime idioms and anecdotes: Origin of the word "marooned."

Nefarious 17th-century pirates, privateers, and buccaneers

---

highjacked all sorts of ships and took captive various sailors and slaves. Early slaves in the transatlantic slave traffic were tribespeople from Cameroon, Africa. When a pirate ship wound up with an excessive number of slaves, they simply set the Cameroons ashore on the remote West Indies islands. They shortened the name from Cameroon to Maroon, and the freed but abandoned Africans became known as Maroons, or marooned Africans. They settled in the hills and mountains of several Caribbean islands. Marooned, as a word, eventually came to mean simply "lost in the wilds," but this is how it started.

On the second day out of Fremantle, I hit the outer deck early to get some laps in before it got too hot. The northern coast of Australia gets mighty hot in midsummer. That's where we were told that the ducks lay fried eggs in February.

Deck hands were unlashing the lounge chairs from the railings as we got away from the storms of the Indian Ocean.

On the afterdeck, the few smokers are clawing their way out through the big doors with their eyes half-open. They have to have that first smoke. There are not many smokers on this ship. Smokers are a diminishing population for more reasons than one.

Maritime idioms and anecdotes: Origin of the term "Loose Cannon."

Back in the days of sailing battleships, there was no hazard to the ship and safety of the crew greater than for a cannon to break loose from its lashing. The security of these wheel-mounted cannons was paramount. On stormy seas, the heavy cannons always tested their lashing. If one came loose during a storm, it could be disastrous. The shout, "Loose cannon on the gundeck," was the feared announcement. Men could not corral it as it rolled back and forth on the pitching deck. There have been cases where the loose cannon actually destroyed the wooden hull and sunk the ship. Loose cannon eventually came to be applied to persons who were "out of control." We have known of some folks like that. They hold prominent positions in government.

We finally started seeing some flying fish. I had been searching the waves for them for 50 days and had about given up. We are told that the flying fish populations have been depleted because Japanese netters have been harvesting them for sushi. I've about had it. I can't help it. First, Pearl Harbor, and now sushi.

The lounge lizards come out to the afterdeck and lie in the tropical sun for hours, just inviting melanoma. They lie on one side until they have a surface adequately broiled, then they wake up, turn over, and fry the other side. Believe me, folks. Skin cancer will respond to the invitation. I don't tempt it anymore. I am now on my dermatologist's six-month rotation.

Maritime idioms and anecdotes: Origin of the term "Taken aback."

Taken aback is used to describe someone who has received surprising or unexpected news, perhaps leaving him speechless or unable to respond. That is one use.

Sailing ships relied upon wind force and direction if they wished to make progress across the water. If either of these natural phenomena were to suddenly change, particularly the latter, it could cause the sails to fill in the opposite direction. This could cause unintended strain on the rigging, and it has been known to break a mast. At best, it would stop the forward progress of the ship and cause it to sail backward. And that is how we got the term "taken aback."

On Monday, February 24th, we reached the port in Darwin.

This little city on the north coast of the island continent has had a hard time. On February 19th, 1942, in two separate waves, 242 Japanese aircraft bombed the town to rubble. Nearly a thousand people were killed in the attacks. There were reports of barges loaded with bodies pulled out to sea, and the bodies pushed into the drink. More than half the population of Darwin left the town permanently during and immediately after the air raids. The bombing of Darwin was the first of over a hundred bombing raids on Australia during the war. Thousands of innocent Australians were killed by Japanese bombs.

Shortly after our 2020 cruise, the California Assembly in

Sacramento officially apologized to Japanese Americans for cooperating with the U.S. Government in sending them to internment camps during the war. The tone of the apology paints the U.S. Government as the bad guy and the Japanese as the victims. Maybe that is somewhat appropriate. We were at war. Our government did what it felt was best at the time. And in doing so, our country won the war that we didn't start, and for that, we are forever thankful.

I wonder if Japan has apologized to Australia for killing thousands of innocent Australians. And even if so, is an apology enough?

On our second day in Darwin, I signed up for a guided excursion to see the jumping crocodiles in the Adelaide River. It could have been similar to an alligator-feeding excursion that I took in South Louisiana several years earlier. No comparison! In Louisiana, they let us feed the jumping alligators. It was a barrel of fun. On this Australian river, our boat guide was a female John Wayne type with a Captain Bligh attitude. We sat where she told us to sit, and we listened to 45 minutes of her blatherskite. I was eager to get back to the ship.

I was also eager, and more than a bit anxious, to find out what we were to expect in the next few weeks. Do we go home? Can we go home? We didn't know.

WORLD CRUISE 2020 – EPISODE 18

Lazing: Pass the time in a relaxed, lazy way

Our second day in Darwin was unmemorable. My diary reminds me that a turban-topped Indian cabbie named Hopi gave us a tour of a botanical garden and then returned us to the port. It seems that we have seen more Indians than Australians on this island continent.

It took four days of cruising to reach our next port. It is a long way around "Straya." It took a full day to sail out of the Timor Sea and another two days of sailing eastward in the Arafura Sea. During the night of the third day, we treaded the shallow strait between New Guinea and the Cape York Peninsula, the northernmost part of Queensland, and headed south in the Coral Sea.

On Friday, we spent the entire day cruising very slowly above the Great Barrier Reef in order to avoid any damage to the coral. The water beneath us was the color of a polished Brazilian emerald.

On Saturday morning, February 29th (Leap Day), we anchored two miles off the shore at Yorkeys Knob. I can only imagine the number of jokes about a place with such a name. I wouldn't dare write one of them in my journal. Two miles was as close as we could get. The water in this area, as in almost the whole Great Barrier Reef, is too shallow for an ocean liner such as the QM2.

The tour of Yorkeys Knob, Cairns, and the area in between, reflects scenes characteristic of the banana plantations of Costa Rica, the sugar cane plantations of Cuba, the flora of Key West, and the seaside sprawl of Jensen Beach, Florida. Much of it was like residential Fort Lauderdale but without the canals. The backdrop was a range of mountains that crowds the western edge of the settlement. This adds to the picturesque presentation. It was peaceful and beautiful.

Cairns is not pronounced in any way that would make sense to any old country boy from, say, Arkadelphia or Lampasas. The pronunciation is given as "Kehrnz." Try saying that.

The region reflects retirement leisure. Our guide said a family could sell their home in Sydney for a million dollars, buy one here for half a million, and live on the rest. Sounds good to me.

It was hot in town. After touring the two downtowns, (Yorkeys Knob and Cairns) residential areas, the beach, and the botanic gardens, I had them drop me in downtown Cairns to do a little shopping and pick up a couple of bottles of Clare Valley Chardonnay. Lazing on the outer deck with a good glass of chilled chardonnay was a good way to contemplate what might happen next to our recently-become abortive world cruise.

Maritime idioms and anecdotes: Origin of the term "A clean bill of health."

During the 17th and 18th centuries, there was a constant fear of "plague," such as the "Black Plague" that depopulated much of Europe. This was long before cures had been found to combat these contagious diseases. Often, merchant ships sailing from port to port inadvertently enabled diseases to spread from one city to another and from one country to another. For this reason, cities would refuse to let a ship land in its port unless it had been declared clear of disease by the port from which it had sailed. It had to carry with it a document known as a "Bill of Health." Further, the ship, as it was approaching port, was required to fly a yellow flag indicating that it had a "Clean Bill of Health." That traditional requirement exists today. The QM2 always displays the yellow flag as it approaches a port, indicating that it has a Clean Bill of Health.

We cruised overnight to another coastal town, Arlie Beach, and again anchored nearly two miles offshore. Arlie Beach didn't have much to offer. But as sailors have always said, "Any old port in a storm." Our storm wasn't weather-related; rather, it was an insidious coronavirus and it had scrambled our itinerary.

Arlie Beach is the jumping-off place for the hordes of people who come here from all over the world to snorkel the Great Barrier Reef. It is also the gateway to Queensland's pristine Whitsunday Islands. James Cook named the islands in 1770 as he believed he passed through the area on the Christian holiday of Whit Sunday. (Pentecost Sunday)

We spent half the morning watching, directly below our balcony, the various excursion boats and tenders loading hundreds of eager tourists, most of them headed for snorkeling adventures on the Great Barrier Reef or at the Whitsunday Islands.

It was noon by the time I reached shore on the tender boat. There is not just a whale of a lot to see in a town of 1,208 people. Airlie Beach boasts a lagoon, a walkway, a reef, and a marina. I shouldn't be critical. The town where I was born, Pocahontas, in Arkansas, is larger than Airlie Beach. But I just can't seem to recall the last time any cruise ship stopped by there.

Cruising in the southern hemisphere will screw with a person's head. We know that down here, their major storms are called cyclones, and they don't rotate correctly. Good old hurricanes rotate counterclockwise. The same kind of tropical storms down under rotate clockwise. We are told that water running down a gurgler (as they call a drain down here) forms a vortex that spins the opposite of what it does in your toilet bowl back at home. An issue about where the sun comes up, passes overhead and goes down where it does starts to play on your brain.

Everybody back in God's country (our USA) knows that if you want your flowers and shrubs to get plenty of sunshine and be protected from cold north winds, you should plant them on the south side of your house. We know that the cold fronts come from the North. No "blue norther" ever came from the South.

Here in the Southern Hemisphere, the cold fronts come from the direction of Antarctica, the south. The north side of homes is the warm side and the south side is exposed to the cold fronts. It is true even on this ship. As we cruise eastward (or when we cruise eastward), the north side of the ship is exposed to direct sunlight. Lounge Lizards who have not yet gotten their skin dark enough to pass for a whole different ethnicity flock to the sunny deck on the north side of the ship because the south deck is totally shaded. Think about that when you transplant your tropical plants in your yard. You would do it differently if you lived in Sydney.

WORLD CRUISE 2020 – EPISODE 19

Untrammeled: Not deprived of freedom of action or expression; not restricted or hampered.

On Tuesday, March 3rd, we made port in the dazzling city of Brisbane. Brisbane is big, about the size of Chicago, and is equally modern in appearance.

We had cruised one day and two nights southward from Airlie Beach, Australia. We were "down under," as they say. Now, we were getting "way down under." We were almost to the Tropic of Capricorn – still tropical but just barely. I am reminded that hot temperatures occur far from the tropics. I have cooked in sweltering heat driving across Kansas in the old pre-air-conditioned days when it was 108 degrees. I also remember working in the building trades in Las Vegas when the mercury reached 114. I chuckle when I hear these Brits complaining about 85 degrees. We were soon to find out what kind of midsummer temperatures Australia would lay upon us.

Queensland is big. There are only six territories on the continent, so they are all big. Hardly anyone lives in Queensland except in the cities along the coast. Think about this for perspective. Queensland is three times as big as Texas, but there are more people in Houston than in the whole state of Queensland.

We were given the full day to explore Brisbane at our own leisure, completely <u>untrammeled</u> by excursions, tour leaders, or deadlines. We hired another turban-headed Indian cabbie to take us to the Lone Pine Koala Sanctuary. The sanctuary contained some 140 bundles of cuteness for us to see. Koalas sleep 18 – 20 hours a day so they hardly noticed that we were there. The sanctuary had as many kangaroos. We bought little sacks of food for the kangaroos, and they ate the food from our hands. Most of them were lying down in the sweltering heat and were too lazy to stand up for the food that we offered. I knew how they felt. I was inclined toward joining them.

One day south of Brisbane was Sydney. We arrived there early on March 5th. It was Day 63 of our cruise.

Morale had deteriorated amongst the guests. There were a lot of angry folks on the ship. Don't get me wrong, they were pleasant to one another as well as to my wife and me. They were angry at Cunard. That is a little funny because Cunard is the cruise line that they love. Here's the story.

We had hundreds, maybe a thousand, folks who had purchased segments of the World Voyage rather than the whole voyage. Those early segment folks were supposed to leave the cruise in Hong Kong, and an equal number of new folks were supposed to come aboard to fill the rooms. That didn't happen. We didn't go to Hong Kong for people to board, so those cruise purchases were canceled. We skipped all the way down to Fremantle, Australia, where those hordes of people left the ship to go home. That left hundreds of rooms vacant after Fremantle.

To avoid cruising with empty staterooms, Cunard ran a promotion offering those rooms at unheard-of prices in Australia. It worked. Aussies filled the rooms for a segment from Fremantle to Sydney. Here's the rub. The 1,100 world cruise folks, including my wife and me, had paid big bucks for our time aboard. And now several hundred Aussies are cruising with us for mere peanuts. The unfairness was obvious. We missed visiting eight ports and several countries, including Thailand, Malaysia, Indonesia, Hong Kong, and Singapore. Of course, it was not Cunard's fault, nor was it ours. We were happy to be safe from the coronavirus.

On our first day in Sydney, we had to anchor in the harbor and tender to the dock if we wanted to go. And we didn't. We had no excursions planned, and it was pouring rain. We were an unscheduled ship, and there was no room at the dock. During the night, dock space was made, and we moved to shore. That made going ashore easier, but it was still raining. After lunch, the rain had appeared to let up so I headed for the gangway. I had to go ashore at least for a bit in order to have something to write about. We had spent two days in Sydney on another world cruise a few years earlier.

About the time I emerged from the port into the downtown of the city, the deluge returned with a vengeance. I had my good duck brolly that I got at the Peabody Hotel in Memphis about 15 years earlier. It gave me good protection for my upper body, but the blowing cloudburst thoroughly soaked me from the knees down.

We said goodbye to our Aussie tablemates in Sydney. Both couples lived in Sydney but had never met until this cruise, where we all shared the same dinner table. The onboard population was thinning.

On Saturday morning, we bade farewell to the iconic Sydney Opera House and the Harbor Bridge, cruised out of the harbor, and headed south in the Tasman Sea.

It was not "smooth sailing." I looked out just after daybreak, and the view that greeted me reminded me of my working days out on Alaska's Bering Sea. But we are on the Tasman Sea, 36 degrees of latitude south of the equator. It was 68 degrees, raining, and the wind was blowing at Force 7 – "Near Gale.". I went to the 7th deck and opened a door to the promenade. The wind nearly sucked me through the doorway. I decided to stay inside.

The Tasman Sea is referred to in Australasian English as "the Ditch;" for example, 'crossing the Ditch means traveling to Australia from New Zealand, or vice versa. The diminutive term "the ditch" used for the Tasman Sea is comparable to referring to the North Atlantic Ocean as "the Pond."

We were losing interest in Australia. We had been there longer than planned and were concerned about what was to happen next. The big "unknown" was hanging heavily on our shoulders.

WORLD CRUISE 2020 – EPISODE 20

Cortège: A person's entourage or retinue

Oddly as it seems, after so many changes to our schedule and the continuing unknowns, we learned that we would visit Melbourne on the exact day that our original itinerary indicated.

It is Cunard's policy to schedule and produce a top-notch gala affair on each world cruise. It is not for everyone on board because many people had just purchased segments. They didn't qualify as "world cruisers." The gala was just for those of us who purchased the whole four-month odyssey.

The gala was in Melbourne. I have been to several galas, but not one like this one. Even the president of Cunard, Simon Palethorpe, flew in from London and brought a <u>cortège</u> of dignitaries and entertainment folks with him.

The Crown Hotel in Melbourne is like a city inside a city. I have never before seen such a complex. I thought our thousand-strong contingent, all gussied up in tuxedoes and formal gowns, would make a splash, figuratively speaking. Shucks! In that grand hotel, I suspect that we were hardly noticed.

As soon as we entered the ballroom, there was an ongoing presentation by an Aboriginal tribesman playing a didgeridoo, among other things. When everyone was properly seated, the program opened with a prayer by our Captain. He then informed us that eleven people had responded to his 2 am request the night before for blood donors. Captain Aseem Hashmi then introduced Simon Palethorpe, the President of Cunard. Mr. Palethorpe's apologies for the changes and missed ports on our world cruise were appropriate, I suppose, but unnecessary. World cruisers are mature and sophisticated enough to understand that Cunard was doing everything possible to provide us with the cruise experience of our lives.

Soon, the entertainment started. Mark Vincent is a classically trained tenor. And what a singer he is! Google up a YouTube of him and hear him for yourself. And ladies, he's good-looking too. You should see him knock out a Tom Jones hit.

I don't know what else to say about the evening. It was the best that either my wife or I had ever experienced. We could think of no way that it could have been better.

It was near midnight when we cast off from Melbourne, and Captain Hashmi set a course through the Bass Strait for Adelaide.

A day at sea between ports is ideal as it gives one the opportunity to reflect and discuss his experiences ashore.

I have hardly mentioned the glittering city of Melbourne. I have been thinking mainly of our gala evening in that city. Eleanor and I were both overwhelmed by the beauty, cleanliness and modernity of Melbourne. All of the cities that we visited in Australia were tidy. What's the secret? Maybe a number of things like budgeting money for beauty and enforcement of laws associated with cleanliness and beauty. I don't know, but I wish our American cities were as attractive.

After a night of cruising the Bass Strait, we entered an area called the Great Australian Bight. You can google "bight" and "Great Australian Bight," and you'll know everything you need to know.

We spent the day sailing on westward courses along the absolute bottom of the "Island Continent." As we skirted the southern coast, we could often see, from our balcony, an irregular horizon. That was mainland Australia. The Captain said he had never sailed all the way around Australia in one trip before. He chuckled as he told us that he couldn't get lost as long as he kept the shoreline off our starboard side.

It was cool below the continent, more than 30 degrees of latitude south of the equator. I suppose you could say we were down under the real "Down Under." It had become difficult to keep a proper perspective of the time difference between our location and the time back in Texas. We had been as many as 17 time zones ahead of our time at home, and at some hours, it was the same day as at home; at other hours, it was not.

On the morning of March 10th, we made port in the beautiful city of Adelaide. We knew that we were working our way back to Perth. We had no idea what was to happen after that.

Adelaide is surprisingly large – somewhat larger than San Antonio. As we know, San Antonio is one of the top ten cities in the USA. Adelaide is a pretty city facing the St. Vincent Gulf and protected from the Southern Ocean by Kangaroo Island. Adelaide has been known as the "City of Churches," referring to its diversity of faiths. Adelaide has been consistently listed in the top 10 of the "World's most livable cities."

Eleanor and I booked an excursion that took us through the city of Adelaide and up into the Mt. Lofty Mountains. Mount Lofty is the highest point in the southern Mount Lofty Ranges. It is about 8 miles east of the city center of Adelaide. The views from the observation points seem to go on forever out over the Adelaide Plains to the west and the Piccadilly Valley to the east.

Fellow tourists could hardly contain their excitement when they saw koalas sleeping in the eucalyptus trees. We had seen plenty of cute little creatures up close at the sanctuary in Brisbane, so I elbowed my way past the dozens of people snapping photographs and went to the observation platforms.

After our visit at Mt. Lofty, we went on to the little German town of Hahndorf. And folks, it really is German – founded by Germans and still populated by Germans. The culture is everywhere:

in the style of the architecture, the vineyards and wineries, and the plethora of German-style eateries and pubs.

After a good tour of the town, Eleanor and I chose the Haus Restaurant for some sustenance and libation. Since it is German, and Eleanor claims to be German, she figured she would drink a beer. I asked for a glass of local beer, and what did we get? It was Sierra Nevada beer from Chico, California.

We had one more port before we would be back in Fremantle. Cunard has to decide by that time. Our future was in Cunard's hands. Or was it controlled by a coronavirus? We didn't know.

World Cruise 2020 – Episode 21

**Uncanny: Strange or mysterious,
especially in an unsettling way.**

It was March 12th, and we were about out of Aussie places to
visit. Frankly, we had seen about enough of Australia. Places were
decreasing in importance. What was going to happen to us was of
greater importance. There was only one port remaining before we
would be back in Fremantle, where our circumnavigation of the
continent started. We would have much to reflect upon if and when
we ever got the nightmare of coronavirus behind us.

Adelaide was fresh in our memories. We must not forget some
of the beauty of Adelaide. A memorable feature of Adelaide was
its Norfolk Pines. Those interesting trees grow well in southern
countries, but we have never seen so many as we did in Adelaide.
Fortunately, our guide explained the phenomenon. Adelaide was
founded during the age of sailing ships. The fierce Southern
Ocean storms often crippled ships by breaking their main mast.
Norfolk pines grew straight, true, and strong, so they made excellent
replacement masts for the ships. In order to prepare for this market,
locals planted thousands of Norfolk pines. The image of the trees
became a characteristic of the city of Adelaide. Now, they line the

streets all over the city as well as along the long straight roads out across the Adelaide Plain.

We sailed west out of the Great Australian Bight back into the Southern Ocean. The Southern Ocean, also called the Antarctic Ocean, is the southernmost waters of the world, and they encircle Antarctica and the South Pole.

During the night, we rounded the southwest corner of Australia at Walpole and entered the Indian Ocean. I don't know how others feel, but when I am in the Indian Ocean, I feel an awareness that I am farther from my home than I have ever been. It can be an unsettling feeling

Our dinner table mates still included Hazel, the talkative one from Windsor, Ontario, and Knut and Regina Kammann, who live in Sydney. Knut and Regina were interesting folks. He is from Germany, and Regina is from Switzerland, so they own a house in Switzerland and one in Germany. They live half the year in Europe and the other half in Australia. Our other table mate, Jennifer, a Brit who lives in Australia, has quit our table. She had some political opinions that didn't jive with those of some of the others, and she didn't like breaking bread with anyone who didn't share her prejudices. So much for the better.

We reached the Busselton Harbor just as the blue nighttime sky was giving way to the morning yellow above the eastern horizon. During this time, the horizon becomes visible, so sailors can use the stars to navigate. It is called Nautical Dawn.

Tender boats were launched soon after we dropped anchor. A couple of boatloads were tendered ashore, and at 9:30, the captain announced that the tender service was temporarily suspended due to rough seas. The wind was Force 7 (Near Gale) on the Beaufort Scale. The captain is being careful. It can be dangerous trying to step from the ship onto a bouncing lifeboat. A man was crushed to death like that on this ship a couple of years earlier. A few years before that, our MS Amsterdam sent a thousand or so folks ashore by tender boat to Port Stanley, Falkland Islands. A sudden storm blew in, and they could not retrieve the guests. The shore-bound tourists had to spend the night in the Falklanders homes as there were not enough hotels in the little town to take care of them. We didn't want that to happen here in Busselton.

Even though it was rough in the bay, it was nothing compared to being out beyond the breakwater in the Indian Ocean, which is notorious for its swells that can raise and toss this quarter-mile-long ship.

I finally got ashore a little after noon. I drank a glass of local beer at a seaside bar and did a little bit of people-watching. I confirmed that Busseltonians don't appear appreciably different From San Franciscans, just fewer tattoos.

Busselton didn't have much to boast about other than its wooden pier, which is the longest wooden pier in the world. At 6,040 feet in length, I suppose it is pardonable vanity if it is the only outstanding feature that the city can proffer. I didn't walk it. What's to see out there except more water?

We hoisted anchor at 5:30 PM and set a course for Fremantle.

May 15th, 2020, Fremantle, Western Australia

It was like a bombshell explosion. We had been wondering what the future of our Grand World Voyage held in store. It had been changing day by day with the effects of the coronavirus and travel restrictions taking effect. We were willing to forego scheduled visits to Tenerife in the Canary Islands and even Funchal on the Portuguese island of Madeira. We were disappointed that we would not visit Reunion Island in the Indian Ocean. We had looked forward to visits to Mauritius, Durban, Port Elizabeth, and Cape Town in South Africa and in Walvis Bay, Namibia in West Africa.

All of that no longer matters. The captain announced that the World Tour was being curtailed. Every guest must get off the ship here in Fremantle and make our way home. The ship, as of the following evening, would revert to function as a merchant ship. No frills. It would set out for its home port in Southampton, England, stopping only as necessary for fuel and stores.

A lot of Brits wanted to stay on the ship to Southampton. Cap says, "No Way!! You cannot claim to be unable to fly. Our medical staff will examine you." He didn't want to mess with guests trying to call their own shots.

It took a full day for the Cunard folks to work out the logistics, but on March 16th, we flew out of Perth, Australia. Although it took the day and the night to fly to Sydney, change planes, fly to Los Angeles, change planes, and fly to Austin, and get home, and even though we crossed the International Date Line again, it was March 17th when we finally got to our house in San Marcos. Our luggage would arrive in another couple of days.

The timing was <u>uncanny</u>. The next day was Day 1 of national quarantine.

So this is the story of our intended World Cruise in 2020. Cunard arranged our travel and reimbursed us for the portion of the cruise that we missed.

As an additional note, a good number of the Brits refused to leave the ship in Fremantle for whatever medical reasons. They wanted to sail back to Southampton. However, the ship didn't immediately return to England. It had to go to several locations in the Indian Ocean and Africa to discharge employees. It was weeks before the ship got back to the UK. The ship's bars, along with the casino, libraries, and dining rooms, were closed, and no one could go ashore when the ship stopped at various ports. I chuckle to think about it. I suspect the Brits didn't.

THE HOLY LAND

**Smote: In the biblical sense, rebuke, as in Jesus
rebuked the storm, per certain translations**

The Holy Land is unique among the countries and regions on
this planet. It is a magnet that draws Christians, Jews, and Muslims
from the far corners of the world. One feels that uniqueness the
moment he steps on that holy soil.

It is the land of Noah, of Abraham, Isaac, and Jacob, of Joshua
and David: It is the land of the Apostles. And most importantly, it is
the land of Jesus, the Christ, the Messiah, the Savior of the World.

It was January 19th, 2020, when I stepped off the gangway into
the port city of Haifa. The first impression is a modern city built on
the slopes of the historic Mount Carmel. Haifa harbors a population
of people from all stripes of Middle Eastern history. Anyone on
the street might be a descendant of Joshua or Esau. Their ancestry
might be from the Israelites, the Canaanites, or the Ishmaelites. It
is fascinating to contemplate the histories of the people of the Holy
Land.

The winter chill would give way to warming sunshine. We
found our prearranged tour and boarded a small bus for our trip to
the interior.

The Holy Land is surprisingly small, less than half the size of
Arkansas. And when scriptures speak of travel to a faraway land, it

is probably equivalent to crossing the state line from Arkansas into Louisiana.

Our destination and primary reason to visit Israel was to tour Galilee, the Jordan River, and as many biblical sites as possible. It is hard to cover a lot in one day if one has to be guided by someone else's program, which was the case.

I particularly wanted to visit Nazareth, the birthplace of Jesus. Nazareth is a city in Israel with biblical history. In the old city, the domed Basilica of the Annunciation is, some believe, where the angel Gabriel told Mary she would bear a child. St. Joseph's Church is said to be the site of Joseph's carpentry workshop. The underground Synagogue Church is reputedly where Jesus studied and prayed.

These are sites that I wanted to visit. Our guide said that Nazareth wasn't safe for a visit. Nazareth is known as the Arab Capital of Israel, and its population is 99.8% Arab. I suppose Ahab was right. Nazareth is not a safe place for Christians. We passed within about four miles of the city and could see it from our tour bus windows.

We made our way across the Southern Galilee region to the ancient city of Tiberius. Tiberias was a young city, just a village actually, when Jesus was born, just 19 miles to the west in Nazareth. It is now a Jewish city of some 50,000 folks.

During the Ottoman period, although the city was 1,500 years old, it was reduced to "ruined and desolate" with only 12 Muslim households. Now, it is a resort town on the shore of the Sea of Galilee. It bears little semblance of the old city that it once was.

At Tiberias, we turned south alongside the Sea of Galilee to the lower end, where the Jordan River resumes and flows further southward into the Dead Sea.

We left the road at Yardenit and visited the baptismal site. It is an uncanny awakening to anticipate visiting a place, for years, with a firm mind's picture of what it looks like, only to find it to be just the opposite. My vision had been built around a wide stream flowing through a desert environment with a wide gravelly beach as an ideal spot for people to wade into the water. What we found was a slow-moving stream in a deep riverbed surrounded by an abundance of tropical foliage. Except for the oleanders and wild banana trees that lined the banks, the stream could have passed for one of the small rivers in North Arkansas where I grew up. It is about the size and flow of the Eleven Point River in Randolph County.

Enough of what the Jordan River looks like. It is the stream, and quite likely the very spot, where Jesus came from Galilee to the Jordan to be baptized by John, but John tried to deter him, saying, "I need to be baptized by you, and do you come to me?"

Jesus replied, "Let it be so now; it is proper for us to do this to fulfill all righteousness." Then John consented.

As soon as Jesus was baptized, he went up out of the water. At that moment, heaven was opened, and he saw the Spirit of God descending like a dove and alighting on him. And a voice from heaven said, "This is my Son, whom I love; with him I am well pleased."

My mind comprehends, only with great difficulty, that I was standing, looking at the very stream where it happened. My eyes were looking at the same river banks, the same stream, that my Savior looked at and waded out within. The thoughts still overwhelm me.

I had a whole new feeling within me as we left the baptismal site and traveled up the road on the east side of the sea.

Still warm inside from my experience at the river, I looked out over the Sea of Galilee. This is the sea where Simon and Andrew were casting their nets when Jesus summoned them to follow Him and become fishers of men. This is the sea where Jesus told the fishermen where to cast their nets. This is the sea where Jesus' disciples set out in a boat for Capernaum, and Jesus walked upon the surface and caught up with them. When the storm blew in and the water got rough, Jesus <u>smote</u> the storm and calmed the water. Yes, this is the very sea.

The lake is not large, only about 8 miles wide and 13 miles long. It is like a big pond, though, with unobstructed shorelines. The windswept waves can get treacherous. Current is only the flow of the Jordan through the lake and is imperceptible.

Our next stop was at Capernaum, the birthplace and home of Simon Peter. A significant town of 1,500 when Peter lived there, it was abandoned prior to the First Crusade in the 11ᵗʰ century. It is still abandoned and, in fact, non-existent today.

There was nothing left of Capernaum to indicate that it was ever a town. Five hundred years of abandonment will do that. But desolate and unpeopled as it was, it was illustrious ground. From Capernaum sprang the tree of Christianity that spread around the world. After Christ was tempted by the devil in the desert, he came here and started his teaching. This place became his home for the next few years. He began to heal the sick, and his fame spread. Sufferers came from Syria, the Transjordan, and even Jerusalem to be cured of their ailments. It was here that Jesus healed the centurion's servant and Peter's mother-in-law. Multitudes of lame, blind, and people who were devil-possessed came to Jesus, and he healed them all.

He chose twelve disciples, all local men, and sent them out to preach the gospel. He cursed Bethsaida and Capernaum for not repenting. Surely enough. They are both in ruins now.

Structures in historical Capernaum are limited to a church, ruins of a 4ᵗʰ-century synagogue, and a modern memorial built over the site of Peter's childhood home.

Less than two miles from Capernaum, we came to the site where Jesus preached to the multitudes and fed them on loaves of bread and fish that he multiplied in order to feed the entire 5,000 folks. Several churches have been built over the centuries to preserve and commemorate the site. The present Church of the Multiplication of the Loaves and Fish, shortened to the Church of the Multiplication, is a Roman Catholic church located at Tabgha on the northwest shore of the Sea of Galilee in Israel. The modern church rests on the site of two earlier churches. We were allowed time to reflect and worship before traveling on.

There are so many other locations in the Holy Land that I would love to visit. It is too dangerous now with militant groups like Hamas in Gaza, Hezbollah in Lebanon, and the Houthis in Yemen, all determined to wipe out the Christians and Jews in Israel and turn the area back into Palestine.

It will not happen, though. The Holy Land was promised to the Israelites as their forever home. I am glad that I have been able to visit at least once. So far.

COLONIAL SALTILLO

**Gentility: Social superiority as demonstrated
by genteel manners, behavior, or appearances**

It was the Yturria family gathering to celebrate the Diamond
Jubilee anniversary of Fausto and Maria Elena Yturria. They
chose the luxurious Camino Real Hotel, situated on the crest of
a hill, looking down upon the colonial city of Saltillo, the capital
city of Coahuila, for the occasion. The setting could not be more
picturesque, with the Sierra Madre Oriental mountains standing
imposingly on the western horizon.

Three generations of Fausto and Maria Elena gathered for the
occasion. They came from locations throughout central and northern
Mexico. It was a happy occasion. They spent the days relaxing around
the swimming pool, visiting, laughing, reminiscing about old times,
and watching the niños and nietos playing in the water.

Several of the older teens spent the earlier hours of the day, with
some playing golf and others playing at the tennis courts. After they
had showered and dressed, they rejoined the others in the pool area.
They, as they had been taught and their culture mandated, went
from lady to lady and kissed each one of them before taking a seat.

The young ladies lounged and visited with the older members.
Occasionally, a young lady would excuse herself, return to her

room, and come back in a bathing suit. After a refreshing swim, she returned to her room, dressed, and rejoined the family gathering.

It was our first trip to Saltillo. It was our first exposure to the relaxed, loving atmosphere and <u>gentility</u> (or gentilidad) of a large Mexican family. That visit was nearly four decades ago. It made a lasting impression on me.

The Old Spanish Trail

Cession: The formal giving up of rights, property, or territory by a state

The Old Spanish Trail is true to its name. It is old, and its origin was Spanish. There is a romantic sound to the name. It was a hundred years before Route 66. I was determined to explore it.

It started in Santa Fe, New Mexico, and although there were divergent routes through some of the segments, some 700 miles later, it finished in Los Angeles, California. The trail ran through areas of high mountains, arid deserts, and deep canyons. It is considered one of the most arduous of all trade routes ever established in the United States. Explored, in part, by Spanish explorers as early as the late 16th century, the trail was extensively used by traders with pack trains from 1830 until the mid-1850s. The area was part of Mexico from Mexican independence in 1821 to the Mexican Cession to the United States in 1848. In order to explore the most direct route, I chose the one opened by the Santa Fe merchant Antonio Armijo in 1829.

Antonio Armijo led a trading party of 60 men and a caravan of mules to Alta California. He departed from the Northern Route at Abiquiu, 48 miles northwest of Santa Fe. That is where I picked up his trail. Before heading west, I camped by the side of Abiquiu Lake on the Rio Chama on May 7th, 2021.

Armijo's group blazed a trade route using a network of indigenous routes, incorporating parts of Jedediah Smith's routes of 1826 and 1827 and Rafael Rivera's route of 1828 to the San Gabriel Mission through the Mojave along the Mojave River. Armijo documented his route in a report to the governor, and this was published by the Mexican government in June 1830.

The first leg of our trip took us to La Plata, 160 miles to the west, on the Colorado state line. We lingered in La Plata to explore the town where my mother "pounded the brass" as a Western Union telegrapher back in the early 1920s. The depot where my mother worked was the Santa Fe Station in those days. It is an Amtrak depot now. The town hasn't grown. Just 612 hardy folks live there now.

Our next stop was inside the Navajo Reservation at Teec Nos Pas, originally Tisnasbas. The population of Teec Nos Pas is holding steady at around 500 folks, all Navajo. The only active businesses are a trading post and a gas station. T'iis Nazbas Community School, like most schools on the reservation, was built by the Bureau of Indian Affairs. Everything else in the area reflects years of neglect.

Our next stop was at Mexican Water. I wondered about the name. We found that a trading post was given that name over a hundred years ago for some wells that provided water for travelers on the Navajo Trail. However, there is no Mexican water in Mexican Water these days. The wells have dried up, and folks get their water from the San Juan River. Interestingly, Mexican Water is in Apache County on the Navajo Reservation. The original Old Spanish Trail was four miles south of us at this point.

We intersected the trail again at Dinnehotso and ran parallel with it to Kayenta. Kayenta is a major town in the northern part of the reservation. It was on my route back in the 1970s when I traveled from my Arizona job to my Arkansas hometown.

Kayenta is different because of its scenic location. It is the gateway to Monument Valley and is en route to Lake Powell, Grand Canyon, Canyon De Chelly, and Mesa Verde. Residents in Kayenta hand-craft much of the silver and turquoise jewelry that is sold in the trading posts of northern Arizona.

Just west of Kayenta, the trail veers north and passes below the lava fields of the Rainbow Plateau and continues to the Colorado River. The Crossing of the Fathers was a series of sand bars on the river a mile west of Padres Butte. The Crossing of the Fathers is named for the Spanish Franciscan priests or "padres" Atanasio Domínguez and Silvestre Vélez de Escalante. They first reported it during an expedition that forded the Colorado River there in 1776. There is only a jeep trail to the crossing so I continued west to Page, where I could cross the river at the Glen Canyon Dam. The Crossing of the Fathers is no more except as a name because it is now under four hundred feet of Lake Powell water.

We lingered a day in Page. I had lived there four decades earlier while building a large electrical power plant on the Navajo Reservation.

Page was known as a "Bureau Town." It was created by the Bureau of Reclamation to support and provide housing for workers building the Glen Canyon Dam in the middle 1950s. It was not a new concept. The Bureau had created Boulder City, Nevada, similarly, in the early 1930s to support the construction of Boulder Dam, later known as Hoover Dam.

We drove down off the windy mesa, upon which the town of Page was built, to the Navajo Bridge to cross Glen Canyon and the Colorado River. I was pleasantly surprised to find that a new bridge had been built since I had lived there. The "New Navajo Bridge" stands alongside the old "Navajo Bridge." All vehicular traffic now uses the new bridge, and the old one only provides a crossing for pedestrians and horses. That is good because I recall how we used to feel the old bridge moving as we drove across it, especially on windy days.

Our next stop was in Big Water, Utah. Here, I found another change from when I lived in the area back in the 1970s. The town of Glen Canyon City, which had sprung up during the construction of the Glen Canyon Dam, no longer existed. It had long been known as a hotbed of polygamy.

Alex Joseph, an outspoken polygamist and founder of the

Confederate Nations of Israel, a Mormon fundamentalist sect, brought his four wives with him and moved to Glen Canyon City in 1983. His following became known as Josephites. They eventually elected Alex to be the Mayor, upon which he changed the name of the town to Big Water.

I had learned snippets of these goings-on over the years but this was my first opportunity to see the town up close and personal.

We drove an hour west to Kanab, then turned south to the town of Fredonia. Here, we picked up the Old Spanish Trail for the first time since it veered away through the desert near Kayenta on the Navajo Reservation.

Kanab is a pretty little Mormon town, as most Mormon towns are. A welcome sign at the edge of town proclaims Kanab, with its proximity to many spectacular rock formations, as "The Greatest Earth on Show," an interesting play on words.

Kanab has long been known as "Little Hollywood" due to the many movie films and television westerns that have been filmed there. The rock formations, mesas, and bluffs make perfect scenery for western filming.

Seven miles south of Kanab and across the state line lies the town of Fredonia. Although small, with just some 1,300 people, Fredonia is still the largest town in the "Arizona Strip," that strip of extreme northern Arizona separated from the rest of the state by the Grand Canyon.

At Fredonia, we turned West and drove to Pipe Spring. Pipe Spring, and the area surrounding the spring, is green with lush vegetation watered by the nearby Virgin River. Antonio Armijo and all the trade trains that followed rested and stocked up on water at Pipe Springs. Pipe Spring is now a National Monument.

There was a dark side to the Old Spanish Trail, not a blame to the trail but how it was used. Dominant Indian tribes, such as the Navajo and the Ute, captured people from the weaker Southern Paiute tribe and sold them as slaves in settlements like Santa Fe. Primarily due to their lack of horses, the Paiute were vulnerable to mounted raiders. In some cases, whole settlements were captured and depopulated.

Our highway split us away from the OST up to St George, Utah. We didn't reconnect to the trail until Mesquite, Nevada, on the Virgin River. Armijo followed the Virgin River bottoms south to the Colorado. From there, several miles of Armijo's route is now under Lake Mead.

Armijo traveled west parallel to the river, over difficult terrain in the Black Mountains, to avoid the deep narrow gorge of Boulder Canyon, to the riverside oases of Callville Wash and Las Vegas Wash. Boulder Canyon is the narrow gorge where Boulder Dam, now Hoover Dam, was later constructed.

I abandoned Armijo's westward trek of 1829 as there were no roads to access it. I elected to follow what became the "Northern Route" at Mesquite southwest through the Las Vegas Valley and across the Spring Mountains. The Northern Route and the Armijo route will converge in the desert near the Nevada-California border.

Spanish Trail travelers through Clark County followed changing routes as they learned shortcuts and new sources of water, but the trail always connected watering holes. Spanish Trail pioneer Antonio Armijo and early fur trappers depended on the Virgin and Colorado Rivers to take them safely to California. In the 1830s, when travelers found the unfailing springs of Las Vegas Valley, caravan leaders opened a new path between the Virgin and Muddy Rivers and Las Vegas Springs. Well-watered Red Rock Canyon became part of the route, though long, waterless stretches remained along the trail. The main trail crossed Clark County from Las Vegas Springs to Cottonwood Spring (Blue Diamond), Mountain Spring, Stump Spring (Pahrump Valley), and on into California.

After visiting the site where the travelers camped in Las Vegas – There is now the Old Spanish Trail City Park at the site – we crossed the Spring Mountains and reconnected with Armijo's route at the Nevada/California state line.

As we crossed Emigrant Pass in the Nopah Range, we found

various vistas where the ancient route is still visible across the benches of the mountains.

Our next and final stop on the Old Spanish Trail was the small town of Tecopa. At this point, the trail turns southward to Fork of the Road on the Mojave River, then turns west over Cajon Pass and on to Los Angeles. We may explore that segment in time to come.

Looking back, we had tracked nearly 500 miles of the most arduous of all trade routes ever established in the United States. The 700 total miles of the Old Spanish Trail was a pack trail in the 1830s, only wide enough for a horse or mule laden with bulky packs of furs or supplies. It later was expanded to a wagon road known as the Mormon Trail.

We explored the route in a modern air-conditioned car. We can only imagine the difficulties encountered by these early pioneers who blazed the trail over mountains and deserts and across raging rivers. One must look upon these sites in order to try to understand.

There is an old expression, "I saw the elephant," which meant that someone had gone west, seen the sights, and returned home. The Spanish of the 17th and 18th centuries who blazed the early trails could certainly lay claim to having "seen the elephant."

THE BIG APPLE

**Dromedary: An Arabian one-humped
camel, like the one in the pictures on
packages of Camel cigarettes.**

It was the third of January 2020 when we flew into New York City. The Big Apple felt like an icebox compared to balmy San Marcos, Texas, from whence we had come just a few hours earlier. Don't expect to gain a great deal of information while you are in NYC. These folks may possess a wealth of information and intelligence, but they don't speak English. The pleasant Bangladeshi lady who helped us at JFK Airport spoke not a word. The turban bedecked cabby whose Chevy bounced like a lame <u>dromedary</u> was from India and spoke only a few marginally understandable words. I didn't get his whole name but I saw his license, and it had Singh in there somewhere. He looked like a guide we had on an earlier trip to Tamil Nadu.

Our hotel check-in lady, Mala Ramdai Deonarine, from Guyana, was not particularly articulate. She had yes and no down pat. Thank you was a little more difficult. The shuttle bus driver was Paul. What a breath of fresh air. He is from Jamaica. He showed me a half dozen ways to shake hands. LeBron James would be proud of me. So here we were in our NYC hotel. From what we had heard, we needed to lock our windows, even though we were four floors above the street. After all, folks, this was New York City.

Yesterday, as we winged our way from Austin to NYC, I sat back in my seat, closed my eyes and reflected on some of my earlier flights when flying was so different. Air travel was relaxed but dignified. People dressed up to travel. They talked with one another. Pretty stewardesses tended to our every need. Even the pilot would walk through the cabin and greet people. There was trust. We had never heard the words - extremism, radicalized, Jihad, terrorists – those words would come several decades later.

I thought of my first commercial airline flight. It was October 1st, 1955. I was 17 years old and had been serving in the Panama Canal Zone for nearly a year. I had my thirty-day furlough papers in my pocket and was giddy with excitement. It was early in the afternoon when my buddy, Harley Franklin, checked a jeep out of the motor pool. He drove me from our post, Fort Kobbe, in the Canal Zone, across the canal into the Republic of Panama and to Tocumen Airport.

Harley accompanied me to the boarding area. We had some time to kill as we were nearly an hour ahead of my boarding time. Presently, a pretty Panamanian lady came through, serving complimentary cocktails. She spoke nearly perfect English with just enough Latin accent to be enticing. I never did learn what the drinks were called, but they were bright rose-colored and were based on rum, the favored liquor in the Caribbean. They were good.

It wasn't long until I climbed aboard the big Pan Am World Airways DC-7B. It was the biggest airliner that I had ever seen. It had four big radial piston engines. I watched a brilliant sunset over the Isthmus as we climbed away and headed north. We flew all night from Panama to Miami, Florida. I can still hear the sound of those big radial engines – a sound that I love – as they droned on through the night. A jet would have been faster, but jet airliners had yet to be invented.

Air travel has changed. It is now faster, more informal, and impersonal. That feeling of romance in air travel is gone, never to return. People are now bringing their "emotional support" dogs on trips. Dogs love it. Other passengers, not so much.

Egypt

Aplomb: Self-confidence or assurance, especially when in a demanding situation

It was 2020, and we were on an all-new grand world voyage. I looked forward to visiting Egypt again after several years of absence.

We had sailed a day and two nights across the southeastern Mediterranean. Most of the passengers, having been abroad for more than three weeks, had lost their fascination for arrivals and departures. Their lively interest and school-boy impatience had worn off. They would take their sleepy heads to the dining room and fortify themselves with coffee and a thousand calories of the ship's victuals. They are content to remain on board and visit ancient Egypt after breakfast. Those old countries do not go away at night; they stay until after breakfast. I, on the contrary, still eagerly anticipate the first sight of land on a new continent and am reliably ensconced on a forward outer deck looking for first sight.

The sun was just rising over the Nile Valley and illuminating the tops of the domes and minarets of Alexandria as we glided into the harbor and sidled up to the broad concrete dock. A convoy of freight trucks was already unloading pallets of everything the ship's kitchens would need for the next several days. I am forever fascinated by the foresight of whomever it is that makes out the shopping list. There are pallets of everything from anchovies to artichokes. Steam is rising into the heavy morning air from the mountains of frozen fruits, poultry, and hundreds of other items.

Soon, the gangway was in place, and the lost tribes of America invaded the ancient world with pent-up excitement that was not evident an hour earlier. There were fleets of modern tour busses for those headed for The Valley of the Kings, Luxor, and Karnak. We wouldn't see those folks for another ten days when they would meet us at a port on the Red Sea. Smaller buses were gorging themselves full of folks headed for scattered locations around the city. Some are headed for the American Consul's office, whatever for I haven't a clue. Others will visit Cleopatra's Needles, Pompey's Pillar, the River Nile, and Bibliotheca Alexandrina, the giant library where I intend to spend a few hours.

Alexandria's ancient library was one of the greatest of all classical institutions, and while replacing it might have seemed a Herculean task, the new Bibliotheca Alexandrina managed it with aplomb. Opened in 2002, this impressive piece of modern architecture is a deliberate attempt to rekindle the brilliance of the original center of learning and culture. The complex has become one of Egypt's primary cultural venues, a stage for numerous international performers, and a home to a collection of brilliant museums.

The building takes the form of a gigantic angled discus embedded in the ground, evoking a second sun rising out of the Mediterranean. The granite exterior walls are carved with letters, pictograms, hieroglyphs, and symbols from more than 120 different human scripts. Inside, the jaw-dropping main reading room accommodates eight million books and 2500 readers under its sloping roof, with windows specially designed to let sunlight flood in but keep out rays that might harm the collection. I was in heaven.

The following morning, we set out for Giza. We chose a guided tour with a small group made up of two couples from Boone, North Carolina, and a couple from Leesville, Florida. Our guide was Nailah, an attractive native of Cairo. We didn't know what to expect. She wore simple but tasteful Western attire. The only thing eastern about her clothing was her hijab, which failed to hide her beautifully coifed jet-black hair. Naila was a licensed guide and an erudite Egyptologist. She could narrate Egyptian history in minute detail from 7,000 BC through the Middle Ages. She was a museum curator moonlighting as a tour guide to make a few extra Yankee dollars.

Naila was an excellent tour guide! We began our tour by heading to the Giza plateau. There, we explored several monuments, including the Great Pyramid of Cheops (the only remaining wonder of the seven wonders of the ancient world dating back to about 2500 B.C, the Pyramid of Chephren (son of Cheops), and the Pyramid of Mycerinus (grandson of Cheops).

It was a long day. We had arisen at 4:30 am, breakfasted in our stateroom, and were on our excursion bus at 6:00 am. We left the pier at 6:30 and drove through the city of Alexandria and then southward for three hours to the city of Giza. Our trip took us across the low marshland of the Nile Delta. As I looked at the tall reeds growing along the water's edge, I could only think "bullrushes." It was easy to imagine a floating basket of reeds and baby Moses inside. We could not stop there either. Our destination was The Pyramids and Sphinx at Giza. The famous pyramids became visible across the desert long before we reached the city. We made our way through the city and up onto the plateau, where the three major pyramids dominate the horizon for miles.

Although there were a few thousand people there and maybe hundreds of buses, it was not horribly crowded. The area is just that big.

Words can hardly describe the enormity of the three major pyramids on the plateau. These have been dated to the year 2,600 BCE, so they are approaching 5,000 years old. The big pyramid is the only remaining wonder of the Seven Wonders of the Ancient World. It is 480 feet high and is constructed of 2,200,000 blocks of limestone, with an average weight of two and one-half tons. The base is square and covers 14 acres.

Off to one side was a villainous-looking group of men dressed in the desert Bedouin attire. Their remuda of Bactrian camels and dromedaries were patiently kneeling behind their masters, chewing their cuds. They were hawking rides for as little as $10.00. None of us had ridden a camel before, but Naila advised that the camel jockeys were an unscrupulous lot and were likely to charge more to have the camel kneel for a dismount than the original fare for the ride. They were downright scary-looking anyway.

It is hard to look at these villains and envision the Grandeur and pageantry associated with the Pharaohs, Ramses II and III Tutankhamun, Cleopatra if you choose, and Khufu. No, these are the descendants of the Egyptians who sat on their asses and camels and watched Israelite slaves making mud bricks to build the vast structures of Egypt that tourists have traveled to see for the last 4,100 years.

We were on our own to wander and snap photos of the giant pyramids and surroundings. There were a number of Egyptian men dressed in blue uniforms riding camels about the area. When we tried to get good we-were-there type photos of ourselves. One of the camel jockeys photo-bombed us repeatedly by placing himself behind us; then, he wanted to be paid for his disservice. We were disadvantaged until Naila came to our rescue and shooed the miscreant away.

We reboarded our bus and drove down off the plateau to a parking lot for the Temple and the Sphinx. It was much more crowded there. No less impressive, this giant and mysterious monolith is actually sculpted from a solid limestone hill. We snapped several pictures in the area. We didn't ride a camel there either.

Amon, our dutiful chauffeur, drove us across the River Nile into Cairo and upstream for nearly a mile, where we boarded a riverboat containing one of Egypt's finest restaurants. We joined the 300 or so from the other tour groups and were treated to a sumptuous Egyptian dinner, music by a large band, and a very entertaining belly dance. I think some of our elderly friends' pacemakers were working overtime to maintain control. All the while, we were cruising the River Nile with the city of Cairo on the east shore and the town of Giza on the west side.

All during our cruise, we were surrounded by Egyptian Police boats with armed policemen looking us over. It was a bit unnerving just to wonder what it was that they were on guard for us. Was it for our safety or theirs?

The sun was setting as we headed back down through the Nile delta to our awaiting ship and some needed rest. While half of our fellow excursionists napped, Naila's narrative had never slowed. She was like the energizer bunny.

I asked Naila to explain the beehive-looking domes that we were passing in the rural farming region. She explained that they were pigeon houses. Pigeons are a delicacy in Egypt and have been eaten there for thousands of years, but they are not a staple food. Pigeons are raised for consumption in conical towers throughout the Egyptian countryside.

The pigeon houses are known as dovecotes and are made from mud brick and are designed to resemble an artificial mountain. Some farms had at least a half dozen of such barracks. We bypassed the town of Mit Ghmar where there were hundreds of these dovecotes in the town, actually more dovecotes than residences.

Back on the ship in time for a shower and clean clothes, we had just enough energy for a snack on the Lido Deck and were quickly back in our stateroom and asleep. We would have a thousand memories to reflect upon the following day.

THE SNAKE

Gig: A long pole with a spear-like tip that has multiple barbed tines

It was back around 1968, give or take a couple of years; I made a trip from my home in the Northwest to my hometown in Arkansas for a visit. My mother, Donna Cates, was still living out on the home place east of the town of Maynard.

The old home place looked pretty good. My mother had remarried a year earlier. Les, my second stepfather, was a blessing to my mother. Les Johnson was slight of build, and at a shade over 70 years old with an advanced case of COPD from a lifetime of smoking Chesterfield cigarettes, he couldn't do any measurable farm work. Nevertheless, Donna and Les had cleared the despicable persimmon and sassafras sprouts that are a bane to pasture lands, and had the place looking pretty good. They had had a well drilled and now had running water and a functional bathroom – a great improvement from the days when I lived there.

On the second day of my visit, I drove into town to pick up a couple of items for my mother.

Maynard was a town of some 300 folks, and its beginnings can be traced back to Civil War days. It was strictly a Bible Belt town. The area's families had very Anglo-British surnames, which mirrored those found throughout the characteristic migration route south from Virginia into the Carolinas and then westward to Oklahoma. Common family names in northern Randolph County included names such as Jones, Brooks, Spencer, Smith, Blackwell, Hunt, Evans, Long, and Turner, as examples. There was not a Scandinavian, Italian, or Spanish name to be seen anywhere in the area.

While shopping in town, I encountered an old friend and classmate that I had not seen in ages. Carman Harris was from the big Harris family that lived up toward the state line. My family had known the Harris Family since my toddler days.

When I say the Harris family was a bunch of rednecks, I say it with a great deal of respect. Most of our neighbors, as well as I, could wear that moniker. The Harrises were the purest of rednecks. They farmed a couple hundred acres of cotton and grain sorghum. They worked hard, played hard, and fought hard. My eldest sister could attest to their fighting. Donna Dean was dating Hartwell Harris when they were in high school. She was visiting in the Harris home on one occasion when two or more of the brothers got into a brawl. One of the boys threw a pair of scissors at his brother, and rather than hitting him, the scissors found their mark in the calf of Donna Dean's leg, leaving a gash that had to be sewed up by the only doctor in the north part of Randolph County.

Carman and I, along with his older brother, Norman, and younger brother, Jesse Neal, had often fished together in neighboring farm ponds back in the early 1950s and had even hunted rabbits in the snow on one occasion.

It was a warm summer morning when Carman and I were visiting in town and talking about old times. Carman shared that he and a couple of friends planned to go frog hunting that evening and invited me to join them. That sounded like fun. It would be like the old days. I had lived out on the West Coast for more than a decade, so I had been far removed from the kind of fun that men and boys still had in rural Arkansas.

Later that day, I arrived at Carman's house just before sundown.

His friends, Aubrey Jones and Olan Samons arrived shortly afterward. I had known Olan in school 15 years earlier but had not met Aubrey.

We checked our flashlights and lanterns, strapped on our revolvers, piled into Carman's old pickup with our gigs and gear, and headed out for the evening.

Our first pond was one behind a barn near Rex Dismang's house. We walked around the pond and shot a couple of nice bullfrogs. Our gigs didn't work with us walking the bank, and besides that, the frogs had the advantage. They would skip across the lily pads to deep water where we couldn't go.

Darkness fell on our party, and it was time to get serious. The sky was clear, and the quarter moon gave us enough light to know where we were, and that was about it.

We went to a large stock tank (or pond in the local Arkansas vernacular) on the Dismang farm across the dirt driveway that passed in front of the Harris home. I had fished that pond many times, but in the last couple of decades, it had silted in to some degree, and lily pads completely covered the surface. One of our group had already staged a nice aluminum john-boat there for us to use.

We loaded into the boat and pushed out through the frog and snake-infested lilies and started scanning the surface with our lights. Our lights picked up dozens of shining eyes among the lilies. Carman informed us that the double eyes were frogs; if we could only see a single eye, it was a snake. The pond was full of eyes.

As we started around the edge of the pond, there was lighthearted chatter about how many snakes were out there and that they had been known to get into a boat. Aubrey stated, without hesitation, "If a snake gets in the boat with me, I am leaving the boat." We were having fun, and there was plenty of laughter. It wasn't like fishing or squirrel hunting, where we would have to be quiet. I had never been on a real frog hunt like this, so it was great fun for me. The pond was productive, and we were harvesting some nice-sized bullfrogs.

As time went on, I was the gig man in the front of the boat. I was on my knees on the aluminum seat, looking forward with the gig in my hand. The guys behind me were paddling the boat, and when we spotted a frog, they kept their lights shining on the frog to blind it and paddled the boat close enough for me to gig the frog. At one point, we had our lights on a particular frog, and the guys were paddling forward to get me in position to gig the frog. I told them. "Just a couple more feet, guys, and I'll have him."

About that time, Aubrey, who was behind me, said, "Allan, there's a snake right between your feet." I thought he was joking, so I kept my eyes on the frog. Suddenly, the boat was rocking violently, and there was a big splash. Aubrey had jumped out of the boat and landed in the water. I looked around, and surely enough, right between my boots was a sizeable cottonmouth. I quickly turned and stood up on the seat away from the big moccasin, trying to keep my balance and not fall into the water among no telling how many other snakes.

My first impulse was to grab my revolver and shoot the snake, but that would be shooting holes in the bottom of the boat. Carman was scrambling to try to beat the snake with a boat paddle. I could do nothing but watch. The hapless snake managed to escape under one of the seats, which was a shaped aluminum seat that went to the bottom of the boat. The snake was safe there, out of our reach.

We made it to the shore and pulled the boat out on the ground. Aubrey was there waiting for us. I said to Aubrey, "You must not have gotten too wet; the water was not more than knee-deep there, was it?"

Aubrey maintains, to this day, that he is the second man in history to walk on water, that he didn't even get his britches wet getting to the bank. Well, maybe.

We could only speculate how the snake got into the boat. There were several scrub willows around the water's edge. We agreed that the most likely answer was that the snake fell from one of the low-hanging branches. That is even scarier.

I have revisited the memory of that summer evening a thousand times, and I have related the story to anyone who might show interest.

In 2016, I was visiting in my hometown during the annual Pioneer Days festival. I had not seen my friends in decades. Suddenly, my friend Levon Cox said, "You wanted to see Carman Harris. There he is under the sweet gum tree." I was elated.

Carman and I visited, and our conversation led to the frog hunt and snake incident. Carman said, "Aubrey and Olan are both here in the park, lets go and talk with them."

We located Aubrey and Olan, and the four of us reminisced about the details of that frog hunt nearly fifty years earlier.

In my eighty-plus years, I have had a lot of experiences, but that moonlit evening when the moccasin visited us in the boat stands out as perhaps the most unique of them all.

Epilogue

Demerit: a feature or fact deserving censure.

Over the years, I have authored two books. The first was a comprehensive autobiography of my life, and the second is a memoir concentrating on my travels to some 73 countries around the world.

My formal education is limited as I dropped out of high school two years before graduation to join the army. I took a few classes in junior college but never had a course in creative writing or a journalism curriculum. I concede that my writing probably deserves censure for literary <u>demerit</u>. However, I hope my friends have found something interesting or entertaining in the previous chapters.

Thank you for staying with me.

Printed in the United States
by Baker & Taylor Publisher Services